Praise for *The Vine Movement*

This is a very useful, brush-clearing book to help both church and parachurch leaders navigate the tension and complexity of moving beyond their individual mission statements to partner together in the mission of the gospel.

Todd Adkins
Co-founder, Lifeway Leadership Podcast Network
Director of Leadership Development, Lifeway Christian Resources, Nashville, TN

Local church leaders can sometimes characterize parachurches as unbiblical, arrogant and distracting. Parachurch leaders can sometimes stereotype local churches as cumbersome, dogmatic and slow. Mikey Lynch offers us a different take. Theologically rich and nuanced, and full of wisdom and practical insight, *The Vine Movement* can inspire us to relate with discernment, appreciation, honour and love for those serving in different parts of the vineyard to us—and to actively collaborate in cultivating a gospel ecosystem.

Peter Dray
Director of Creative Evangelism, UCCF: The Christian Unions, UK

Hilarious, provocative, biblical, historical, concrete and extremely helpful. It is my prayer that Mikey's book will help both denominational churches and parachurches to understand one another better and to work brilliantly together to proclaim Christ.

Ben Pfahlert
National Director, Ministry Training Strategy, Australia

Mikey Lynch brings a winsome blend of intellectual curiosity and generosity to the thorny problem of church and parachurch ministry. As someone who frequently works in the intersection of these kinds of organizations, I found this book to be a rare combination of careful theological insight and practical wisdom. The clarity of Lynch's discussion of the doctrine of church in the opening section is worth the price of the book alone. I've already found myself recommending it to campus ministry workers and church pastors who are wrestling with how their different ministry models fit together to serve the kingdom.

Dan Anderson
Director, The Lachlan Macquarie Institute, Canberra
Chair of the Board, Australian Fellowship of Evangelical Students
Former Anglican Chaplain, Robert Menzies College, Macquarie University, Sydney

Mikey Lynch has written a brilliant book on a vital topic for anyone concerned about the mission of Jesus. Good material on the relationship between the church and the parachurch is surprisingly rare. What is written can sometimes come from a narrow theological perspective, arguing for the value of the one over the other without a practical sense of how mission actually proceeds in the world. Or they can be highly pragmatic, promoting 'whatever works' over what is true and biblical. Mikey, by combining a first-rate theological mind with long and fruitful experience in both church and parachurch ministry, has brought together what is too often apart: theological depth and practical mission experience. I firmly believe this will become the one-stop, go-to book on the subject for years to come.

Rory Shiner
Senior Pastor, Providence City Church, Perth
Network Director, Providence Church Network

As someone with a foot firmly planted in both my local Chinese church and the parachurch that employs me, I've always been fascinated by the relationship between churches and parachurches. Is the parachurch something to be avoided or embraced? Thanks to Mikey Lynch's detailed analysis, I am all the more excited to see how I can best serve God's kingdom in both my church and parachurch.

Sam Chan
Public Speaker, City Bible Forum, Australia

Partnerships between local churches and parachurch organizations provide wonderful opportunities for the growth of the gospel, but too often are fraught with tension and misunderstanding. Mikey Lynch has done us a great service by giving a clear theological foundation for these relationships. He establishes the priority of local church ministry and explores the relationship between local churches and denominational and parachurch organizations in a range of contexts.

David Williams
Director of Training and Development, Church Missionary Society, Australia

As someone who trains Christian people for chaplaincy and pastoral care ministries, both within the public sector and parachurch organizations, I see people struggle to know where their ministries connect with more traditional church ministries. In this important project, Mikey Lynch explores the assumed (but largely unexamined) relationship between churches and parachurch organizations and ministries. *The Vine Movement* is a helpful attempt to describe existing parameters that differentiate between church and parachurch, and then to demonstrate faithful ways of integrating both ministries in a way that honours each one's alignment with Christ and his mission while respecting the remit of the other. This work would be of interest both at an organizational level, and for individuals wishing to understand their place in a larger whole.

Kate Bradford
Chaplain and Pastoral Supervisor, Anglicare, Sydney

The Vine Movement is an ambitious but careful examination of the relationship between the local church and various parachurch ministries. Mikey Lynch demonstrates that, while the local church has spiritual authority, parachurches can deepen the growth of the kingdom in unique and vital ways. This book explains all this and also provides practical advice for how to productively navigate the relationship between the local church and parachurch ministry in the midst of our fallen world.

Luke Isham
Minister, St Kilda & Balaclava Presbyterian Church, Melbourne

The Vine Movement

SUPPORTING GOSPEL GROWTH BEYOND YOUR CHURCH

MIKEY LYNCH

matthiasmedia
SYDNEY · YOUNGSTOWN

Matthias Media
(St Matthias Press Ltd ACN 067 558 365)
Email: info@matthiasmedia.com.au
Internet: www.matthiasmedia.com.au
Please visit our website for current postal and telephone contact information.

Matthias Media (USA)
Email: sales@matthiasmedia.com
Internet: www.matthiasmedia.com
Please visit our website for current postal and telephone contact information.

ISBN 978 1 925424 75 1

Cover design and typesetting by Lankshear Design.

Acknowledgements

N ikki and the kids, for the friendship and support through the production of this 'difficult second album'.

Kate Bradford, for generous, constant and thoughtful input to my blog's Facebook Page as I developed ideas for this book. Arthur Davis, for energetic input, and for being a stimulating foil for my ideas. Chase Kuhn and Jerry White, for some thought-provoking conversations early on in the writing process. Pieter Tuit, for the loan of a massive reading list and some helpful mentoring early on in the project.

Nick Gross, for designing the classy diagrams.

Kate Bradford, Renae Godden, Luke Isham, Dan Shepheard and Rory Shiner, for reading through the whole manuscript and giving encouragement and feedback.

Murray Campbell, Andrew Heard, Chase Kuhn and Pieter Tuit, for help on chapters 1-3; Harriet Connor, for help on chapter 7; Gary Millar, Tim Patrick, Megan Powell du Toit and John Woodhouse, for help on chapter 10; and John Zechendorf and Nathan Campbell, for help on chapter 14.

Geoff Robson, for his thoughtful and thorough editing, including lots of probing questions and good humour along the way.

To David N Jones, whose life and library was a formative model for my Christian mind and ministry. His churchmanship, his commitment to gospel growth beyond any one church or denomination, and his confidence that Christ will build his church all embody the central ideas of this book.

To K John Smith, a creative, compassionate and courageous pioneer of Australian church and parachurch ministry, from whose legacy we all benefit.

Contents

Foreword

Where would we be today without the many parachurch movements that began to either reform or enhance the organized church? Some of these became formally connected to churches, while others stimulated local churches to develop new ministries and outreaches. But many became long-term organizations of their own.

In 1530, St Ignatius of Loyola led a movement of people who wanted to be more deeply committed, so formed the Soldiers of Christ. In 1540, the Roman Catholic Church, seeing their strength and growth, brought them into the fold as an order.

In 1517, Martin Luther nailed his 95 theses to the church door in Wittenberg, Germany. This time, the Roman Catholic Church was unable to contain the division, resulting in the Reformation.

In the 1780s in Britain, Anglican evangelical Robert Raikes and others created the Sunday School movement to minister to children caught in the Industrial Revolution. At first, it was not readily accepted in the church. But soon this parachurch movement became an integral part of local churches in Britain and America.

In 1179, Peter Waldo, an ordinary layman, asked Pope Alexander III for a preaching licence. It was granted as long as he was under the supervision of local clergy. This became the Waldensian Movement, which, notably, was a movement of laymen. In 1184, Waldo was excommunicated by Pope Lucius III.

In the late 1700s, William Carey (often called the father of modern missions), a layman and shoemaker, had a vision for sending missionaries to India. He left the Anglican Church, became a Particular Baptist pastor, and founded the Particular Baptist Society for the Propagation of the Gospel Among the Heathen (later the Baptist Missionary Society). He took his mission outside the local church.

In the 1930s and 40s, there was an explosion of parachurch organizations such as The Navigators, Intervarsity Christian Fellowship, Campus Crusade for Christ (now Cru), Young Life, Youth for Christ, and many others. Notably, again, most were begun by laymen.

Indeed, many of today's parachurch organizations were started and are staffed by laymen and women. The parachurch movement has become an avenue of ministry for those who did not have the benefit of theological education or ordination. To be fair, of course, local churches and denominations desperately attempt to engage laymen and women meaningfully in a myriad of ministries; they are not opposed to significant lay involvement.

In 1983, I wrote *The Church and the Parachurch* at the direct request of Dr Joe Aldrich (then President of Multnomah School of the Bible and Multnomah Press). I asked him, "Why would I write a book that neither church or parachurch leaders will like?" He said simply that the topic needed to be addressed. At the time, there were about 10,000 Christian parachurch organizations. I predicted that this would increase to several times that. Some wrote in response that the parachurch movement would die. Today, there are more than 90,000 such groups in the United States alone.

Mikey Lynch has produced a wonderfully written and researched book to address both the theological and practical aspects of the tensions, realities and complementary ministries of the local church and the parachurch. My early research pales in comparison to the detailed and definitive research that Lynch has done. He is thorough, balanced, critical, discerning and articulate in presenting the theological foundations, or lack thereof, of both structures.

I initially planned to scan the book then write this foreword. But I was irresistibly drawn to read it in great detail. It is so carefully researched and even-handed in presenting opposing viewpoints as well as being intensely theological. At the same time, it is profoundly practical, with cogent suggestions and warnings for both church and parachurch.

This is the most definitive and insightful book that has been written in recent history on this very important aspect of God's kingdom work. At a time when churches are proliferating outside denominational control and when parachurches continue to form, we must learn how to work together for the cause of the gospel. Conceptually, there is a broad agreement across the body of Christ that both structures are valid and needed. But as we say, theologically, "the devil is in the details"!

Like the saying that all politics are local, so all applications of church and parachurch dynamics are local. We can agree on general principles and even theology, but struggles ensue at the local level where personalities and programs dominate, and conflict and misunderstandings can result. Lynch rightly emphasizes the importance of relationships and communication.

Ultimately, we need to see all of these issues from the perspective of the kingdom of God. No one church or parachurch meets every purpose of the kingdom. God works in ways beyond our understanding or plans. He is at work far beyond any structures that we create—church or parachurch. Finally, most fundamentally, we must not focus on organizations or churches, but on individuals who come to faith and are discipled to maturity. It is individual men, women and children who are reached with the gospel and who mature in the faith. They are not pawns in our systems, but the very heart of what we as the body of Christ are about. We are guided by Paul's words in Colossians 1:

> To [his saints] God chose to make known how great
> among the Gentiles are the riches of the glory of this

mystery, which is Christ in you, the hope of glory. Him we proclaim, warning *everyone* and teaching *everyone* with all wisdom, that we may present *everyone* mature in Christ. For this I toil, struggling with all his energy that he powerfully works within me. (Col 1:27-29, ESV)

Our work is profoundly personal.

May we in churches and parachurches keep this in mind as we pursue our mission and vision, realizing and committing to the gospel in all its fullness, and proclaiming it to every person.

That's why this book is so important. Mikey Lynch has given us both a roadmap and detailed guidelines, buttressed with a sound biblical foundation, to help us in the task.

Jerry E White, PhD
International President Emeritus, The Navigators
Author, *The Church and the Parachurch: An Uneasy Marriage*
Major General, United States Air Force, retired

Introduction

The *Trellis and the Vine* gives a vision for word-centred disciple making in the local church and beyond.[1] It is something of a manifesto for a simple, biblical view of Christian ministry. The central metaphor of the book describes spiritual disciple-making ministry as the 'vine', which is helped to grow by the 'trellises' of infrastructure and governance. Colin Marshall and Tony Payne explain their central metaphor like this:

> The basic work of any Christian ministry is to preach the gospel of Jesus Christ in the power of God's Spirit, and to see people converted, changed and grow to maturity in that gospel. That's the work of planting, watering, fertilizing and tending the vine.
>
> However, just as some sort of framework is needed to help a vine grow, so Christian ministries also need some structure and support. It may not be much, but at the very least we need somewhere to meet, some Bibles to read from, and some basic structures of leadership within our group. All Christian churches, fellowships or ministries have some kind of trellis that gives shape and support to the work.[2]

1   C Marshall and T Payne, *The Trellis and the Vine: The ministry mind-shift that changes everything*, Matthias Media, 2009.
2   Marshall and Payne, *The Trellis and the Vine*, p 8.

For many who have read and loved this book over the past ten years, *The Trellis and the Vine* has given an affirming clarity as they read in print convictions they were already working out in practice. Others have been jolted into focus as they realized how they had drifted from the core priorities of Christian ministry. For as the authors warn, "that's the thing about trellis work: it tends to take over from vine work".[3] Many have found it useful to pass on to their church leadership teams and pastors-in-training, to also establish them in its ministry mindset.

The power of *The Trellis and the Vine* lies not so much in Marshall and Payne pioneering new ideas, but in the way they express basic truths in a sharp and direct way and tease out the necessary implications of these truths with a kind of delightful, challenging and inspiring inevitability.

In *The Vine Project*, Marshall and Payne both build on and deepen the theological convictions in *The Trellis and the Vine*, but also lay out a helpful process by which leaders can review, renew and refocus a local church around these convictions.[4]

Building trellises for the global vine

Both books are clear that the rule of Christ extends to the ends of the earth and that the individual Christian and the local church should be concerned about global mission: "The parable of the trellis and the vine is not just a picture of the struggles of my own local church; it's also a picture of the progress of the gospel in my street and suburb and city and world."[5]

After all, most of us are the fruit of the global mission: we *are* 'the nations' to which those original disciples were sent.[6] Our primary concern, therefore, ought not to be a narrow conception of local church growth, but rather 'gospel growth':

3   Marshall and Payne, *The Trellis and the Vine*, p 9.
4   C Marshall and T Payne, *The Vine Project: Shaping your ministry culture around disciple-making*, Matthias Media, 2016.
5   Marshall and Payne, *The Trellis and the Vine*, pp 10-11.
6   Marshall and Payne, *The Vine Project*, p 130.

INTRODUCTION

It's interesting how little the New Testament talks about church growth, and how often it talks about 'gospel growth' or the increase of the 'word' ... Returning to our vine metaphor, the vine is the Spirit-empowered word, spreading and growing throughout the world, drawing people out of the kingdom of darkness into the light-filled kingdom of God's beloved Son, and then bearing fruit in their lives as they grow in the knowledge and love of God ...

This results, of course, in individual congregations growing and being built. But the emphasis is not on the growth of the congregation as a structure—in numbers, finances and success—but on the growth of the gospel, as it is spoken and re-spoken under the power of the Spirit.[7]

This requires not just thinking about the 'vine work' in our local church, but also the process of transplanting new 'vines', and the building of new 'trellises' to support these vines in new areas—locally, regionally and globally; in other words, church planting. As Marshall and Payne write: "the gospel is growing throughout the world like a vine whose tendrils keep spreading across the fence, and over the fence, and into the neighbour's backyard."[8] Such 'vine work' will require new 'trellises' to equip, send and support new works. And eventually they create new networks of trellises and vines, whether informal connections or formal denominations and mission societies.

The focus of *The Vine Project* is purposefully and unapologetically the local church. The church is central to God's ultimate purposes and so of vital importance to our faithful and fruitful obedience to his Great Commission.

This means, however, that there remains plenty of space to explore further the implications of a word-centred disciple-making 'vine' ministry beyond the local church. The organic focus on disciple making rightly opens us to thinking beyond the local

7   Marshall and Payne, *The Trellis and the Vine*, p 37.
8   Marshall and Payne, *The Trellis and the Vine*, p 81.

church or the denomination—for wherever the people of God can go with the word of God, there the vine can spread. It is fitting for our trellises to have to play catch-up to the wonderful ways in which Christ works through his people in building his church in the world.

The gospel ecosystem

When this larger vine becomes healthy and vigorous, we end up with a whole 'gospel ecosystem', as Tim Keller calls it:

> Just as a biological ecosystem is made of interdependent organisms, systems, and natural forces, a gospel ecosystem is made of interdependent organizations, individuals, ideas, and spiritual and human forces. When all the elements of an ecosystem are in place and in balance, the entire system produces health and growth as a whole and for the elements themselves.[9]

Such an ecosystem, Keller writes, includes not only "church planting and church renewal movements" but also "a complex set of specialty ministries, institutions, networks, and relationships", including:

1. a prayer movement uniting churches across traditions in visionary intercession for the city
2. a number of specialized evangelistic ministries, reaching particular groups (business people, mothers, ethnicities, and the like)
3. an array of justice and mercy ministries, addressing every possible social problem and neighbourhood
4. faith and work initiatives and fellowship in which Christians from across the city gather with others in the same profession

9   T Keller, *Center Church: Doing balanced, gospel-centered ministry in your city*, Zondervan, 2012, p 371.

5. institutions that support family life in the city, especially schools and counselling services
6. systems for attracting, developing, and training urban church and ministry leaders
7. an unusual unity of Christian city leaders.[10]

Those of us who give and pray and serve and lead need to reflect together on how we can help tend this complex ecosystem. This is more than pruning a single vine or even managing a single suburban garden. Just as there is a global ecology, there is a global *gospel* ecology. Alongside the practical complexity of tending wisely to this gospel ecosystem, there is also the theological complexity of thinking faithfully about it. This challenge is felt even by the keen individual Christian: what stuff should I get involved with?

About me

My Christian life and ministry have been entangled with both church and parachurch work all the way along. I was baptized as a child in an Anglican church, but my family were not regular churchgoers. I attended church schools and learned much about the gospel in religious education classes, chapel services, and conversations with chaplains. In fact, it was at an evangelistic event hosted during one of Scotch College Melbourne's school mission weeks that I was first truly shaken to seriously consider the gospel by guest speaker Ian Powell. I came to faith several years later, after my family moved to Hobart. This was through a combination of: attending church on Sunday at St John's Presbyterian Church; informal evangelistic Bible studies (Scripture Under Scrutiny, or SUS for short) with Jo, a woman from the church; involvement in events hosted by the Australian Fellowship of Evangelical Students (AFES) ministry at the University

10 Keller, *Center Church*, pp 374-376.

of Tasmania; and reading books by CS Lewis, John Chapman, Francis Schaeffer, Josh McDowell, and others.

Since then, I have been involved in all sorts of ministries: teaching Scripture in a local primary school under the umbrella of the Tasmanian Council of Churches; leading on Anglican Camping Tasmania Youth Camps; and serving as a member of an open-air preaching circus group, 'The Trinity Troupe.' I was a founder and editor of a short-lived, small-circulation zine called *Regurgitator* in the early 2000s. I have blogged at Christian Reflections since 2006, published a couple of books, and helped launch a few podcasts. I served for seven years as an ordained elder and unordained pastor ('Home Missionary') of the church I helped to plant, Crossroads Presbyterian Church, and so was also a member of the local Presbytery of Derwent and General Assembly of Tasmania.

I have now worked for ten years on staff for AFES at the University of Tasmania. I became a founding director of The Vision 100 Network (Tasmania) and The Geneva Push (National)—both church-planting networks—in 2002 and 2008, respectively. I served as the Tasmanian Network Coordinator for the Ministry Training Strategy (MTS) from 2008 until 2018, and as a chaplain for Jane Franklin Hall residential college from 2009 until 2020. In 2005, I gathered together a team of Christian IT volunteers which has since grown into the not-for-profit ministry New Front Door: the Church IT Guild.

In all of this, I have struggled practically and theologically with how church and parachurch work together well, fielded all sorts of suggestions and objections, and have at various times been either deeply frustrated or profoundly inspired.

In this book, I draw on all of these experiences, together with the experiences of my friends and colleagues and the lessons I have been able to glean from the practical and theological reflection of others throughout church history. This is very much a practical book, not merely a theoretical book.

What does healthy vine work look like when applied to the local university Christian Union? The combined evangelistic effort of a regional town? The global mission society? How can our trellises help or hinder this wider work? How do we uphold the value of the local church even as we unleash God's people with the gospel word? And what do we make of other Christian enterprises that spring up in the church and beyond—those that are not focused primarily on the ministry of the word? As God's people eager to do good, we will be busy not only with disciple making, but also with all sorts of good deeds in charity, community, art, education, health and politics. Where do these deeds belong, and how do they relate to our disciple-making ministries? These are the types of questions that this book attempts to answer.

How do we serve beyond the local church?

There are so many ways we could serve the cause of the gospel. Look on any brochure table or noticeboard in almost any church foyer across the country and you will find conferences, workshops, outreaches, mission societies, fellowships, collectives and lobby groups to address a whole range of internal and external needs. You can grow in your Bible knowledge, be supported in your parenting, overcome an addiction, reach out to prison inmates, fund clean water, advocate for refugees, engage in open-air preaching, reconnect with your manhood or womanhood, be refreshed as a pastor, evangelize and equip university students, start prayer teams in the workplace, form your Christian worldview, and on and on it goes. And each of these groups wants you to pray for them, give to them, and roll up your sleeves and get involved with them.

So how do you choose where to put your time, energy, money, prayers, and passion?

In the first place, this is a question of Christian wisdom, freedom, and decision making—matters I covered in my previous book, *The Good Life in the Last Days*.[11] In that book, I argued that

11 M Lynch, *The Good Life in the Last Days: Making choices when the time is short*, Matthias Media, 2018.

God made the world complex, so that there will usually be competing priorities and no easy answers for what exactly we should be doing. It's complicated, but that's the way God made the world to be. We can attain some clarity about the best way to live when we think about our individuality and our unique circumstances. Since we are not omnipresent and omnipotent, we have particular responsibilities and abilities; we don't have to care about and do something about absolutely everything. But we are also blessed with genuine Christian freedom to choose between multiple good things. This means that I get to—and *have* to—wisely exercise my Christian freedom in choosing which conferences and ministries I get involved with, and how much I give and serve. There is no single ratio of family life, secular work, recreation, Bible convention attendance, charitable work, political advocacy and parachurch evangelism I must conform to.

But to fully inform my Christian freedom so I can make a wise choice, I must reflect not only on my unique context and circumstances, but also on the unique nature of the various activities I could be involved in. What is Christian charity work? What is a university Christian Union (CU)? What are these things we often group together with the term 'parachurch'?[12] For that matter, what is a local church? And how are the church and parachurch different or similar? Is one more important or less important than the other?

I think most Christians have a hunch that the local church has a special place in God's purposes, but what does this mean for all the other Christian organizations I could be involved with? Without having clarity on these kinds of questions, it's difficult to see the way forward.

In fact, there are questions that are even more complicated:

- What is the relationship between the missionary society, the indigenous church, and the sending church?

---

12 The word 'parachurch' simply means 'alongside the church' (the Greek preposition 'para' means 'alongside').

- What is the responsibility of the church for organizing works of charity in the community? What is its responsibility for political advocacy? What should be its connection to external Christian organizations that do these things?
- What is the nature, authority and importance of the denomination? Is the denomination properly seen to be the 'regional church', or is it in fact a kind of parachurch?
- What account should Christian publishing houses, theological colleges, bloggers, podcasters and YouTubers be held to?
- How should the biblical principles about church discipline, leadership appointment and the ordering of church gatherings apply to the membership, leadership and meetings of parachurch groups?

It is important for all mature Christians to wrestle with these issues. As we all live out our faith by being active in the work of the Lord, we all have to think through how to serve the gospel both within and beyond the local church. The Lausanne occasional paper on church/parachurch relationships describes the range of people for whom it was written:

> ... for those actually involved out there in "striving side by side for the faith of the gospel" ... for the pastor in a small town, the organisation staff member in a city suburb, the denominational leader in danger of getting out of touch, and the Bible school or seminary teacher whose seed thoughts will grow into fruit-actions, whether they are right or wrong.
>
> It is a down-to-earth document, grappling positively with the facts of disharmony and disunity. It is for those of us desperately concerned and deeply involved in the task of world evangelization, often "you in your small corner, and I in mine."[13]

---

13 Lausanne Committee for World Evangelization Commission on Co-operation, *Cooperating in World Evangelization: A handbook on church/para-church relationships*, Lausanne Occasional Paper 24, The Lausanne Movement website, 1 March 1983, p 14, accessed 6 September 2022 (lausanne.org/content/lop/lop-24).

This very much reflects my purpose, too—although I would add that, as well as writing for staff and ordained leaders, I am also writing for anyone who participates in and benefits from parachurch ministries.

About *The Vine Movement*

In part 1 of this book, I lay down some theological foundations to help us think clearly about the nature of the church, the parachurch, denominations, and the kingdom of God. While some might be tempted to skip over part 1 to get to 'the practical stuff', it is a very important basis for all the practical recommendations that follow.

In part 2, I draw together these ideas and provide principles and suggestions for how to establish healthy patterns of relationship between church and parachurch ministries, both locally and globally. The focus of my recommendations is not how to start and manage a parachurch ministry,[14] but rather the healthy interaction between church and parachurch.

Lastly, in part 3, I will go into more detail about particular kinds of parachurch organizations, seeking to draw from the biblical teaching, learn from historical case studies, and provide some practical principles for every Christian. This section is 'applied missiology, ecclesiology and ethics', with a good dose of church history thrown in. At many points, it is not so black and white; it's a synthesizing of theological and moral principles into practical recommendations. You don't need to read the whole of part 3 from beginning to end; perhaps you will prefer to find the category of parachurch that you are most engaged with and read that chapter. While *The Vine Movement* can be enjoyed as one long book, it can also be used (especially part 3) as a collection of discussion papers as needed.

---

14 For practical advice in this area, see WK Willmer, JD Schmidt and M Smith, *The Prospering Parachurch: Enlarging the boundaries of God's kingdom*, Jossey-Bass Publishers, 1998.

The exciting possibility is that the gospel might spread more rapidly, believers might become more Christlike, and good deeds might abound, all through the partnership of churches and para-church ministries. The book is written to help God's people be principled, strategic and generous, so that para-churches might be effective in a way that also honours and encourages healthy local churches, and so that local churches might proactively support the wider work of God's people in the world.

PART 1 //
THEOLOGICAL FOUNDATIONS

Chapter 1: What is the church?[1]

Yumin started to crochet when she broke her leg. She had nothing to do. She couldn't go bushwalking or kayaking like she normally did; she was stuck sitting down. It was a strange hobby for her, not the kind of thing she imagined herself ever doing. But her sister was expecting a baby and she thought she'd make her a cute little hat. And besides, it was short term, just while she healed up and got back on her feet and into the great outdoors again.

Except that it wasn't. She'd caught the bug.

Of course, Yumin got back into her active hobbies when the cast was removed and the doctor gave her the green light. But she didn't put away the crochet hook, either. She started working on more ambitious patterns, and sniffing around for other people to make things for. Eventually, at the urging of friends and family, she launched a website—Leaf & Lark—to sell some of the items she was making. And it began to do quite well. She was not only covering the costs of materials but was making more money besides, which was nice because it didn't feel like

1   An earlier version of this material was delivered in seminar form in 2018 for the University Fellowship of Christians, Hobart, and in sermon form in 2019 at Crossroads Presbyterian Church in Hobart.

work. She was being paid for doing something she'd do anyway. She was living the dream!

But was her new crochet site a business or a hobby? She didn't even think this was a question worth asking, until an uncle raised the question at a family gathering: "Do you have an ABN?"[2] Oh dear. Ignorance was bliss, but suddenly a whole new world of questions opened up before her. Yumin used Google to help her figure out if Leaf & Lark qualified as a business or a hobby. She began to drown in fact sheets and online self-assessment checklists, each covering slightly different factors and each annoyingly vague and occasionally kind of contradictory. The Australian Tax Office is reluctant to give a simplistic answer to the question "When does a hobby become a business?" but it recognizes that there is a difference between the two. Rather than offering a simple definition, they provide information that is intended to add up to a clear answer.

In these next two chapters, I will argue that the difference between a church and a parachurch is quite similar to the difference between a business and a hobby. If our theological principles and definitions are too simplistic, then we end up reaching quite extreme conclusions such as 'every parachurch really is a church' or 'all parachurches are bad'. Instead, we need to have a clear understanding of how the Bible defines a church, and then think carefully about how this understanding helps us to define all the other activities and organizations Christians might be involved in.

So what is the church?

The universal church

When we think about the church, we must not immediately jump to thinking about Sunday services, parish councils and crèche rosters. The church is very different to a secular business at this point.

2   Australian Business Number.

In the first place, the church is *the heavenly gathering of all those saved by Christ*. The Greek words translated in most of our English translations as 'church' mean 'assembly', 'gathering' or 'congregation'. The particular 'gathering' that is the church of Christ is spiritual, heavenly, universal and glorious. This is pictured beautifully in Hebrews 12:

> You have come to Mount Zion, to the city of the living God, the heavenly Jerusalem. You have come to thousands upon thousands of angels in joyful assembly, to the church of the firstborn, whose names are written in heaven. You have come to God, the Judge of all, to the spirits of the righteous made perfect, to Jesus the mediator of a new covenant, and to the sprinkled blood that speaks a better word than the blood of Abel. (Heb 12:22-24)

How can it be said that we "have come" to the heavenly Jerusalem —not that we are "going to come", but we "have come"? In what sense are we Christians, scattered throughout the world, actually assembled with the "church of the firstborn", together with God and his angels? It doesn't feel like that. I'm sitting on my couch, with a cup of coffee on my left and my dog curled up asleep on my right. Is this just a statement of the future reality we share—a reality so certain that we can say it has come, because God has promised it to us?[3]

I think it's stronger than that. There is a genuine sense in which we *really have come* to a heavenly assembly. The answer lies in our spiritual *union with Christ* by his Spirit. Because of our spiritual union with Christ, we are spiritually "seated ... with him in the heavenly realms" (Eph 2:6). And because all Christians are united with Christ, we are also all united to one another. To be saved is to be united with Christ together with all his people in Christ.

---

3   Chase Kuhn unpacks various approaches to this question in CR Kuhn, *The Ecclesiology of Donald Robinson and D. Broughton Knox: Exposition, analysis, and theological evaluation*, Wipf and Stock, 2017, pp 105-110, 187-190.

Consider the way in which the book of Ephesians speaks about the church. The church is made up of those who are "blessed ... in the heavenly realms with every spiritual blessing in Christ. For he chose [them] in him before the creation of the world to be holy and blameless in his sight" (1:3-4). The blessings we have received in him are listed in verses 4 to 14: election for holiness; predestination for adoption; redemption and forgiveness; revelation of his end-time purposes; and sealing by the Holy Spirit. All these blessings came to us when we were "included in Christ" (v 13).

This union with Christ is explored further in the next chapter:

> But because of his great love for us, God, who is rich in mercy, made us alive with Christ even when we were dead in transgressions—it is by grace you have been saved. And God raised us up with Christ and seated us with him in the heavenly realms in Christ Jesus, in order that in the coming ages he might show the incomparable riches of his grace, expressed in his kindness to us in Christ Jesus. (Eph 2:4-7)

This glorious spiritual union is what lies behind the reality of the universal church that we read about in Hebrews 12. The church is the full number of all those who are truly united to Christ by faith and have truly received all the benefits of his death for sins and resurrection to new life. Those for whom Christ died ought to be thought of together, as his church whom he loved:

> Christ loved *the church* and gave himself up for her to make her holy, cleansing her by the washing with water through the word, and to present her to himself as a radiant church, without stain or wrinkle or any other blemish, but holy and blameless. (Eph 5:25b-27)

The church is a spiritual reality constituted by Christ and his gospel.

This same reality is described in Ephesians with other words: Christ's "body" and "one new humanity" (2:15-16), and "God's people", God's "household" and "a holy temple" (2:19-21). Not only are we 'in Christ', but Christ is 'in us' through the Holy Spirit (2:22; 3:16-17, 19; 5:18).[4]

Other terms used elsewhere in Scripture include "vine" (John 15:1-17), "flock" (Acts 20:28), "olive tree" (Rom 11:17-24), "Abraham's seed" (Gal 3:29), "royal priesthood" and "holy nation" (1 Pet 2:9), "foreigners and exiles" (1 Pet 2:11), "the lady chosen by God" (2 John 1), and "bride" (Rev 19:7). Each image contains its own emphasis, and therefore we must not assume that they refer to precisely the same thing. For example, not every term contains the idea of 'gathering', as the word 'church' does; and some of them, such as 'foreigners', describe God's people only as we are in this age, rather than as we will be in eternity. But taken together, these descriptions give us a fuller picture of who God's people are.

The ancient Nicene Creed describes the church less metaphorically as "one holy catholic and apostolic church", a string of adjectives that unpack for us the church's nature. There is only *one* church, gathered around Christ, and so it must be *catholic* (i.e. universal): all those who have faith in Christ are included in his church, no matter who they are, where they are from, or what they have done. The church belongs to God, and so it is *holy*: it is credited with the righteousness of Christ, and so declared to be holy, and its members are called to live holy lives—a calling which will reach its perfection in our resurrection and glorification. And the church is constituted and ruled by the *apostolic* word about Christ and his saving work: "built on the foundation of the apostles and prophets, with Christ Jesus himself as the chief cornerstone," as Ephesians 2:20 puts it.

So what is the church? The Westminster Confession of Faith summarizes it well:

> The catholic or universal Church, which is invisible, consists of the whole number of the elect, that have been, are, or shall be gathered into one, under Christ

4 Miroslav Volf describes the church as "the mutual personal indwelling of the triune God and of his glorified people" (M Volf, *After Our Likeness: The church as the image of the Trinity*, Sacra Doctrina, Eerdmans, 1998, p 128).

the head thereof; and is the spouse, the body, the full-ness of him that fills all in all.[5]

When we think about church and parachurch ministry, we must begin with this reality of the universal church: "whatever other meanings the word may bear, *this* ... must be its *leading, guiding* meaning—that which must to some extent regulate and modify the rest."[6]

But this still leaves us with the question of the nature of local churches. How does this glorious and eternal reality relate to First Baptist Church, Albury, or Magnify Church, Lexington? What is the place of the local congregation in God's purposes?

What is the local church?[7]

The local church is a faithful, formal community of Christians who gather for the purpose of meeting God in his word, praying to him, praising him, building up each other in the faith, building unbeliev-ers into the faith, loving one another, and managing the affairs of the church. The Thirty-Nine Articles of Religion (a statement of faith used by the Anglican denomination) describe the local church this way:

> The visible Church of Christ is a congregation of faith-ful men, in the which the pure Word of God is preached, and the Sacraments be duly ministered according to Christ's ordinance in all those things that of necessity are requisite to the same.[8]

5   The Westminster Confession of Faith, 1647, XXV.1.
6   W Cunningham, *Historical Theology: A review of the principal doctrinal discussions in the Christian church since the Apostolic Age*, vol 1, Banner of Truth Trust, 1969, pp 12-13, emphasis original.
7   An earlier version of this material was published as an article in the newsletter of The Vision 100 Network in September 2018.
8   The Thirty-Nine Articles of Religion, XIX, 1562. Note, however, that, in context, article XIX is probably referring to the wider church institution rather than simply a local fellowship; see L Gatiss, 'A congregation of the faithful', *Church Society*, 3 September 2019, accessed 6 September 2022 (churchsociety.org/resource/a-congregation-of-the-faithful).

It is important to notice that the local church is a church in the same kind of sense as the universal church: it is *the gathering of God's people around Christ*. The local church is a visible expression of this invisible heavenly reality (see Diagram A).[9] During his earthly ministry, Christ taught, "For where two or three gather in my name, there am I with them" (Matt 18:20). And the apostle Paul describes a solemn gathering of the Corinthian church in these striking terms: "When you are assembled and I am with you in spirit, and the power of our Lord Jesus is present ..." (1 Cor 5:4). What you see and experience in a local church is an imperfect but genuine display of the ultimate spiritual reality of the universal church. So it is mysterious, fearful, profound and wonderful.

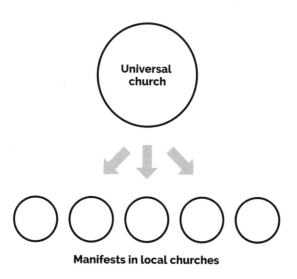

Diagram A: Local/Universal

9   The social distancing restrictions applied by governments to manage the COVID-19 pandemic in 2020 and 2021 led many churches across the world to start online church services (as well as online small groups and other meetings). This has forced us to be explicit in our reflection about the nature of church, and about whether by 'gathering' we mean 'physical gathering'; see A Heard, M Lynch and L Windsor, 'Is church online church?' [video], *Reach Australia*, YouTube, 18 May 2020, accessed 1 September 2022 (youtube.com/watch?v=JWo7DEhmW4w).

Importantly, Scripture gives no other Christian institution this kind of recognition. Fundamentally and essentially, there are not many churches, but one church of Jesus Christ (Eph 4:4-6); and this one church is then expressed in many local gatherings.[10]

A few elements of my definition need to be expanded upon. Firstly, *a true local church is faithful to God's word*. A church that departs from the fundamentals of God's word has forfeited its right to be a true Christian church in any spiritually meaningful sense. This is what is meant by 'the marks of the true church'. These marks, as outlined in The Belgic Confession, are:

> The true church can be recognized if it has the following marks: *The church engages in the pure preaching of the gospel*; it makes use of *the pure administration of the sacraments* as Christ instituted them; it *practices church discipline for correcting faults*. In short, it governs itself according to the pure Word of God, rejecting all things contrary to it and holding Jesus Christ as the only Head. By these marks one can be assured of recognizing the true church—and no one ought to be separated from it.[11]

Christ constitutes his church through his Spirit by his word. Where Christ is through his Spirit by his word, there is the church.[12]

---

10 "These local gatherings, whether at Corinth or in the cities of Galatia, or in Jerusalem, were manifestations of the one church of Christ. Christ had gathered them, and he himself was present according to his promise where two or three were met together in his name. Thus they were gathered round Christ through his Spirit, and consequently nothing was lacking for a complete church of Christ. They were never spoken of as part of Christ's church because they were Christ's church, gathered by him round himself at a certain time in a certain place. They were manifestations of the supernal [heavenly] church of which every member of the local church was at that very time a member" (DB Knox, 'The church and the denominations', *The Briefing*, 1994, 144:1-6, pp 3-4, accessed 6 September 2022 [thebriefing.com.au/1994/10/the-church-and-the-denominations]). That said, I don't think it's necessary to go so far as to say that each local church is somehow "the *whole* church" of Christ; cf. Volf, *After Our Likeness*, p 154, emphasis original.

11 The Belgic Confession, XXIX, 1619 [1561], emphasis mine.

12 Volf makes the point that the church is constituted by both the proclamation and the confession of the faith; it is constituted "from below" by the Spirit dwelling in each member, not "from above" by its leadership and their ministry (Volf, *After Our Likeness*, pp 149-152). He argues that the presence of Christ is not somehow "added" to the gathering, but present in each believer (p 156). See also GJ Spykman, *Reformational Theology: A new paradigm for doing dogmatics*, Eerdmans, 1992, pp 452-453.

Secondly, the use of the word *formal* in my definition needs unpacking. This point will become very important when we begin to think about a definition of 'parachurch' in chapter 2. By 'formal', I mean to say that the church is not just any occasional gathering of Christians that involves prayer and Bible study. A church is a gathering that formally and self-consciously calls itself 'church'. Gathering around Christ's word is a *necessary* condition for an assembly to be a Christian church, but it is not a *sufficient* condition. To be a local church, it needs to be 'formed', 'constituted', 'instituted', 'covenanted', 'planted' or 'particularized'—whatever your convictions about church government and your preferences of terminology dictate (see Diagram B).

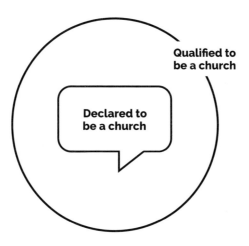

Diagram B: Declared/Qualified

As Donald Robinson writes, "Local churches are not lightly or arbitrarily formed".[13] Just as those with sound doctrine, godly lives and the ability to teach—all the necessary qualifications for eldership—still need to be appointed to eldership (1 Tim 4:14,

13   D Robinson, 'The church in the New Testament', in *Donald Robinson Selected Works*, vol 1, *Assembling God's People* (PG Bolt and MD Thompson eds), Australian Church Record, 2008, p 221.

5:22), so too does the local church require formal recognition to be a genuine local church.

Problems arise when we confuse necessary and sufficient conditions to *qualify* with necessary and sufficient conditions to *be*. Just because someone has the gifts and character to qualify as an elder doesn't automatically make them an elder. Being faster than any other person over a hundred-metre stretch might be all that is needed to win a gold medal at the Olympic Games, but this fact doesn't make you a gold medallist; you must compete (according to the rules) in the Games.

So it is with the local church. A local church is a definable entity in the New Testament. For example:

- It has leaders appointed to it (Acts 20:17).
- It has a recognized roll of widows (1 Tim 5:9-16).
- It can "come together" in a way that suggests a recognizable membership (1 Cor 5:4; 11:17-20, 32; 14:26).
- It can expel people from its midst (1 Cor 5:13).[14]

All of this demonstrates that local churches have definable boundaries—so we can meaningfully speak of *the church* of Thyatira, or *the church* that meets in the house of Priscilla and Aquila, and so on.

Thirdly, *a local church has continuity in authority, identity and relationships beyond the gathering itself.* This is why I have described the local church as a "formal community of Christians who gather", rather than "a formal gathering of Christians".

A view of church that has been immensely influential in Australia and beyond has been called the 'Knox-Robinson Corrective', due to its origins in the teaching of Broughton Knox

---

14 Even when Jesus says "where two or three gather in my name, there am I with them", the immediately preceding verses have distinguished "two or three others" who might confront a "brother or sister who sins" from "the church", to which you ultimately must go: "If they still refuse to listen [to two or three of you], tell it to the church; and if they refuse to listen even to the church, treat them as you would a pagan or a tax collector" (Matt 18:16-17); cf. M Reeves, 'What is a church? What is a CU?', *UCCF*, 11 August 2020, p 3, accessed 13 September 2022 (uccf.org.uk/about/cu-and-church); and Volf, *After Our Likeness*, p 137, fn 37.

and Donald Robinson from Moore Theological College.[15] According to Robinson, the New Testament's teaching on the local church focuses fundamentally on an activity rather than an organization. He writes:

> The church on earth ... is also *intermittent* and not continuous in character, since its every meeting involves the necessity of dispersal when the time comes ... On earth the church comes and goes, having no abiding city and no temple. Christians never know exactly who they will meet at their next assembly; and no church has any certainty that it will ever meet again. In the midst of life it is in death.
>
> It is not too much to say that the church on earth does not exist or is not visible, except in the actual assembly of believers.[16]

Taken on face value, this creates a sharp boundary around the way we think about the local church—a boundary that is difficult to work out in practice.

Do we cease to think of ourselves in relationship to others in our church as soon as the gathering is over? Does the authority of the church's leadership extend over its members beyond their time of gathering together? Doesn't the act of gathering together create a pattern of relationships that endure during the week?

While perhaps a very occasional 'assembly' might have no enduring identity, such an important, purposeful and regular 'assembly' as a Christian church is a different matter. Students don't cease to be a part of the school outside of the classroom. Politicians don't cease to operate as members of parliament out-

---

15 See Kuhn, *The Ecclesiology of Donald Robinson and D. Broughton Knox*. It must be noted that the views of Donald Robinson and Broughton Knox on the church aren't exactly the same, nor do they remain unchanged over time. Nevertheless, there are sufficient commonalities and stability to be able to speak about the 'Knox-Robinson' view of church.

16 D Robinson, 'The church of God: Its form and unity', in *Donald Robinson Selected Works*, vol 1, p 236, emphasis original.

side of its session. Teams don't cease to identify with their club when they are off the sports field.[17]

Thankfully, and to be fair, Knox and Robinson concede this (to some extent):

> Concepts of continuance do, of course, exist, in the New Testament, including continuance in the relationship established between Christians by their coming together 'in church', but such continuance is not coextensive with the activity 'the church.'[18]

> But because of our human nature and the way we do things, [fellowship] forms patterns. It is for this reason that it is possible to speak of elders of a gathering or a church when there is no gathering going on at the moment, as in Acts 20.[19]

But throughout their writings, such comments are occasional, compared to an overwhelming emphasis on the local church existing only when gathered, often expressed in absolute terms that don't easily allow for these concessions. In fact, the ongoing reality of the church as community should be more than conceded. Michael Jensen argues along these lines:

> [The Knox-Robinson model] is certainly a linguistic analysis of the usage of a particular word in the New Testament texts. Is this sufficient to provide for a proper

---

17 "I would say a basketball 'team' is still a 'team' even when its members are spending the night in different hotel rooms or cities. And they are a team in the first place, of course, because they consistently come together and do the things which constitute them as a basketball team" (J Leeman, 'Theological critique of multi-site: What exactly is a "church"?', *9Marks*, 30 September 2010, accessed 13 September 2022 [9marks.org/article/theological-critique-multi-site-what-exactly-church]).

    Graham Cole argues that the wider category of the 'people of God' is needed, otherwise the risk is that 'church' exists in a kind of "conceptual isolation" (cited in D Robinson, '"The church" revisited: An autobiographical fragment', in *Donald Robinson Selected Works*, vol 1, pp 268-269). Robinson notes Cole's suggestion with approval in a retrospective written later in his ministry. See also Kuhn, *The Ecclesiology of Donald Robinson and D. Broughton Knox*, pp 103-104.

18 Robinson, 'The church of God: Its form and unity', p 234.

19 DB Knox, 'De-mythologizing the church', in *D. Broughton Knox Selected Works*, vol 2, *Church and Ministry* (K Birkett ed), Matthias Media, 2003, p 31.

theological description of the concept of the "church"? ...
What Scripture says about the concept of "church" is
not merely confined to the way it uses the particularly
[*sic*] word "church."[20]

The church is a community of Christians who gather. This is
captured by theological descriptions of the local church that
speak of it as "the assembly of God's people—a *society* of Christians".[21] A simple example of this might be found in Acts 9:31,
which possibly refers to the scattered members of the Jerusalem
church as "the church".[22] This way of thinking about the community and gathering of God's people is also seen in the
different words used in the Old Testament to describe the community of Israel. One of these words, the Hebrew word *edah*,
"seems to refer to the congregation of Israel, whether assembled or not". This word is almost always translated by the
Septuagint Greek Old Testament with the word 'synagogue', and
is often translated as 'community' in our English translations
(see, for example, Exodus 16).[23] The activity of gathering is

---

20 Cited in Kuhn, *The Ecclesiology of Donald Robinson and D. Broughton Knox*, pp 104-105,
  emphasis original. Kuhn admits that Robinson did not fully integrate his findings with
  broader systematic theology, but questions whether this would overturn his claims
  (p 105). Jensen's point is that the biblical description of local church implies, or even
  requires, a continuity of relationship and identity for these communities. See also GR Allison, *Sojourners and Strangers: The Doctrine of the Church*, Foundations of Evangelical
  Theology, Crossway, 2012, pp 313-314, fn 47.

21 T Witherow, *The Apostolic Church: Which Is It?*, Free Presbyterian Publications, 1997 [1856],
  p 13, emphasis mine. See also Cunningham, *Historical Theology*, vol 1, p 12; and Volf, *After
  Our Likeness*, p 137.

22 Robinson says that this is "still the Jerusalem church, attenuated or dispersed through
  persecution" (Robinson, 'The church in the New Testament', pp 216-217). But this explana-
  tion undermines his insistence that 'church' must refer to a gathered assembly.

23 RL Reymond, *A New Systematic Theology of the Christian Faith*, Thomas Nelson, 1998,
  pp 806-807. On the distinction and relationship between *edah* and the Hebrew word more
  commonly used for the Israelites gathered in an assembly (*qahal*), see Kuhn, *The Ecclesiology of Donald Robinson and D. Broughton Knox*, pp 100-105. Both Hebrew words are even
  found together in the expression "the whole assembly of the congregation" (ESV) or "all the
  members of the community of Israel" (NIV; Exod 12:6; Num 14:5). Knox and Robinson draw
  on a biblical theology of gathering across the Bible as background to the New Testament
  usage of the word 'church': to be saved is to be 'gathered', while to be 'scattered' is to come
  under judgement. This background actually further enriches our appreciation of the reality
  that 'church' carries with it a broader concept of 'community'. For Israel remained 'gathered'
  (as opposed to 'scattered') in the promised land, in a sense, even when they were not
  assembling in a local synagogue or at the temple in Jerusalem.

essential to the local church, but its life and character need not be restricted to the time of gathering. Even when we are not actually gathered together, we continue to think of ourselves and live together as 'the people who gather'.

Fourthly, *caught up in this definition of what the church does are other related activities* such as baptism, the Lord's Supper, church discipline, ordaining leaders, and collecting money for use in God's work and good deeds. All these things are implied in the definition but need to be drawn out. The Lord's Supper and baptism are sometimes described as 'the sacraments' and are spoken of separately from 'the ministry of the word'. But they can also be seen as a particular kind of 'meeting God in his word': they are 'visible words'.[24] Church discipline is really a sad, negative consequence of our duty to build each other up through correcting and rebuking. Ordaining leaders and collecting money are just two examples of the kinds of things churches do when they gather that are part of "managing the affairs of the church", which go on to facilitate further meeting with God, building each other up, and loving one another.

Fifthly, *a mature local church has its own formally recognized leadership.* Christ gives the gifts of leaders to his church so that the church may be built up (Eph 4:7-13). These leaders are called various things in the New Testament, including elders, overseers, ministers, teachers and pastors. Another group are called deacons (e.g. 1 Tim 3:8-10). None of these leaders are necessary for the formation of a local church, for we are told that it was well after the churches in Lystra, Iconium and Antioch were planted that Paul and Barnabas returned and "appointed elders for them in each church" (Acts 14:23). A church is a church

---

24 "Augustine calls a sacrament *a visible word* (August. in Joann. Hom. 89), because it represents the promises of God as in a picture, and places them in our view in a graphic bodily form (August. cont. Faust. Lib. 19)" (J Calvin, *Institutes of the Christian Religion* [H Beveridge trans], IV.14.6, 1845, emphasis original, accessed 15 September 2022 [ccel.org/ccel/calvin/institutes]).

before it has its own human leaders.[25] After all, Christ is as much the head of any local church as he is of the universal church, and he rules it by his Spirit through his word. The apostle John can even provocatively declare:

> As for you, the anointing you received from him remains in you, and you do not need anyone to teach you. But as his anointing teaches you about all things and as that anointing is real, not counterfeit—just as it has taught you, remain in him. (1 John 2:27)

Even though a local church does not need its own local leadership to be a true church, it has not reached the mature state God intends for it until it has appointed its own leaders. Paul writes to Titus: "The reason I left you in Crete was that you might put in order what was left unfinished and appoint elders in every town, as I directed you" (Titus 1:5). It would be a stubborn and foolish thing for a church to resolve, like Peter Pan, to never grow up in this way. It would be a disappointing and possibly shameful thing for all its suitably qualified members to continually shirk the privilege and responsibility of formal leadership.

Sixthly, *not everyone in a local church is truly a Christian, and not every genuine Christian is a member of a local church*. The church on earth is a mixed assembly: those who are truly born again, and so are members of the universal, heavenly assembly; those who profess to be Christians, but are not truly born again; children of Christians, who may not have a formed faith of their own; and those who don't claim to be Christian, but who attend for any number of other reasons. Moreover, in the messiness of lived experience, there are genuine Christians who may not always be active members of any local church, or who may be members of churches that are not truly faithful churches at all

---

25 Depending on what you think about the connection between congregations, it could be argued that when a church doesn't have its own particular local leadership, it still has the leadership and oversight of the wider network of churches of which it is a part. We'll discuss this more in chapter 3.

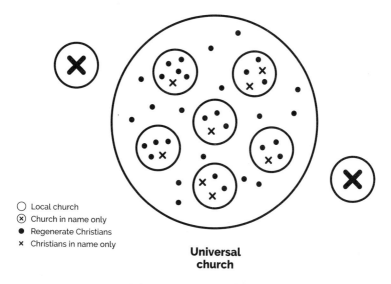

○ Local church
ⓧ Church in name only
● Regenerate Christians
✕ Christians in name only

Universal church

Diagram C: Invisible/Visible

(see Diagram C).[26] These are not ideals to be celebrated, but realities to be recognized. This is the mixed nature of the visible church in this present age.

Finally, *a local church is not simply a means to an end*. It would be easy to read my definition and see the local church as a very functional thing: a body that meets to satisfy certain purposes, and then, once the desired outcomes are attained, simply adjourns its meeting. But this misses the fact that the gathering of the local church is a good thing in itself.

God's purpose is to gather his people to himself and to dwell among us. This purpose can be traced across the whole Bible. God gathers Israel to himself at Sinai and then brings the nation into the promised land, where he intends for them to regularly gather at the temple for the great feasts. Later, his judgement on their godlessness was to scatter them to the

---

26 This is one of the important points that the concept of 'invisible church' is seeking to make: the true church is never fully contained by the institutional church; see Westminster Confession, XXV.1-2 and 4-5. As Augustine said, "there are many sheep outside and many wolves inside" (cited in H Bavinck, *Reformed Dogmatics* [J Bolt ed], abridged edn, Baker Academic, 2011, pp 593, 600-601). Although see warnings about the dangers of the invisible/visible distinction in Spykman, *Reformational Theology*, pp 438-439.

nations through the conquests of Assyria and Babylon, by which process they become "not a people".[27] And yet, the prophetic hope was that he would one day come and gather them to himself once more, in a kind of new exodus.

This final 'gathering' is what Jesus is bringing about as he builds his church. When God's saved and glorified people meet together in loving fellowship, with God in their midst, God's purposes reach their fulfilment. So there is something wonderful about the very fact of gathering. These purposes of meeting God, building each other up, and loving each other are not mere 'SMART Goals' for which we assemble out of mere pragmatic efficiency.[28] They are the fulfilment of the very things that God saved us to be: people who love the Lord our God with all our heart and mind and soul and strength and love our neighbours as ourselves.[29] As John Stott writes:

> We are not only Christian people; we are also church people. We are not only committed to Christ, we are also committed to the body of Christ. At least I hope so. I trust that none of my readers is that grotesque anomaly, an un-churched Christian. The New Testament knows nothing of such a person. For the church lies at the very centre of the eternal purpose of God. It is not a divine afterthought. It is not an accident of history. On

27 1 Peter 2:10; cf. Hosea 2:23.
28 'SMART' is a management acronym which stands for 'Specific, Measurable, Achievable, Relevant and Time-framed Goals'.
29 However, I don't agree with Donald Robinson and Broughton Knox that since the church is the end goal of God's mission, the church itself therefore cannot have a mission of its own—in other words, that mission is the activity of *Christians* but not of *the church*; see DB Knox, 'Heaven is people' in *D. Broughton Knox Selected Works*, vol 2, p 248; and Robinson, 'The church of God: Its form and unity', p 242. The end goal of the church is a dynamic, not a static, reality. We manifest our being both as we enjoy loving fellowship with God and one another, and as we serve his purposes in the world. As those entrusted with God's word in the world (1 Tim 3:15; 1 Pet 2:4-10), local churches—not merely individual Christians—are responsible for the proclamation of that word. See MD Thompson, 'Does the local church have a mission?', in *Exploring the Missionary Church* (BG Webb ed), Explorations 7, Anzea Publishers, 1993, pp 1-25; and DA Williams, *Relocating Holism: A theology of care for the poor in conversation with Sydney Anglicanism* [dissertation], Fuller Theological Seminary, 2017. Removing evangelistic mission from the responsibilities of the church leaves this vital work without the oversight of any biblical institution.

the contrary, the church is God's new community. For his purpose, conceived in a past eternity, being worked out in history, and to be perfected in a future eternity, is not just to save isolated individuals and so perpetuate our loneliness, but rather to build his church, that is, to call out of the world a people for his own glory.[30]

The importance of gathering

I want to take a moment to pause to reflect positively on the fact that the local church is a community of Christians *who gather*. This will be important in some of the chapters that follow, especially chapter 3 (on denominations) and chapter 12 (on megachurches and multi-site churches). As we have already seen, the local church manifests the ultimate reality that Christ has gathered his people to himself by his work of salvation. So the act of gathering is not merely a matter of practicality or tradition; it is in itself a significant spiritual act. We are the church of God and we express that by gathering on earth as the church of God. While there are all sorts of exceptions due to health and special needs, work, living arrangements and unusual circumstances, the normal and regular pattern of the Christian life involves the church community gathering weekly and then scattering to serve God throughout the week, still connected with one another as the community which gathers, and gathering in all sorts of smaller groups in between.

The weekly gathering of God's people with their local church is a vital part of the normal way that God's people worship God, grow in their faith and minister to one another. These gatherings also become powerful ways in which unbelievers can not only hear the gospel but also see it at work in the life of the

---

30 J Stott, *Living Church: Convictions of a lifelong pastor*, IVP, Downers Grove, 2011, pp 19-20. See also the critique of "secularizing the church ... as a voluntary society" in DW Taylor, *Like a Mighty Army? The Salvation Army, the church, and the churches*, Pickwick Publications, 2014, pp 133-134.

church community. The New Testament also teaches at several points that there is an authority properly entrusted to the local church community as a gathered entity. For example, the stern responsibility of church discipline involves a declaration by the church as a gathered congregation (Matt 18:17-18; 1 Cor 5:4-5).

The social-distancing restrictions imposed in response to the COVID-19 pandemic have forced Christians to think about these things on a large scale. The power of modern livestreaming and video conferencing technology has meant that Christians could still connect with one another even when unable to meet in person. How are we to think about these online events? Are they not church at all? A poor substitute for the real thing? Or just as much church as a pre-COVID, in-person gathering? Is it appropriate to celebrate the Lord's Supper over Zoom? Is it a good idea to continue offering livestreaming as a normal way to participate in church? These were questions that some churches had already considered as they adopted livestreaming 'online church' or multi-site congregations primarily using a large amount of video content. But they suddenly became questions that almost every church had to think about.

I have weighed into these discussions on various occasions, arguing that the kind of gathering assumed and expected in the Scriptures is *physical* gathering, while realizing that online meetings are "kind of church", but in a sub-optimal way.[31] Our embodied existence matters: we are saved by an incarnate, resurrected Saviour and called to a glorified resurrection hope, and we live out that salvation in our bodies in this age. In the light of these discussions, the definition of the local church provided above could be clarified by saying that "the local church is a community of Christians who gather *physically*". There is great potential to use video conferencing technology to make some kind of fellowship possible for those who would otherwise

---

31 Heard, Lynch and Windsor, 'Is church online church?'; and M Lynch, *The Knox-Robinson View of Church and Livestreaming* [audio file], University Fellowship of Christians website, 24 March 2020, accessed 23 March 2022 (ufcutas.org/content/knox-robinson-view-church-and-livestreaming-%E2%80%94-episode-1).

struggle to attend church meetings in person, but it is not fitting to build the whole pattern of church life around physical gathering being an optional extra.

The centrality of the church

The church is enormously important to God's purposes in salvation history. No other Christian institution is given such importance in God's word. Ephesians 1 tells us that Christ rules all things with an interest in the wellbeing and glory of the church: he rose from the dead and ascended "far above all rule and authority, power and dominion, and every name that is invoked, not only in the present age but also in the one to come"; and this resurrection and ascension to rule as the "head over everything" was "*for* the church" (1:21-22). That is how important the church is to Christ's purposes in the universe. The church is the focal point of a larger work of God "to be put into effect when the times reach their fulfilment—to bring unity to all things in heaven and on earth under Christ" (v 10).[32] The church is so identified with Christ and his work that it is called "his body, the fullness of him who fills everything in every way" (v 23).

God gathers the church not only for our good, but also for his glory. The repeated idea in Ephesians 1 is that we are blessed "to the praise of his glory" (v 14; cf. vv 6, 12). Chapter 2 tells us we are saved together with Christ "in order that in the coming ages he might show the incomparable riches of his grace" (v 7). Paul presents a similar idea in chapter 3: "His intent was that now, through the church, the manifold wisdom of God should be made known to the rulers and authorities in the heavenly realms, according to his eternal purpose that he accomplished in Christ Jesus our Lord" (vv 10-11).

---

32 The Greek word translated here "bring unity" includes the word translated "head" elsewhere in Ephesians. So the NIV 1984 translation: "to bring all things in heaven and on earth together under one head, even Christ."

PART 1: THEOLOGICAL FOUNDATIONS

The universal church, manifested on earth in local churches, is of great importance in God's purposes. When we see the church in the light of God's work, we see more than an imperfect institution or an awkward fellowship. The church is, as CS Lewis has his fictional devil Screwtape describe it, "spread out through all time and space and rooted in eternity, terrible as an army with banners ... a spectacle which makes our boldest tempters uneasy".[33]

~

Where, then, does the church end and other Christian activity begin? Is there such a thing as a Christian ministry that is *not* church, and, if so, how should we think about such ministries? This is where we turn in chapter 2.

33 CS Lewis, *The Screwtape Letters with Screwtape Prepares a Toast*, Harper Collins, 2002, p 5.

Chapter 2: What is the parachurch?[1]

We are faced with the reality of a great deal of Christian ministry that does not take place in the weekly gathering of the local church, is not sponsored or governed by the local church, and is sometimes not even sponsored or governed by any denomination. In their book *The Prospering Parachurch*, Wesley Willmer, J David Schmidt and Martyn Smith include an appendix of a dizzying taxonomy of sixteen types of parachurch ministries.[2] These organizations present all sorts of practical complications, as well as more abstract theological complexities. Worse still, our practical experience can confuse our theological reflection, so that we slip into arguing on the basis of our fond personal experiences with this or that parachurch, our personal commitment to our local church, or simply 'what works'. On top of this, lack of theological clarity can lead to further practical difficulty as we use words

1   An earlier version of the material in this chapter was delivered in seminar form in 2018 for the University Fellowship of Christians, Hobart; and in sermon form in 2019 in Hobart at Crossroads Presbyterian Church.
2   Arts/culture; associations; audiovisual/media; camps/conferences; constituency-based ministries; consulting; counselling/guidance; education; environmental/agricultural; evangelism; health care; legal assistance/political action; missions; printed media; relief and development; social services. See Willmer et al., *The Prospering Parachurch*, pp 201-214.

in slippery ways, which lead us into a tangle of confusions and contradictions.

How are we to think about such groups? In this chapter, I want to begin by proposing a broad definition of 'parachurch' before exploring whether such a definition is even sustainable (is there such a thing as a parachurch?) or justifiable (should there be such a thing as a parachurch?). Lastly, I argue that parachurch ministries are, in fact, desirable for the wider Christian community and 'gospel ecosystem'.

What is a parachurch?[3]

A simple definition of 'parachurch' is *organized Christian activity that is distinct from the visible, institutional church*. This definition is extremely broad: it doesn't clarify whether the church should be understood as local or regional, and so it forces us to consider whether denominations (and denominational organizations) are a kind of parachurch.[4] It speaks of "organized Christian activity" rather than "Christian organizations", and so forces us to consider whether 'little churches within the church',[5] informal fellowships, or even the Christian household might be considered as parachurches. It doesn't clarify what kind of distinction from the church is needed, and so potentially includes within its scope meetings of church elders and church small groups— or any meetings that are distinct from a local church in its

---

3   There is little clarity gained by studying the Greek origins of the prefix 'para' (so N Jason, 'The relationship between church and para-church: Biblical principles', in BJ Nicholls [ed], *The Church: God's agent for change*, Paternoster, 1986, p 200). The prefix in 'parachurch' most likely just means 'auxiliary' and/or 'ancillary', such as in similar words like 'paramilitary' and 'paramedic'.

4   We will return more fully to questions surrounding denominations in chapter 3.

5   *Ecclesiolae in ecclesia* was an expression used by Martin Luther in the 16th century to describe deliberate smaller fellowships in which more thoroughgoing spiritual reformation might take place. This concept found expression in the conventicles or *collegia pietatis* in 17th-century German Pietists and the Dutch Nadere Reformatie. See DM Lloyd-Jones, 'Ecclesiola in ecclesia', address given at the Puritan and Westminster Conference, 1965, accessed 13 September 2022 (the-highway.com/ecclesia_Lloyd-Jones.html).

entirety but are subgroups of that church.

Some definitions of parachurch build conclusions into the definition. Willmer, Schmidt and Smith cite two definitions before providing their own, which consists of four tests:

Test 1:   Is the group organized as a non-profit?

Test 2:   Does the group have a Christian mission statement?

Test 3:   Is the group independent of traditional church structures?

Test 4:   Does the group work at one or more specific ministries or services?[6]

While very useful, this is far too narrow for a starting definition. It rules out, for example, consideration of denominational parachurch organizations and informal, organic parachurch ministries.

In his book *The Church and the Parachurch*, Jerry White proposes a definition for the "para-local church" (his term) which is deliberately broader: "Any spiritual ministry whose organization is not under the control or authority of a local congregation."[7] This doesn't require formal organization of a parachurch, which is helpful. But White's definition adds slightly different limitations. For example, he potentially rules out a Christian soccer league by defining the parachurch as a "spiritual ministry". He also excludes the possibility of a local church overseeing a parachurch ministry—such as a school founded and governed by a church. White simply asserts that denominational associations and agencies are ultimately not significantly different from any other parachurch, an assertion we will properly evaluate in chapter 3 below.[8]

In his article 'Nine marks of a healthy parachurch ministry', Mack Stiles says a defining characteristic is that "parachurch

---

6   Willmer et al., *The Prospering Parachurch*, p 14.

7   JE White, *The Church and the Parachurch: An uneasy marriage*, Multnomah Press, 1983, p 19.

8   White writes: "*We must recognize every ministry structure other than a local congregation as a para-local church structure* … Denominational structures … are all para-local church structures." At this point, White has shifted his definition from "any spiritual ministry whose organization is not under the control or authority of a local congregation" to "any ministry structure other than a local congregation" (*The Church and the Parachurch*, p 65, emphasis original).

ministries have only a narrow slice of the church's responsibilities and prerogatives".[9] But by confusing what *is* with what he believes *should be*, he doesn't include the (unhealthy?) parachurch that is all-encompassing.[10] Stiles's description also starts by making a judgement about those who argue that the church can legitimately be said to exist in forms other than the local church—such as the regional church, or the 'sodality' (we will talk about 'sodalities' under the heading 'Is there such a thing as a parachurch?' below).

Philip Schmutz's definition is also very broad, while acknowledging the existence of denominations. Parachurch, according to Schmutz, is "a Christian organization with one or more specific Christian purposes functioning with a large degree of independence from any one local church or denomination".[11] My main concern with his definition is that it makes independence a key marker of the parachurch, where I will argue that a parachurch might be seen as distinct from the local church in other ways.

Like others, my definition is extremely broad by design: I want to start with a description that captures all the various phenomena that might in some way be considered parachurches, and even include other activities and groups we would ordinarily *not* think of as parachurches. This will force us to think with theological clarity about the whole. Here, then, is my definition:

> A parachurch is organized Christian activity that is distinct from the visible, institutional church.

This definition has three components. First, a parachurch is *organized activity*. A parachurch need not be formally organized

---

9   JM Stiles, 'Nine marks of a healthy parachurch ministry', *9Marks*, 1 March 2011, accessed 13 September 2022 (9marks.org/article/journalnine-marks-healthy-parachurch-ministry)

10 This is also the problem with those who use the term 'sodality' to describe parachurches, if the 'sodality' is defined as being restricted in membership and/or purpose. Such a definition excludes holistic parachurches with open membership. See 'Is there such a thing as a parachurch?' below.

11 P Schmutz, *Para-Church Organizations: A blessing and a curse for the local church*, Xulon Press, 2018, loc 118.

and constituted; it need not be an organization in some technical sense. Nevertheless, a 'parachurch' must be, in some sense, more than just "everything Christians do that isn't church". It is the element of purposeful, organized effort that makes us consider the activity as a thing with its own identity. A parachurch need not be communal activity. A solo Christian might write a blog or organize a neighbourhood soccer game with deliberate intent, but these should at least be considered as possible parachurches.

Second, a parachurch is *Christian activity*. Willmer, Schmidt and Smith's second test, "Does the group have a Christian mission statement?", is useful here.[12] For example, a group of Christians might start a not-for-profit organization with no explicitly Christian purpose *for the organization*. While their own motives will, of course, be shaped by a desire to do all things for the glory of God—and they may even hope and pray that this not-for-profit venture will open doors for evangelism or some other specifically Christian goal—the fact that they did not consider their activity to be explicitly Christian in any sense means this is not rightly regarded as parachurch. Likewise, a young adults Bible study group might plan a LAN party with no intention of this being an extension of the study group itself.[13]

On the other hand, consider an example where a group of Christians organize a more focused activity—such as a book club or a food van—where the activity has no explicitly religious component, and yet it has been very deliberately organized by Christians, acting as Christians, for Christian motivation. Such activities, I believe, could be rightly considered as parachurches. I recognize that I am establishing a fuzzy boundary here, but I think some ambiguity is necessary given how much Christian activity is relatively informal. Remember the illustration about the tax office and the definition of a business? The nature of 'Christian motivation' is a bit like that: there is usually a series of

12 Willmer et al., *The Prospering Parachurch*, p 14.
13 A 'Local Area Network' party is where computer-gaming enthusiasts gather to play multi-player games together across a local computer network.

clues that something might meaningfully be considered a para-church. A parachurch is a consciously organized Christian activity, but this doesn't mean that all parachurches need to be primarily concerned with the central activity of making disciples.

Third, a parachurch is *distinct from the visible, institutional church*. Since, as I showed in chapter 1, all true believers are part of the universal, invisible, heavenly church, there is no way Christians can be distinct from the universal church, whether they are in bed, at work, in a Sunday church meeting, or at a parachurch soup kitchen. But there is a range of ways in which a Christian activity might be distinct from the *visible, earthly, institutional church*.[14]

But what makes it distinct?

How is a parachurch distinct from the visible, institutional church?

Appeals are sometimes made to the 'marks of the true church' as a useful tool in determining the line between church and parachurch.[15] These marks, as outlined in The Belgic Confession, are:

> The true church can be recognized if it has the following marks: *The church engages in the pure preaching of the gospel*; it makes use of *the pure administration of the sacraments* as Christ instituted them; it *practices church discipline for correcting faults*. In short, it governs itself according to the pure Word of God, rejecting all things contrary to it and holding Jesus Christ as the only Head. By these marks one can be assured of recognizing the true church—and no one ought to be separated from it.[16]

14 I have not included the term 'local church' here because whether you consider a denomination to be in some sense a 'church' needs to be considered. More on this in chapter 3.
15 For example, Paul Rees is quoted at length arguing for this position in appendix A of LCWE Commission on Co-operation, *Cooperating in World Evangelization*, pp 103-105.
16 Belgic Confession, XXIX, emphasis mine.

If these things mark out a church, then might the lack of some of these marks be proof that we are dealing with a parachurch? For example, if the group doesn't practise excommunication, is it not a church? If it conducts the Lord's Supper, is it a church after all?

While I personally believe that it is appropriate to restrict the sacraments and church discipline to the church, I nevertheless want to argue that these things are not an adequate measure of what makes something a church or parachurch. Rather, these things are not practised in a parachurch because it has already been determined that it is not a church. A church might neglect these things, and so be an *unhealthy* church. But it would still be an unhealthy *church*.[17] Or a parachurch might presume to practise these things and so be a presumptuous parachurch, but it has not by that presumption suddenly become a church (see Diagram D). Using the marks of the true church to define or distinguish a church from some other Christian activity is to

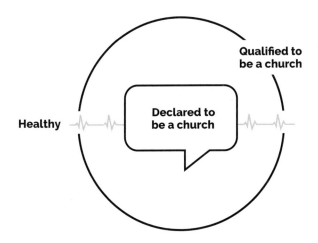

Diagram D: Healthy/Unhealthy

17 Consider the difficulty that the Society of Friends and the Salvation Army, neither of which administer the Lord's Supper or baptism, present for the World Council of Churches; see Taylor, *Like a Mighty Army?*, pp 102-111.

misunderstand the purpose of these marks.[18] They were not intended to be a *complete definition* of the visible church, nor a *full description* of the visible church, let alone a *clarification* of what makes the visible church different from other Christian activity. Rather, they were intended to be *an evaluative test to see whether a church was true or false*; a way to discern the purity and legitimacy of a local church. As The Belgic Confession says:

> We believe that we ought to discern diligently and very carefully, by the Word of God, what is the true church— for all sects in the world today claim for themselves the name of "the church" ... we are speaking of distinguishing the body and fellowship of the true church from all sects that call themselves "the church".[19]

What, then, are the ways in which a parachurch might be distinct from the visible church? A few possible distinctions:

- formal constitution
- governance
- being a subset of the whole church community
- having a narrow purpose or restricted group of participants
- not being engaged in a necessary function of the church
- not being conducted by or benefitting the church.

18 John and Charles Wesley discouraged the leaders of their movement from administering the Lord's Supper. But the issue was not fundamentally because the sacraments were a mark of the church; the issue was proper authority: unordained administration would be schismatic. See MA Noll, *The Rise of Evangelicalism: The age of Edwards, Whitefield and the Wesleys*, Downers Grove, 2011, p 146. The Salvation Army didn't formally adopt the identity of 'church' until the late 20th century, and yet they administered the sacraments from the 1860s. They ceased to administer the sacraments in 1883, not primarily because they were not a church, but because the sacraments were not essential to the Christian life; cf. HIW Hill, *Officership in the Salvation Army: A case study in clericalisation* [PhD thesis], Victoria University of Wellington, 2004, pp 74-77; and Taylor, *Like a Mighty Army?*, pp 76-77. Ironically, it seems that their decision to cease was more controversial than their administration, as it was seen by some as devaluing the sacraments. It was also rightly perceived that this decision would undermine rather than uphold ordained administration in local churches; cf. Hill, *Officership in the Salvation Army*, pp 77-99; and R Hattersley, *Blood and Fire: William and Catherine Booth and their Salvation Army*, 2017, loc 4960-4987.
19 Belgic Confession, XXIX.

The most fundamental distinction is that of formal constitution: *a parachurch is distinct from the local church when it is not established as a local church.* Just as we saw in chapter 1 that a local church comes into existence when it is deliberately formed, so it is that a parachurch (whether separate from, governed by, or housed within a local church) can be formally structured to explicitly not be a church. Sometimes, a pastor or parachurch leader smirks, leans in, and says something like: "But is this network *really* a denomination?" Or: "Is this discipleship ministry *really* a church?" My answer to such curveball questions is: "No, because they don't call themselves a denomination/church." There may well be presumptuous networks and parachurches that over-reach and begin to behave as de facto denominations or churches. But, in the first place, such parachurches remain presumptuous *parachurches* (see Diagram E).

The most obvious expression of this distinction is that of governance or control: a parachurch is often under leadership that is distinct from that of any church or denominational structure. To illustrate this point, Jerry White provides a diagram, which distinguishes parachurches based on their degree of independence from local churches, as he sees it, from least independent to most independent:

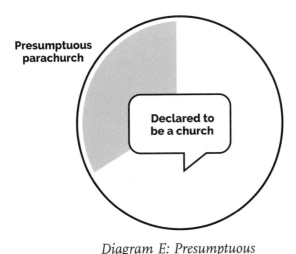

Diagram E: Presumptuous

- direct relationship to local congregations (like denominational structures and associational structures)
- church supplying (like seminaries and Christian schools)
- church planting (whether denominational or independent)
- church renewal and service (like evangelists and other service organizations)
- specialist ministries (like youth ministries, publishing houses and relief agencies).[20]

The more independent an organization's governance, the more clearly distinct it is. But there are, in fact, a range of ways to create separation between church and parachurch beyond creating an entirely separate organization. At the smallest level of distinction, a unique committee or ministry structure under the direct oversight of the local church or denomination can be established. A further step removed is to set up a separate parachurch organization, with the church or denomination retaining some degree of control through the organization's constitution.[21] But there remain many other ways in which organized Christian activity might be distinct from the church, because not all parachurches are separate organizational entities.

Some ministries are a subset of a local church. There are any number of classes, groups, activities, teams and programs that a local church (or denomination) might establish and oversee, and which can be seen as in-house parachurch ministries. These may never be seriously considered as parachurches—we normally use the word 'ministry' rather than 'parachurch' for these subgroups. But it can be enlightening to look at them through the lens of 'parachurch', for they, too, need to be conscious of their relationship and interaction with the church of which they are a part. Even those structures that are more fundamental to the operations of the church—such as a small-group structure

---

20 White, *The Church and the Parachurch*, p 65.
21 Some possibilities include: 1. some/all church officials sit on the board, and church leaders have power to appoint some/all board members; 2. church leaders have power to veto board appointments; 3. certain key decisions must be ratified by church leaders.

or an eldership meeting—could be helpfully considered as para-churches for the purposes of some types of analysis.[22] For example, there is nothing fundamental that distinguishes a small group Bible study from a house church; and yet, by continuing as a ministry *of a larger church*, it remains a kind of 'parachurch ministry' of the larger church and therefore needs to remain aligned with the larger church. Or consider that a local church's eldership meetings are just as much a 'presbytery' as a regional presbytery, since 'presbytery' simply means 'body of elders'.[23] Perhaps this shift in terminology can help us look at church elders' meetings with fresh eyes. Just as what we normally call a 'presbytery' (i.e. the regional body) needs to be careful not to undermine the individual local churches, so also even the local church's 'presbytery' needs to be conscious that it acts in service of its congregation. Similarly, just as what we normally call a denominational 'synod' or 'assembly' can give time for prayer, singing, and ministry of the word, so also even a local church's 'assembly of elders' should give time to such spiritual activities, and not devolve into a mere board meeting.

Parachurches can also be distinct by *having a narrow purpose or restricted group of participants*. The local church is responsible for a holistic ministry to all its members. Even if it may be limited in its reach by geographical and practical factors, the local church should, in principle, be open to all. Parachurches, however, might be formed to have a deliberately narrow focus (such as theological education, evangelism, or strengthening marriages) or a deliberately restricted target group (such as a particular age group or life stage, or strict membership requirements). Such restricted mem-

---

22 As another example (alongside small groups and eldership meetings), one could almost include a 6pm congregation of a large suburban church. When congregations are part of a 'local church' and do not have the autonomy to (for example) choose their own leaders or set their own budget, they operate in a strange and somewhat ambiguous conceptual space.

23 Earlier in the development of Presbyterianism, the English word 'presbytery' did have this breadth of meanings; see H Powell, *The Crisis of British Protestantism: Church power in the Puritan Revolution, 1638-44*, Politics, Culture and Society in Early Modern Britain, Manchester University Press, 2015, p 11.

bership and purpose would be unhealthy for a local church but is entirely appropriate for a specialized organization.

Yet another kind of distinction is where *a parachurch's primary activity is not a necessary function of the church*. There are many good and godly things that churches and denominations may offer which are not mandated: charitable organizations, theological colleges, demographic-based ministries, short-term missions, and many more. It can be helpful to distinguish that which is necessary and central to church life from that which is optional and peripheral. Such peripheral ministries can be seen as parachurches, and might sometimes be best established as separate organizations.

There are many other distinctions that could be relevant, but a final one worth mentioning is *whether those involved in the activity of the parachurch are members of one particular church*. A denominational nursing home or school might be founded and owned by a church but have no members of that church on its board, no members involved in the day-to-day running of the work, and no members benefitting from the organization. This entirely outsourced ministry is different from that conducted by and for the members of the church. These kinds of ministries could be cut loose without any impact on the life of the local congregation or denomination.

So in summary, there are many possible ways in which a parachurch may be distinct from a local church:

- having a formal constitution
- being governed independently
- being a subset of the whole church community
- having a narrow purpose or restricted group of participants
- not being engaged in a necessary function of the church
- not being conducted by or benefitting the church.

We can also express the range of parachurch ministries, and their varied relationship to the local church, by considering their purpose and their intended participants:

	Holistic disciple-making purpose	Narrow disciple-making purpose	Other purpose
Whole-church participation	Public church meeting (not a parachurch)	Church-wide training program	Church-wide charitable fundraiser
Narrow group of participants	Youth group	Marriage enrichment course	Political advocacy group in a local church
External participants	Christian union	Theological college	Childcare centre

Table 1: Types of parachurches

So far, then, we have a definition of the local church and a starting definition of the parachurch:

> A local church is a faithful, formal community of Christians who gather for the purpose of meeting God in his word, praying to him, praising him, building up each other in the faith, building unbelievers into the faith, loving one another, and managing the affairs of the church.

> A parachurch is organized Christian activity that is distinct from the visible, institutional church.

Now it is time to begin thinking about how these two phenomena interact. How substantial are the things that distinguish the parachurch from the church? Are they enough to meaningfully separate the parachurch from the church? For example, how watertight is the requirement that a local church formally define itself as a church? Are parachurches really just crypto-churches, and would we be better off calling them what they really are? Or do we need to change our patterns of governance and membership to make room for a broader and more diffuse idea of church? On the other hand, if we grant that the category of parachurch is substantial, how biblically legitimate are such activities and organizations? Should a meaty and thoroughgoing doctrine of the church motivate us to absorb these functions into the church, or else abandon these organizations as inappropriate, no matter how effective and well intentioned they may be?

Is there such a thing as a parachurch?

In 1974, Ralph Winter published an extremely influential article entitled 'The two structures of God's redemptive mission', in which he argued that, in the Bible and throughout Christian history, there have been two structures for God's work in the world.[24] In addition to the synagogue-type "New Testament church" (which he also called a 'modality') there is the "missionary band ... organized out of committed, experienced workers who affiliated themselves as a second decision beyond membership in the first structure" (which he also called a 'sodality').[25] Such missionary bands had a certain self-sufficient independence from any one local church, while often drawing practical and spiritual support from local churches. In his passionate and visionary book *Beyond the Local Church: How apostolic movements can change the world*, Sam Metcalf draws on Winter's work with fierce, prophetic boldness:

> The church in its apostolic, missionary form is just as equally 'church' as the church in its local, parish form. God never designed or intended either to do the work of the other.[26]

24 RD Winter, 'The two structures of God's redemptive mission', *Missiology: An International Review*, 1974, 2(1):121-139.

25 Winter, 'The two structures of God's redemptive mission', p 123. Sodality (from *solidalitas*, Latin for 'fellowship') was used very early on to describe monastic communities. Used in a general sense, sodality/fellowship is another legitimate synonym for 'parachurch'; cf. Reeves, 'What is a church? What is a CU?', p 12. I am personally reluctant to use 'sodality', as it might seem that I am therefore supporting a particular formulation of the sodality/modality framework.

26 S Metcalf, *Beyond the Local Church: How apostolic movements can change the world*, IVP, Downers Grove, 2015, p 28.

Para can mean 'not quite.' So calling something 'para' implies it's not the real or total deal ... While they may serve and be alongside, someone who is labelled 'para' never has total legitimacy in the eyes of the ones they serve ... 'The supremacy of the church local' is the view that the church in its local form is the only legitimate expression of the body of Christ ... The concept of para-church flows directly out of this truncated, inadequate concept of the church.[27]

In this way, Metcalf goes further than Winter's article by arguing that the missionary band is *as much 'church' as the local church* and that "parachurch terminology reinforces an aberrant ecclesiology—what I call 'the supremacy of the church local'— that is detrimental to the health and vibrancy of the Christian movement no matter where it is expressed".[28] It is one thing to say that parachurch ministry is as much a legitimate part of God's work in the world as church ministry is; it is something different to say that parachurch 'sodality' is as much a *church* as the local church 'modality'.

There is much to admire in Metcalf's book: his zeal for pioneering mission and leadership development; his understanding of the peculiar needs and gifts of pioneering leaders; and many of the historical examples he unearths of various kinds of 'sodalities' through the centuries. But I am not convinced that he makes a strong biblical or theological case for the necessity of seeing all these ministries as being every bit as much a mode of church as the local congregation. The weight of evidence for this approach rests much more on historical and sociological description than it does on theological principle.[29] In fact, Winter's article laid the groundwork for Metcalf's pragmatic

---

27 Metcalf, *Beyond the Local Church*, p 65.
28 Metcalf, *Beyond the Local Church*, pp 63-64. Although he was inconsistent on this matter, William Booth sometimes spoke of the Salvation Army this way: "We are, I consider, equal every way and everywhere to any other Christian organization on the face of the earth ... We hold 'the keys' as truly as any Church in existence" (cited in Taylor, *Like a Mighty Army?*, p 98).
29 cf. JS Hammett, 'How church and parachurch should relate: Arguments for a servant-partnership model', *Missiology: An International Review*, 2000, 28(2):200.

approach by arguing that the New Testament structures of church and mission were "borrowed patterns" that were not "'let down from heaven' in a special way".

For Winter, it was God's intention to model for us this kind of principled borrowing.[30] The biblical justification for this view is largely taken from the descriptive, narrative parts of the Bible, rather than the explicit teaching in the New Testament letters. The problem with this approach is that it risks reading pre-existing ideas into the Bible and drawing too many conclusions from what the text doesn't say.[31] In practice, it is not clear that sodalities need to be defined as one of 'two structures of God's redemptive mission' in order to harness the best of their dynamics. Moreover, such a framework does not remove the challenges of negotiating the relationship between the local church and other structures for ministry and mission.[32]

Another example of a similar impulse is found in the theology of Broughton Knox and Donald Robinson, which we considered in chapter 1. Knox and Robinson make much of the presence of Christ constituting the church: "For where two or three gather in my name, there am I with them" (Matt 18:20).[33]

---

30 Winter, 'The two structures of God's redemptive mission', p 123.

31 cf. BK Camp, 'A theological examination of the two-structure theory', *Missiology: An International Review*, 1995, 23(2):197-209.

32 Even in the era of the "medieval synthesis" (Winter, 'The two structures of God's redemptive mission') of diocesan church and monastery, the relationship was complex and often difficult—arguably no less than in Protestant history. Orders were started entrepreneurially, sometimes gaining approval or sanction at a later date. At various stages, the formal church hierarchy sought to exercise more control over religious orders. For example: "we strictly forbid anyone henceforth to found a new religious order. Whoever wants to become a religious should enter one of the already approved orders. Likewise, whoever wishes to found a new religious house should take the rule and institutes from already approved religious orders" ('Canons of the Fourth Lateran Council', 1215, sec 13, accessed 15 September 2022 [papalencyclicals.net/councils/ecum12-2.html]).

33 Robinson: "In view of Jesus' word [in Matthew 18:20] ... it is difficult to deny the propriety of a similar churchly expression to groups of a less regular and more informal character even than the household" (Robinson, 'The church of God: Its form and unity', p 236). Knox: "Christ had gathered them, and he himself was present according to his promise where two or three were met together in his name ... consequently nothing was lacking for a complete church of Christ" (DB Knox, 'The church and the denominations', p 3). Chase Kuhn uses the concept of a 'quorum' to describe Knox's use of Matthew 18:20; see Kuhn, *The Ecclesiology of Donald Robinson and D. Broughton Knox*, pp 156-157.

Their writings on the church are neither extensive nor systematic.[34] Moreover, it seems to me that they are not always entirely consistent in their various statements. As a result, it is not clear whether Knox or Robinson really thought that all such informal assemblies must by necessity be considered 'church'. Whatever their personal views, others clearly draw the conclusion that every single Christian fellowship is rightly called 'church'. For example, Phillip Jensen and Tony Payne write:

> In fact, any gathering in which [the preaching of God's word to the assembly of God's people] takes place is a Christian gathering (or church). When you have an Intervarsity cell group that meets together weekly, reads the Bible, prays, evangelizes their friends, cares for each other, and encourages each other, in what sense is it not a Christian church? Because it doesn't have the sacraments? Well, why doesn't it? Because if it did, we'd have to call it church. And if it became a church, we'd lose our nondenominational status and arouse conflict in the Christian community.
>
> We find ourselves in the unfortunate position of denying what we essentially are for the sake of ecclesiastical politics. It is time we came clear—the parachurch has very little that is para about it. It is a church movement. It participates in the heavenly gathering of Jesus Christ, and it gathers locally in expression of that to hear and respond to Christ's Word. It is a church.
>
> What is slightly crazy is our ongoing insistence that this midweek activity is somehow not church, and hence our dutiful occupation of pews on Sunday in order to fulfil all righteousness ... Call it church and be done with it. Stop trying to pretend that you aren't a church, when you transparently are.[35]

---

34 See Kuhn, *The Ecclesiology of Donald Robinson and D. Broughton Knox*, p 200 for an attempt to fill in the gaps on how Knox might relate Matthew 18 to the role of church leaders.

35 PD Jensen and T Payne, 'Church/campus connections: Model 1', in DA Carson (ed), *Telling the Truth: Evangelizing postmoderns*, Zondervan, 2002, pp 201-202.

When this approach is worked out consistently, we have to say that every Christian actually participates in multiple churches of different sizes, often with overlapping leadership and membership. This conclusion becomes confusing and unwieldy in practice, and we find ourselves having to label these various 'churches' with extra phrases and qualifiers:

- This local-congregation church is the kind of church that everybody considers to be their primary church (or one of their primary churches).
- This mid-week-growth-group church is in formal submission to a local-congregation church's leadership and expects everyone to ordinarily be active members of that local-congregation church.
- This is a Christian-Union-supplementary church, which we don't organize in such a way that we expect it to be a primary church community.

To work out this theology in practice also forces us to clarify different kinds of authority relationships between all these different 'churches'. For a local church to stop being involved in a local 'evangelical gospel fellowship' (and so to stop attending a combined service once a year) might ruffle feathers, but it's a legitimate decision. But for a growth group leader to announce that the group he leads will no longer participate with the local congregation it is associated with would be seen as schismatic. Why is that? If they are all equally 'church', aren't they both examples of the same thing? What I am trying to show here is that, in effect, this view ends up making even the simplest local church a kind of 'presbytery' or 'diocese' of tightly associated 'churches'.[36]

Such a position can be sustained, but *in practical outworking and everyday language* it ends up operating in line with the definition I suggested in chapter 1:

---

36 Again, this brings us into the theological territory of thinking about denominations, which we will consider in chapter 3.

> **A local church** is a faithful, formal community of Christians who gather for the purpose of meeting God in his word, praying to him, praising him, building up each other in the faith, building unbelievers into the faith, loving one another, and managing the affairs of the church.

In day-to-day life, we rightly treat this kind of local-congregation-church-that-everybody-considers-to-be-their-primary-church with a particular privilege among other kinds of 'church'. As argued in chapter 1, there are theological reasons for seeing this as a right, biblical approach. In the end, to reserve the term 'local church' for those congregations which are formally recognized as 'church' is not only theologically appropriate; it also makes talking about things much simpler and clearer.

On the other hand, a parachurch might begin to behave so much like a church, taking on so much of its function and primacy, that it has become a sort of de facto church. Like the distinction between a hobby and a business, there comes a point where a parachurch is distinguishable from a local church in name only. In such cases, hard questions must be asked about whether the parachurch needs to explore the processes that would be required for it to become a formally recognized church, or whether it should consider how it might change the way it operates to wind back the holistic scope of its ministry. Later in this book, we will consider some historical examples of parachurch ministries—like the Methodists and the Salvation Army—which ended up becoming separate denominations.

Is there such a thing as a parachurch? Yes, there is. A parachurch is the kind of organized Christian activity that is distinct from the visible, institutional church. The category of 'church' is not so broad that it necessarily swallows up all organized Christian activity. Rather, Christian activity can be organized in various ways that are practically and/or theologically distinct from the local church.

Should there be such a thing as a parachurch?

Perhaps it's true that there is such a thing as a parachurch. But just because something *is* doesn't mean it *should be*. Are these things called 'parachurches' legitimate things, let alone desirable things? Hendrik Kraemer "argued that the maintenance and extension of missionary societies amounted to the perpetuation of a deformity of the Church".[37] And Sam Metcalf wrote that "parachurch terminology reinforces an aberrant ecclesiology".[38] Is this correct?

Some parachurch activities might be undesirable because of their particular goals or approach—they are ill conceived. Some parachurches might be poorly organized, an unnecessary duplication of what already exists, or, worse still, they might be the fruit of schism or ungodly vanity.

But others might be ill conceived at an even deeper level. A parachurch seeking extremely broad-based ecumenical[39] unity could be considered a fool's errand that will inevitably compromise true doctrine and godliness, undermine proper church governance, or, at the very least, distract from productive Christian ministry. For example, a Christian tradesmen's guild could be considered a redundant cause for Christians to gather around —why not just participate as good citizens in the secular guild?

But although we might disagree on which parachurch enterprises are ill conceived, we can recognize that this does not make the very concept of parachurch a bad thing.

Some might argue that, wherever possible, organized Christian activity must be owned by the visible church community and governed by the visible church and its leadership. In this view, it is an abdication of the church's responsibility when it surrenders some of its key roles to external ministries, or perhaps even to secular groups. Steve Timmis and Tim Chester make a strong case for

---

37 LCWE Commission on Co-operation, *Cooperating in World Evangelization*, p 19.

38 Metcalf, *Beyond the Local Church*, p 64.

39 Meaning 'worldwide', ecumenical has come to describe efforts to unite all true Christians together under one umbrella organization. We will discuss this more in chapter 12.

this kind of approach in their book *Total Church*. They say that the church is the divinely mandated institution, entrusted with God's word and work, bound to love one another in everyday life:

> Whether we are thinking about evangelism, social involvement, pastoral care, apologetics, discipleship or teaching, the content is consistently the Christian gospel and the context is consistently the Christian community. What we do is always defined by the gospel, and the context is always our belonging in a church.[40]

The saying "the parachurch only exists because the local church has failed" captures this view well.[41]

Such a 'big' view of the local church is excellent in what it affirms. It is, indeed, tragic when the local church is reduced to a *mere* assembly, where people gather to passively mumble through some songs, take a shot glass of communion wine and a crouton of bread, possibly stick around for a glass mug of instant coffee, and then leave. Our assemblies can facilitate more of the mutual edification we glimpse in 1 Corinthians 14:26, and our church community life can extend into more meaningful relationships throughout the week.[42] What a shame it is when we don't live out the fullness of who we are!

---

40 T Chester and S Timmis, *Total Church: A radical reshaping around gospel and community*, Inter-Varsity Press, 2007, p 16. See also quotes from Steve Tibbert in Reeves, 'What is a church? What is a CU?', p 1.

41 Although, as Calvin Chen helpfully observes, there is no time in history when the church was doing everything that parachurches now do. In the case of university ministries, he points out that parachurch campus ministries were established at the same time that modern universities came into existence: "Parachurch college ministries don't exist because churches weren't doing their job; they came about because the university came about. People needed to hear the gospel or sought people to pray with in these brand new contexts" (C Chen, 'Move, parachurch—get out the way! (Part 1 of 4)', *Calvin's Chronicles*, 22 September 2015, accessed 15 September 2022 [calvindc.wordpress.com/2015/09/22/move-parachurch-get-out-the-way-part-1]).

42 See Tony Payne's explorations of such things towards the end of T Payne, 'The gathering: thinking afresh about church', *The Briefing*, 2003, 302:13-18, accessed 15 September 2022 (matthiasmedia.com/briefing/2003/11/worship-iii-the-gathering-thinking-afresh-about-church). Or at much greater depth in his PhD thesis: T Payne, *A Theological Ethic of 'One-another Edifying Speech' in the Christian Community* [PhD thesis], Moore Theological College, 2019.

But this 'big' view of the local church is problematic in what it denies; therefore, it has certain dangerous tendencies. The in-house teaching and training of all church leaders can become vulnerable to eccentricity and groupthink. The immersive intensity of a gospel community can begin to bear the marks of a dangerous 'cult', where leadership and community expectations become more and more invasive and demanding. The attempts at counselling, world mission and practical support can suffer from a lack of the specialist expertise required to truly care for people. Normal human preferences for demographic-based relationships (like those provided in youth groups) and personal friendships (such as holidaying with those around whom one feels relaxed) can be smothered or neglected. The overall experience can become so burdensome upon the church that the whole church collapses under the strain.[43] Ultimately, I question the assertion that all mission and ministry should properly be conducted by the local church wherever possible.[44]

A similarly unhelpful view can be held at the denominational level, especially by those who believe in the authority of the denominational structure over local churches. It is the denomination that is entrusted with the ministry of the word and the care for God's people, they argue, and so any ministry activity separate from the visible church is a rogue ministry, trespassing on its territory.

---

43 An example of the unrealistic idealism is where Chester and Timmis suggest that a full-time pastor feeling the need to have a day off from the members of his local church is as dysfunctional as if a husband felt the need to have a day off from his family; see Chester and Timmis, *Total Church*, p 121. Not only do they ignore the fact that even nuclear family members have various levels of preference for time and space from one another, but the comparison also clumsily transfers aspects of the nuclear biological family to the local institutional church family without justification. The biblical usage of 'family' does not imply or require the same kind of intimacy and comfort that a happy nuclear family experiences. I return to this in chapter 13 below.

44 Pieter Tuit provides the distinction between a "church-shaped mission" and a "mission-shaped church" approach: "the former believes there is life and also Christian and kingdom life outside the church. The latter sees all of life in all its relationships only within the confines of the church." He argues the church-shaped mission approach is more biblical. See PC Tuit, *A Study and Comparison of the Relationship Between Church and Kingdom in the Missiologies of Johan H. Bavinck and David J. Bosch*, Calvin Theological Seminary, 2000, pp 155-159, 186-191.

In his theological preamble to the Lausanne occasional paper on church/para-church relationships, John Stott provides a slogan: "independence of the church is bad, co-operation with the church is better, service as an arm of the church is best."[45] Stott is not explicit about what he means by 'church' in this slogan, but the context suggests that he must mean the denomination rather than the local church. Denominational opposition to the parachurch often focuses on slightly different factors than the local church objections we have already considered: it focuses on unity and control.

In the first place, parachurches can be perceived to be antisocial, blazing ahead with their independent work and turning their backs on the fellowship of God's people.[46] While this is, of course, true of many parachurches, it is not unavoidably true, as if the very establishment of a parachurch is divisive. As Stott concedes, "co-operation with the church is better".[47] The blanket accusation of disunity really assumes certain things about the authority of the local church or denomination.[48] It's not a particularly big deal if you step out from under an optional structure; but if you step out from under a more formal structure, you are making a statement of defiance in some way—much as leaving a social cricket game early is different than leaving work early. The accusation of divisiveness assumes that all Christian ministry must be conducted under the leadership of the visible church.

This leads us to the second common denominational objection to parachurches: *they are accused of unauthorized ministry.* This objection is especially focused on those parachurch ministries that have a strong Bible-teaching or discipleship component. Some people argue that Christ gave 'the ministry of the word'

---

45 LCWE Commission on Co-operation, *Cooperating in World Evangelization*, p 11.

46 RB Kuiper argues that one reason "why evangelistic activity should ordinarily be supervised and directed by the organized church … [is t]hus every believer by virtue of his being a church member will automatically have at least some part in evangelism, and it will not be left to a few who have a special liking for it" (RB Kuiper, *The Glorious Body of Christ*, Eerdmans, 1966, p 242).

47 LCWE Commission on Co-operation, *Cooperating in World Evangelization*, p 11.

48 This concern is heightened when there is an established state church, such as the Church of England.

only to the ordained elders of the church. It is highly irregular, if not completely out of order, for an unlicensed person to presume to be a teacher of the word of God.[49] This can seem especially alarming when such teaching comes in the context of a parachurch ministry that also has an intensive pastoring component or a proactive leadership development component. These problems become acute when a parachurch accepts in fellowship someone who is under discipline by their home church or endorses in ministry someone who is deemed unfit for leadership by their home church.

But, as I will argue in the next section ('The benefits of parachurches'), not all Christian leadership and discipleship can or should be restricted to the ordained eldership of the church. It is helpful to single out the ordained teachers and leaders of the church and give their leadership roles a particular priority and authority in the life of God's people on earth. But it is not biblical to say that Christian teaching and leadership must be restricted exclusively to the ordained teaching and leadership of the church.[50] While John Stott is right to say that "independence of the church is bad" (if by 'independence' he really means 'isolation'), he goes too far when he says, "service as an arm of the church is best".[51] Service as an arm of the church can certainly be good in all sorts of ways. But is it necessarily *best*?

A former professor of missiology recently commented, while smiling, sighing, and shrugging: "The theological case in favour

49 This was one of Charles Wesley's great concerns with regard to the Methodist movement that he helped lead with his brother John. He often quoted in his letters to John the principle that "ordination is separation" (JR Tyson, 'Charles Wesley and the Church of England: A commemorative essay', *Anglican and Episcopal History*, 2007, 76(4):472).

50 Edmund Clowney writes: "The church, shattered by denominational division, dare not label parachurch organizations illegitimate. In part, they are simply activities of church members. In an undivided church, there would be 'lay' organizations, under the broad oversight of the government of the church, but not the immediate responsibility of the government of the church officers (as there are in the Catholic Church). In part, they represent shared ministries across denominational barriers. That such ministries may be regarded as irregular in denominational polity may reveal more about sectarian assumptions in the polity than about violations of New Testament order" (cited in Reeves, 'What is a church? What is a CU?', p 13).

51 LCWE Commission on Co-operation, *Cooperating in World Evangelization*, p 11.

of a denominational world missions board is much stronger, but practically the non-denominational missionary societies have won the day."[52] Must we resign ourselves to this as a sub-standard reality? Are we left with a dirty compromise of *realpolitik*? Or could it be that our neat, tidy, well-argued systems are too neat—neater than the prescriptions of God's word? On this level, the view of Jensen and Payne outlined above may be unwieldy and impractical, but it serves us well by driving us back to the biblical material: what does the Bible *actually* say about 'church'? In many ways, those who want to give para-churches the label 'church' are also trying to make everything neat and tidy (see the previous section: 'Is there such a thing as a parachurch?'). In fact, more than simply tolerating para-churches, we can appreciate that they are, in fact, a good thing.

The benefits of parachurches

There is, in fact, an important theological place for para-churches, not to mention many practical benefits that flow from their existence. Parachurches are the many and varied manifes-tations of Christian fellowship, within and between local churches, for the cause of the gospel and the practice of all sorts of good deeds in the world. Such fellowship flows from the uni-versal authority of the Lord Jesus Christ, and is spiritually grounded in our (i.e. the universal church's) fellowship with God in Christ by the Holy Spirit, and in all the blessings and promises of God.[53] This fellowship is manifested and enjoyed not only in the formal community of the local church, but beyond it in many and various ways.[54]

Parachurches facilitate broader forms of Christian unity and fel-lowship than local churches can and than denominations should.

52 Personal conversation with the author.
53 On our fellowship with God in Christ by the Holy Spirit, see 1 Cor 1:9; 2 Cor 13:14; Phil 2:1; 1 John 1:3, 6. On the blessings and promises of God, see 1 Cor 10:16; Gal 3:14; 1 Pet 5:1; 2 Pet 1:4.
54 Acts 2:42; Rom 15:26; 2 Cor 1:7, 8-9; Gal 2:9; Phil 1:5; Phlm 1:17; Heb 10:33, 13:16; 1 John 1:3, 7.

Given our deep spiritual union with all true Christians, there is a godly desire to reach out to fellow Christians in our neighbourhood and around the world; it is part of living in the light of eternity. We hope that demonstrable harmony, despite massive diversity, will adorn the gospel, and we expect that broad collaboration will make all sorts of great things possible for the kingdom of God. There are good reasons why local churches and denominations make narrow doctrinal statements and specific practical rulings: they do this so they can carry on communal life together and agree on a deep understanding of biblical doctrine, so that the truth can be faithfully passed on. They are not claiming that agreement on all these matters is required for someone to be a genuine member of the universal church.[55] But at the very least, full participation in the leadership of a church normally requires agreement to the church's doctrinal statement. By contrast, parachurches can facilitate a broader kind of fellowship—one which does not depend on the same level of agreement. Mack Stiles writes: "Parachurch ministries often have the luxury of ignoring secondary doctrines. After all, I didn't care that much about the mode of someone's baptism when I was in a parachurch ministry."[56]

It is important to stress that no particular kind of broad unity and interdenominational fellowship is commanded in Scripture; these parachurch partnerships are simply diverse attempts

---

55 In fact, many churches welcome members who do not subscribe to the finer points of their own doctrinal confessions. For example: "A communicant member is a person who has been baptised and has made a credible declaration of their faith in Jesus Christ as their Saviour" (*An Introduction to the Presbyterian Church of Australia*, Code Committee of the General Assembly of the Presbyterian Church of Australia, 2004, p 7, accessed 15 September 2022 [presbyterian.org.au/images/downloads/about-pca/An-Introduction-to-the-PCA-Booklet.pdf]). Independent congregational churches often require more complete doctrinal agreement because of the power of the congregation in their view of church government.

56 Stiles, 'Nine marks of a healthy parachurch ministry'. Stiles warns: "But this luxury can lead to an open dismissal of church doctrine, as if secondary doctrine is unimportant. When I became an elder of a new and growing church plant, those doctrines which I had set aside as a parachurch worker suddenly took on great importance. How do we handle people whose divorce was unbiblical? What will church discipline look like? What should the requirements for church membership be? What is our church's responsibility to the poor? How do we teach on baptism? What is our position on women in ministry?"

at cooperation. We have to restrain our hopes with realism that such efforts can become an aimless waste of time and that loving relationships and effective ministry might be better promoted by carrying on ministry in parallel, rather than constantly trying to thrash out (or paper over) our points of disagreement. Nevertheless, broad association is one of the great things about parachurches.

Somewhat paradoxically, parachurches facilitate broader fellowship than the church, and yet they can also *facilitate narrower forms of Christian unity and fellowship than local churches or denominations should.* There are very few, if any, denominations that formally affirm and deny everything that a Christian might want to affirm or deny. Perhaps the most controlling local church might aspire to make a ruling on every possible matter, but that would not be a good thing at all. This means that there are matters of belief, ministry style, and broader Christian living that probably won't find focused expression in the structures of the local church. Parachurches, though, can facilitate Christian unity, collaboration and support around these kinds of disputable and incidental matters: for example, Christian theories of free market economics, the implications of supralapsarianism, house church models, and so on. Such things can create a toxic tribalism that disrupts the life of the church and distracts us from a proper focus on the things of first importance in faith, life and ministry. Yet if they are kept in their proper place and proportion, such narrow fellowships based around secondary matters can be desirable for fruitful reflection, exploration and activity.

Parachurches protect the visible church from mission drift and worldly entanglement. There are many good and right things that Christians ought to do as we live out our faith in all areas of our lives. But not everything that Christians ought to do is required of the church itself *as the church.* The church is especially charged with those things mentioned in my definition: meeting God in his word, praying to him, praising him, building up each other in the faith, building unbelievers into the faith, loving one another, and managing the affairs of the church.

The church may, from time to time, extend into other forms of activity. But these are neither required of it, nor central to its reason for being. Mack Stiles writes:

> [The parachurch] exists primarily to protect the church ... The church has a unique and high ministerial calling that stands above all others: the right teaching and preaching of the Word. So when the many good things begin to encroach on the primary task of the church, the parachurch can take that good ministry onto its own shoulders and so protect the church.[57]

Although I wouldn't go so far as Stiles in saying that this is the *primary* purpose of the parachurch, he is right that the parachurch can help the church to focus on its primary task. A side benefit of this kind of protection is that the church can thereby protect itself from some forms of worldly entanglement. To take one example, the history of Christianity shows how easy it is for political and economic interests to interfere with the pure ministry of the church. By deferring certain concerns to parachurches, the local church *as church* can remain aloof from the potentially compromising and corrupting concerns of this world.

More than this, *there are some aspects of gospel ministry and practical good deeds that are best done beyond the bounds of the local church.* Cross-cultural mission and theological education are two obvious examples of vital gospel ministry that will be best pursued beyond the ordinary operations of local church life. This is usually because these ministries require a significant level of specialization and focus that would be difficult for a local church to achieve.[58] They are, therefore, better left to a denominational or non-denominational parachurch.

---

57 Stiles, 'Nine marks of a healthy parachurch ministry'. See also PY De Jong, *The Church's Witness to the World*, vol 2, Paideia Press, 1980, pp 296-297.

58 "Church-based ministries simply cannot do targeted outreach, evangelism, student community, and academic engagement like parachurch groups … [church] ministries will never have the paradigm and scope of seeking to redeem the entire national or global university context nor develop and replicate context-specific strategies and methods" (Chen, 'Move, parachurch—get out the way!'). Part 3 of this book considers several examples of these types of ministries, such as university student ministry and political advocacy.

Arthur Davis provides three illustrations which emphasize the specialization and mobility of parachurches, in contrast to the local church:

Infantry vs. Special ops: home base, inclusive and mandatory versus voluntary and specialized;

Well vs. Bucket: permanent versus mobile;

Computer vs. Flash drive: multi-purpose versus limited purpose.[59]

Not all parachurches are necessarily specialized like this.[60] But this is definitely one of the main reasons for the establishment of parachurches. Another aspect of this specialization is targeted engagement with particular demographics and institutions. A local church ministry to university students, for example, is possibly less likely to be focused on and committed to the overall wellbeing of the university as an institution and a community.[61] Parachurch structures facilitate the full flourishing of God's saving work in the world.[62]

---

59 A Davis, *One Body, Two Hands: An ecclesiology infographic* (provided personally to the author). William Booth reflected this outlook in his justification of the Salvation Army: "What is your attitude towards the 'Fire Brigade?' or if you live on the sea coast, what is your attitude towards the 'Lifeboat crew?' or, again … what is your attitude towards the Volunteers in the killing armies? You cheer them on, encourage them, subscribe to their funds, go to their assemblages and bless them … DO THE SAME WITH US" (cited in Taylor, *Like a Mighty Army?*, p 94).

60 This is one reason why the framework of modality/sodality is not sufficient to cover the full range of parachurches. I explain this framework under 'Is there such a thing as a parachurch?' above.

61 "Additionally, local churches almost by definition will not seek to redeem and witness to a whole campus or all its structures and subcultures as their core mission. Then how about the entire global context of modern secular academia and 'the university'?" (C Chen, 'Gifts of college parachurch ministries to the church [Move, parachurch—get out the way! Part 3 of 4]', *Calvin's Chronicles*, 24 January 2016, accessed 15 September 2022 [calvindc. wordpress.com/2016/01/24/gifts-of-parachurch]).

62 Some suggest that the biblical metaphor of 'the body of Christ' is a helpful way of describing the diverse ministries of the wider Christian community. I'm not so sure. The application of the 'body' metaphor can drift beyond the biblical teaching. So someone might say, "evangelical churches are the head, charismatic churches are the heart, the mission society are the feet, and charitable organizations are the hands of the body of Christ". But the body metaphor is applied in the New Testament to individual gifts in a local congregation, not to institutional entities.

Parachurches recognize that the lordship of Christ and the work of the Spirit relativizes any human institution, including the visible church. While it is true that Christ himself established the institution of local churches and authorizes their human leaders, they remain subordinate to his lordship. The local church has a dual identity as both a spiritual and secular institution. Christ can describe human church discipline in the most frightfully spiritual terms:

> "Truly I tell you, whatever you bind on earth will be bound in heaven, and whatever you loose on earth will be loosed in heaven. Again, truly I tell you that if two of you on earth agree about anything they ask for, it will be done for them by my Father in heaven. For where two or three gather in my name, there am I with them." (Matt 18:18-20)

And yet at the same time, he can recognize that our human judgements cannot be comprehensive:

> The servants asked him, "Do you want us to go and pull them up?"
>
> "No," he answered, "because while you are pulling the weeds, you may uproot the wheat with them. Let both grow together until the harvest." (Matt 13:28b-30a)[63]

In light of this, we should not necessarily expect the work of Christ to be always restricted to or controlled by the human institution of his visible church. We see something of this in Acts 8-12 (and beyond), where the formal leaders and structures of the church are playing catch-up to circumstances, opportunities, spontaneous and informal ministry, and divine interventions.

This reminds us that Acts should be properly called 'The Acts of the Lord Jesus' rather than 'The Acts of the Apostles'.[64]

---

63 In my book *The Good Life in the Last Days* (pp 42-43), I also point out that immediately before the apostle Paul speaks about church discipline in 1 Corinthians 5, he says "I do not even judge myself" (4:3) and "judge nothing before the appointed time" (4:5).

64 See Acts 1:1—if Luke's Gospel describes what Jesus "*began* to do and teach", then surely Acts describes what he *continues* to do.

Before there is a formally constituted church, Christ is at work giving new life to unbelievers by his Spirit through the preaching of the gospel. Before leaders are formally ordained, Christ leads these converts to maturity and gives them gifts of teaching and leadership. Far more foundational than the doctrine of ordination to ministry is the doctrine of the priesthood of all believers.[65] All of us are anointed and empowered to serve the Lord Jesus Christ and build his church (1 Pet 2:4-10; 1 John 2:27). Moreover, often God will work outside the normal structures of the church:

> Throughout biblical history, especially in times of widespread apostasy among his people, God has called individuals (e.g., prophets) to challenge the establishment, and even to stand over against it. Such individuals are uncomfortable to live with, as are the groups they form around them. Yet we should be extremely wary of surrendering to our natural desire to bring them under control. For we may find ourselves *quenching the Spirit of God*.[66]

Almost by definition, movements of reformation begin as parachurches. The ministry of parachurches keeps the church from the hubris of claiming there is a one-to-one correspondence

---

65 Bavinck, *Reformed Dogmatics*, pp 619-620. It is sad that the Westminster Assembly assumed that the 'dissenting brethren' (Congregationalists) would agree with them that women shouldn't have a part in electing church officers any more than children should; see Westminster Assembly (1643-1652), 'The answer of the assembly of divines, unto the reasons of the seven dissenting brethren, against the proposition of divers congregations being united under one presbyteriall government', in *The Reasons Presented by the Dissenting Brethren Against Certain Propositions Concerning Presbyteriall Government; And the Proofs of Them Voted by the Assembly of Divines, Sitting by Authority of Parliament, at Westminster; Together with the Answer of the Assembly of Divines to Those Reasons of Dissent*, Humphrey Harward, 1648, p 21, accessed 15 September 2022 (archive.org/details/present00west).

66 LCWE Commission on Co-operation, *Cooperating in World Evangelization*, p 12-13, emphasis original. The paper immediately goes on to say, "On the other hand, whatever initiatives an individual or group may believe themselves called by God to make, they should wherever possible seek the counsel, goodwill, support and co-operation of the church. Indeed, they should desire to be a part of the church's work rather than independent of it. They should not be over-hasty in pronouncing it dead, washing their hands of it. For they may find themselves sinning against the Body of Christ." See also White, *The Church and the Parachurch*, pp 55-56, 58.

between the work of Christ and the ruling of his local churches and earthly denominations.[67]

Lastly, *parachurches have proven to be enormously effective at investing in Christians through discipleship and training, and at releasing Christians for evangelism and good deeds.* Parachurches make possible a broad pooling of resources, not only across churches, but also through support-raising efforts across countries and even across continents. Because of their narrow focus, they have the luxury of specialization, which means they can excel in an area of exegesis, evangelism or event management in a way that few churches can. Because of their interest in more informal patterns of ministry, they provide many opportunities for fruitful ministry for a range of people, some of whom might not have much opportunity in the structures of the local church.[68] In addition, parachurches are able to be more flexible and efficient in their decision making and execution. Sometimes, this is because they are younger organizations (newly planted churches often experience the same dynamic). Sometimes, parachurches find it easier to 'stay young' because their membership (and even leadership) is more transient than a church. Sometimes, they have (rightly or wrongly) adopted forms of governance that don't include the same cumbersome processes as a local church or denomination. Flexibility and efficiency are by-products of their narrow focus: it is easier to make decisions when you are not responsible for the holistic care of a church community.

For this range of reasons, parachurches in their various manifestations have been the means by which extraordinary things

---

67 See Kuiper, 'Ecclesiastical evangelism' in *The Glorious Body of Christ*, pp 237-243, for a balanced discussion of the freedom of Christians to evangelize and participate in voluntary associations beyond the explicit oversight and consent of the local church, while also upholding the proper place for church accountability and discipline. This chapter was first published as an article during the first decade of the Billy Graham crusades.

68 White, *The Church and the Parachurch*, pp 50, 56-57, 107, 122; cf. W Kuan, 'Learning from the past: (2) Churches and societies', *The Gospel Coalition Australia Edition*, 27 October 2016, accessed 20 September 2022 (au.thegospelcoalition.org/article/learning-from-the-past-2-1).

have been done in the name of Christ. As Willmer, Schmidt and Smith write, "parachurch groups are religion gone entrepreneurial, as God expands his work by enlarging the boundaries of Christian ministry".[69] At various times in church history, parachurches have proliferated to meet a growing need that formal church ministry could not keep up with—such as 13th-century friars meeting the needs of growing medieval towns,[70] the 18th- and 19th-century Methodists meeting the needs of the frontiers of the American colonies,[71] the 19th-century voluntary societies meeting the needs of the urban populations of the Industrial Revolution,[72] and the 19th-century mission societies seizing the opportunity of accessibility to the nations of the world.[73]

All of this generally results in local churches and denominations being strengthened and renewed. The best parachurches don't ultimately erode local churches and denominations, but enrich them. Through their ministries, there is greater zeal and maturity, more ministry competence, more theological depth, and more human beings saved from hell by the gospel of our Lord Jesus Christ.

69 Willmer et al., *The Prospering Parachurch*, p xii.
70 D MacCulloch, *A History of Christianity: The first three thousand years*, Allen Lane, 2009, pp 401-405.
71 Noll, *The Rise of Evangelicalism*, p 138.
72 DW Bebbington, *Evangelicalism in Modern Britain: A history from the 1730s to the 1980s*, Routledge, 1995, pp 117-125.
73 AR Vidler, *The Church in an Age of Revolution: 1789 to the present day*, Penguin History of the Church (O Chadwick gen ed), vol 5, Penguin Books, 1990, p 247.

Chapter 3: The local church and the denomination

As a zealous, impatient and sometimes angry young Christian, converted into a Presbyterian church, I used to cynically joke with my friends that there should be a board game called 'Presbytery', in which you move your token around the board, aiming to grow a fruitful gospel ministry. To complete the game, you have to spin a 'wheel of fortune'—but in this game, no matter where the pointer lands, the answer is always variations of the word 'No' ("A committee has been convened to explore things further", "Presbytery awaits a properly worded overture", and so on). That's how it felt at the time: presbytery seemed like a council of men who gathered to unearth new ways for The Code to impede gospel ministry. The comfort of the local church was the relative freedom to carry on with the 'real work', and the encouragement of the church planting network I helped establish—The Vision 100 Network[1]—was that we could make decisions about the things that 'really mattered' with speed and agility. Rather than feeling suffocated by cau-

---

1   Originally 'Vision 100', inspired by the vision to plant 100 new churches of 200 people in southern Tasmania and so reach 10% of the population. The network and its vision quickly became statewide. Later, the name was changed to 'Vision 100 Resources' to clarify its supporting, resourcing function, and then later still 'The Vision 100 Network'. See vision100.org.

tion, pedantry, and suspicion, we felt united with others around trust, affection, and commitment to a common cause.

About ten years later, by the grace of God, that same presbytery had split into two regional presbyteries. One of the two, the Presbytery of Derwent, had grown through church planting efforts: instead of three churches in southern Tasmania, there were now seven. A similar multiplication had taken place among the Christian Reformed Churches of southern Tasmania, one of which helped establish (and most of whom were affiliated with) The Vision 100 Network. One pastor in the presbytery and the network began to ask whether Vision 100 might now be redundant. With the growth and renewal in our denominational courts, surely it had done its job. Shouldn't the responsibility for networking, training, vision-casting and resourcing now be passed on to the denominations, who might then work in partnership towards the same common cause?

All of this raises several vital questions about one very important aspect of our discussion. In between the church and the parachurch lies another entity, which is not clearly one or the other: the *denomination*.

We have touched on the nature and role of denominations already, but it is time to delve more deeply. What place does the denomination have in our understanding of church, ministry, life and mission? Is it a necessary expression of the church of Christ? Is it perhaps even a kind of 'regional church' that should receive something of the same dignity as local churches? Would it be best, wherever possible, to hand over parachurch functions to denominational oversight?

Or are denominations themselves just another kind of parachurch network, like the local pastors' prayer breakfast or an evangelical coalition? And if so, is it invasive and inappropriate for a denomination to legislate for local churches—declaring what is and is not sound doctrine, deciding how to train and ordain pastors, and overruling on matters of discipline when an appeal is made to their courts?

In this chapter, I begin by asking if there is any theological justification for denominations. I then consider their relationship to local churches: is the denomination more important than the local church, or less? Does it come first, or is it somehow brought into being by the coalition of local churches?

In this discussion, I have tried to mark out the issues as best I can without pushing too hard the specifics of my own convictions, because my aim is for this discussion to be as helpful as possible to as many readers as possible. My goal is to provide clarity on the key issues so that we can better articulate our own convictions and so make decisions about church and parachurch with integrity, in line with our convictions. I also hope that this clarity will help Christians from various church, parachurch or denominational backgrounds to understand each other better, so that we can work together in ways that don't subtly trample on each other's consciences. Collaboration between churches from different denominations is often clumsy because it thoughtlessly imports assumptions about these issues into the parachurch work.[2] Greater clarity could therefore be an important step towards fruitful gospel cooperation.

Before we think specifically about denominations, we need to lay some foundations by first considering another aspect of the meaning of 'church'.

Church as collective noun for Christians?

If you want to have a laugh, google 'collective nouns for animals'. Not only is it funny that we have separate names for each specific type of animal, but the names that the English language has settled on are wonderfully colourful and silly. A murder of crows, a busyness of ferrets, a paddling of ducks, a parcel of

---

2   For example, a recent interdenominational collaboration was titled 'Heads of Churches', which might be a perfectly satisfactory title for the Roman Catholics and Anglicans, but was unhelpful for the Baptist and Presbyterian leaders involved—the moderator of the Presbyterian General Assembly of Tasmania is not the 'head' of the Presbyterian Church of Tasmania in the same way as the Anglican Bishop is 'head' of the Anglican Diocese of Tasmania.

deer, a bask of crocodiles, a coalition of cheetahs, a kaleidoscope of butterflies, a sleuth of bears, a shrewdness of apes, a gulp of cormorants, a flamboyance of flamingos, a kettle of hawks, a cackle of hyenas, a smack of jellyfish, an exaltation of larks, a labour of moles, a barrel of monkeys, a parliament of owls, a pandemonium of parrots, a congregation of plovers, an unkindness of ravens, a crash of rhinos, a squabble of seagulls, a murmuration of starlings, an ambush of tigers, a committee of vultures, a wisdom of wombats, a dazzle of zebras. I couldn't help myself: I had to include all the ones I loved the most.[3]

So what is the collective noun for a group of Christians? Is it a *church* of Christians? Is it right to speak of 'the worldwide church today'? Or 'the church in Manado'? Is this a proper use of the word 'church'? Are there any risks with this usage?

There are certainly some people who think of 'church' this way. If they want to describe the duties all Christians share, they speak of 'the duties of the church'; if they want to characterize the state of Christianity in a certain country or region, they talk about 'the church' in that country or region.

On one level, using a word in a range of ways is neither here nor there; plenty of words can have multiple meanings. But there is a significant shift of meaning when we use the word 'church' like this: it loses sight of the sense of 'gathering' or 'assembling' together. While a local church might still retain its identity as a church when it is scattered from Monday to Saturday, it remains a community of people who gather regularly. By contrast, this 'global church' of all those throughout the world never gathers, nor does 'the church of Western Australia' nor 'the church in South America'.

This lack of precision can create confusion about the powers of the broad community of Christians and about the duties of the local congregation. *Firstly, by using the word 'church' for a large group of Christians, we can unthinkingly transfer too much*

---

3   I know there are too many, but my editor has kindly allowed me to print them all (he must share my love of bizarre names).

churchly power to this larger community. Does 'the church of New York' have some kind of governing responsibility over all the churches within its city boundaries? Should it ordain and discipline? If it gathered, would it be right to celebrate the Lord's Supper? Is it a necessary part of church life to establish and edify citywide (or national or global) fellowships?[4] That may be so, but such conclusions shouldn't be reached by accident.

Secondly, this usage can impose upon the local congregation the expectation that it be formally committed to all the good things that Christians might possibly do. Christians should indeed show concern for the poor of their neighbourhood, participate in the political process of their nation, and worship the Lord in their everyday work and recreation. If we are in the habit of referring to any group of Christians as 'church', we can slide into assuming that all these things must somehow be facilitated by every local church. Isn't this what 'the church' should be doing, after all? But is it true that local churches should be as responsible for political activity as they should be for preaching the gospel? Both are duties of Christians, but are both equally duties of *the church*? We will return to this issue in chapter 4.

That being said, it is possible that the New Testament itself occasionally speaks of the worldwide 'church' (1 Cor 10:32, 12:28-31; Eph 4:1-16; 1 Tim 3:15).[5] These passages appear to speak of the 'worldwide community of Christians'—which is given spiritual gifts, is gradually maturing, faces the risk of stumbling, and is the pillar and foundation of truth in the world. These could simply demonstrate that an extension of meaning is acceptable, even if it's not the primary meaning of the word 'church'. This is how the authors of The Savoy Declaration understand it:

> The whole body of men throughout the world, professing the faith of the gospel and obedience unto God by Christ according to it ... are, and *may be called the visible*

---

4   I will look in more depth at the ecumenical movement in chapter 12.

5   While Ephesians 4:1-16 speaks of 'the body' rather than 'the church', Paul begins the letter by saying "the church, which is his body" (1:22-23; see also 5:23).

catholic church of Christ; although as such it is not entrusted with the administration of any ordinances, or have any officers to rule or govern in, or over the whole body.[6]

So while there are risks associated with using the word 'church' to talk about the larger Christian community, this doesn't mean it's completely wrong to do so. The idea of the 'worldwide church' does not necessarily imply that there should be any institutional shape to this entity.[7] Moreover, we will be well served by being thoughtful, and perhaps even a little cautious, in how we use the word 'church'.

The universal earthly church is a part of the universal heavenly church

Far from being merely an extension of the meaning of 'church' beyond any sense of gathering or assembly, there is a true sense in which the so-called worldwide church (whether visible or invisible) is an assembly. The worldwide church is not a separate church from the invisible, heavenly church. It is not as if we should think of three layers of different churches—first the universal, heavenly church, then the worldwide church, and finally all local churches. Rather, we must remember that fundamentally there is only one church of Christ, which is embodied in various ways.[8] Here's how The Second Helvetic Confession clarifies it:

> **Parts or forms of the church:** The Church is divided into different parts or forms; not because it is divided

---

6 The Savoy Declaration of Faith and Order, 1658, 26.2, emphasis mine. This declaration was adapted from the Westminster Confession by those who didn't agree with Presbyterian church structures. But note that, 30 years later, The Baptist Confession of Faith of 1689 avoids using the word 'church': "All persons throughout the world, professing the faith of the gospel … are and may be called visible saints; and of such ought all particular congregations to be constituted" (26.2).

7 "Whether all those Congregations growing so numerous, and those Presbyteries thus divided should have been called *one Church* still; we know not, nor is it of any moment. We say again, we are not inquiring for names and things" (Westminster Assembly, 'The answer of the assembly of divines', p 10).

8 L Berkhof, *Systematic Theology*, Banner of Truth, 1971, p 566.

or rent asunder in itself, but rather because it is distinguished by the diversity of the numbers that are in it.

Militant and triumphant: For the one is called the Church Militant, the other the Church Triumphant. The former still wages war on earth, and fights against the flesh, the world, and the prince of this world, the devil; against sin and death. But the latter, having been now discharged, triumphs in heaven immediately after having overcome all those things and rejoices before the Lord. Notwithstanding both have fellowship and union one with another.[9]

In this sense, 'global church' really means 'those members of the invisible, heavenly church who are currently still alive on earth'. It is not essentially a different church from the heavenly church; because its members are also members of the heavenly church, they are in that sense truly assembled. Likewise, the 'visible global church' means 'those who publicly identify as and organize as members of local church expressions of the heavenly church' (see Diagram F).[10]

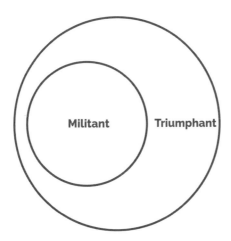

Diagram F: The two modes of the universal church

9   The Second Helvetic Confession, 1566, XVII. Allison refers to these as two 'aspects' of the universal church; see Allison, *Sojourners and Strangers*, p 31.
10   See Westminster Confession, XXV.2.

One key application of this truth is that it ought to give us great confidence. We struggle and groan in our daily battle with sin, weariness and sickness, all the while feeling implicit and explicit pressure to walk away from Christ and join the crowd on the wide road. Our individual faith and communal existence can appear so fragile, vulnerable and pathetic; we are truly a smouldering wick and a bruised reed (Isa 42:3). And yet we saints still on earth are united in Christ, together with the saints who are at rest in glory; we are, in a sense, already triumphant with them. Giving us this vision—which can only come with the eyes of faith—is one of the main goals of that (seemingly) bizarre and frightening book of Revelation. It invites us to rejoice in the reality:

> "Now have come the salvation and the power
>> and the kingdom of our God,
>> and the authority of his Messiah.
> For the accuser of our brothers and sisters,
>> who accuses them before our God day and night,
>> has been hurled down.
> They triumphed over him
>> by the blood of the Lamb
>> and by the word of their testimony;
> they did not love their lives so much
>> as to shrink from death.
> Therefore rejoice, you heavens
>> and you who dwell in them!
> But woe to the earth and the sea,
>> because the devil has gone down to you!
> He is filled with fury,
>> because he knows that his time is short."
> (Rev 12:10-12)

Realizing that the 'global church' is merely one form of the universal church also helps us to understand that the 'global church' doesn't need some additional institutional structure, because it is not, in fact, a separate entity. Its existence is fundamentally spiritual, and it is governed by Christ himself. There is no necessary structure that must be established and edified to ensure that the worldwide body of Christ is built. The worldwide body of Christ is built in the same way as the universal church: primarily through the edification of individual Christians and local churches.[11]

Of course, this is not to say that local churches have no interest in one another. So then, what of the cooperation between local churches and the organizations that facilitate that cooperation? Are denominations 'a thing', theologically speaking, at all? And what authority and importance should they properly have?

Connection, cooperation and leadership between local churches

It goes without saying that there is a deep bond between every true local church: we are all in communion with Christ and with one another, all manifesting the one, holy, catholic, apostolic church in the heavenly realm: "There is one body and one Spirit, just as you were called to one hope when you were called; one Lord, one faith, one baptism; one God and Father of all, who is over all and through all and in all" (Eph 4:4-6). There is a very deep connection between every Christian and every Christian church, a connection that goes beyond our interchurch activities or our form of church governance. Tertullian says that our unity is proved "by fellowship in communion, by the name of brother, and the mutual pledge of hospitality".[12] Our unity with every Christian and every church is a reality that doesn't need to be created or negotiated, but rather recognized and celebrated.[13] It is right for me to have a deep affection for

11 The Westminster Confession even says, "Unto this catholic and visible Church, Christ has given the ministry, oracles, and ordinances of God" (XXV.3). But this does not deny that the proper exercise of ministry and administration of ordinances should be in the local church.
12 Cited in Bavinck, *Reformed Dogmatics*, p 592.
13 Robinson, 'The church of God: Its form and unity', p 233; and Volf, *After Our Likeness*, pp 155-158.

all my brothers and sisters in Christ and a keen spiritual interest in the welfare and maturity of all Christians.

This connection unavoidably creates all kinds of overlap between local churches, which the formal structures of local churches should acknowledge rather than somehow presume to legislate. Total isolation and independence are a kind of sickness. Welcoming a fellow Christian who comes to us is not an advisable option for us to consider, nor is it a recommendation for our church leadership to evaluate and interrogate (and perhaps resolve to act on); it is a joyful duty. Our instinct and stance should be one of open generosity rather than suspicion.

So also welcoming a gospel minister: the default response should surely be one of honour, shouldn't it? A commendation for a gospel minister, of the kind we find throughout Romans 16 or in Philippians 2:19-30, is not in the first place a reference to be weighed and possibly endorsed by you or your local church— as if the one being commended won't be a pastor in your territory until you issue a working visa. Rather, a commendation for a gospel minister is a call to recognize a pre-existing reality —we are *receiving* more than merely *considering an application*.[14] Church discipline, likewise, has a universal scope (Matt 16:19, 18:18-20), for a local church would need extraordinary reasons to welcome as a church member someone who was still under discipline for unrepentant sin or serious doctrinal error in their previous church.

Church membership and ordination won't necessarily translate to an individual Christian's formal membership of our local church, or to a gospel minister's full activity in our denomina-

---

14 For example, 3 John 5-8; cf. Westminster Assembly, 'The answer of the assembly of divines', p 2. Contrary to Knox ('The church, the churches and the denominations of the churches', in *D. Broughton Knox Selected Works*, vol 2, p 90) and Robinson ('The church of God: Its form and unity', pp 244-245), recognition does not grant direct authority to presume to lead individual Christians or local churches wherever they go. Recognition of prior ordination is distinct from induction into a specific church.

tion, as there are extra considerations.[15] But the fact remains that there is a Christian fellowship and ministry that goes beyond our local church or denomination's formal organization. You could say there is an unavoidable kind of 'mutual authority' that local churches have over one another in that their decisions have an impact on each other. Things like ordination, membership and discipline have something of a universal character about them: when a church member or ordained elder moves from one country to another, we can welcome them for who and what they already are (see Diagram G).[16]

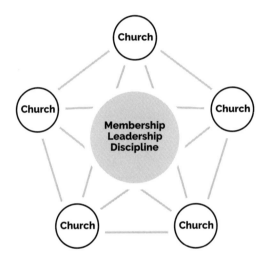

Diagram G: Mutual recognition

15 Each church or denomination will clarify which doctrinal, ethical and practical matters it seeks in good conscience to uphold and pass on. Narrow requirements for eldership ensure that they will remain faithful to these matters. In a congregational church, even the church member is an 'officer of the church' with ultimate decision-making power, expressed in their votes, and so the principle is similar. A narrow confession of faith ensures that members who join together in a particular local church share a common understanding of the Scriptures in the exercise of their duties as members. On a practical level, it can be unhelpful for ministers and elders who are not currently serving in any local ministry to have too much governance power in a denomination, as there is a risk that they will lose touch with the practical reality and needs of church life.

16 See J Bannerman, *The Church of Christ: A treatise on the nature, powers, ordinances, discipline, and government of the Christian church*, Still Waters Revival Books, 1991, pp 317-319.

This connection between all Christians and churches also necessarily motivates cooperation in a variety of ways, which we see in the New Testament (see Diagram H):

- prayer for one another (Rom 15:30-31; Col 4:2-4; 2 Thess 3:1-2)
- financial support for ministry (Acts 18:1-5; 2 Cor 11:7-9; Phil 4:10-19)
- financial support for practical needs of fellow Christians (Acts 11:27-30; Rom 15:25-29; 1 Cor 16:1-4; 2 Cor 8-9)
- sending and receiving of ministry leaders (Acts 11:22-26; 13:1-3; 15; 18; Rom 15:23-24, 16:1-2; Titus 1:5)
- sharing of apostolic letters (Col 4:16; Jas 1:1; 1 Pet 1:1; 2 Pet 3:15-16; Revelation 2-3)
- meeting for consultation, encouragement, correction, and decision making (Acts 11:1-18, 15:1-33, 21:17-25).[17]

Diagram H: Loving fellowship

Two questions of clarification are needed regarding cooperation. First, is inter-church cooperation optional? And second, is it authoritative?

There are endless possibilities for all the different *ways* churches

17 See Westminster Assembly, 'The answer of the assembly of divines', pp 3-4 and 77.

might cooperate with one another, multiplied further by the *degrees* of possible investment. But individual Christians and local churches are finite, bound by time and space, and restricted by physical energy, financial capacity and political power. An authoritative decree would be required to make a specific cooperative activity—the apostle Paul's collection for the poor in the Jerusalem church, for example—compulsory for every church. Unless there is some specific compulsion, a church could express a concern for other churches in an entirely different way. But this observation doesn't mean cooperation is therefore entirely optional. Local churches might be bound by the *principle* of cooperation, even if they are not bound by a *specific* 'cooperative project'.

It helps to think of this duty as being a particular expression of the duty to love. Romans 13:8 urges us: "Let no debt remain outstanding, except the continuing debt to love one another, for whoever loves others has fulfilled the law". On the one hand, many specific possible acts of love are optional, while on the other hand I can never exhaust my duty to love. There is no single, precise recipe for how exactly I am to fulfil the second-greatest commandment, but I am bound to love people as they are, where they are, and when they are, while also taking into account who I am, where I am, and when I am.[18]

A similar principle applies to churches in their relationships with one another. In rare cases, there might be some opportunities to care for another church that we are almost compelled to act upon. It seems that Paul is making a strong appeal along these lines in Romans 15:26-27. Because of the peculiar indebtedness that the young Gentile churches have to the Jewish people as the (human) origin of gospel ministry, and because of the dire need of the Judean churches, they "owe it to the Jews to share with them their material blessings" (v 27). In most cases, however, there are many possible ways in which we might cooperate with other churches; the leadership of each church will

18 Lynch, 'Devotion, diversity and the day-to-day' in *The Good Life in the Last Days*, pp 45-64.

need to weigh those opportunities with the wisdom God gives, according to their peculiar circumstances.

But the picture becomes slightly different when there are formal, authoritative connections between churches.

Are denominations just parachurches, or do they have authority over churches?

This is one of the key points of disagreement between different denominations—episcopalian, presbyterian or congregationalist.[19] Most people acknowledge the value and importance of cooperation between churches, but disagree with each other about whether such cooperation can ever lead to binding declarations on the individual congregations involved. For a congregationalist, each local church is ultimately independent of every other local church. Any cooperative decision is simply a matter of counsel or opportunity, never command; each individual church may choose to reject the counsel and to not participate in this or that opportunity. In this view, denominations are seen as "'parachurch' organizations".[20]

By contrast, the presbyterian and episcopalian believes that assemblies, presbyteries, synods and possibly bishops have a legitimate power over certain aspects of local congregations. They consider it appropriate to bind local congregations to stan-

---

19 Throughout this section, I am using these terms not as nouns (to refer to specific denominations such as 'Episcopalian' or 'Presbyterian'), but as adjectives to describe various types of churchmanship.

20 Knox, 'The church, the churches and the denominations of the churches', p 95. See also Allison, *Sojourners and Strangers*, p 297. See also Howard Snyder, who argues: "But in attempting to make a biblical (rather than merely pragmatic) analysis [of the question of parachurch structures], I encountered a basic difficulty. I could find no *biblical* basis for a fundamental distinction between denominational structures and para-denominational structures. The more basic distinction seems to be between *the Church* as the body of Christ and the community of God's people, and all *institutional structures*, including denominations. Thus I would make a basic distinction between the Church and all para-church structures, and then sub-divide such institutional structures into *denominational* and *non-denominational* structures" (cited in LCWE Commission on Co-operation, *Cooperating in World Evangelization*, p 113, emphasis original).

dards of doctrine, ordination and procedure, to tax local congregations for the operations of the wider denomination, and to function as a court of appeal for complaints against the leadership of the local church (see Table 2).

	View of the denomination	Nature of cooperation	Source of authority
Independent	Association or parachurch	Voluntary association	Wisdom, trust and persuasion; administrative compliance and ongoing affiliation
Bottom-up	Federation of churches	Exists to serve the needs of local churches and regions	Ceded to denominational councils by local churches; limited in scope
Top-down	Denomination as church	Distinct local churches are formed by necessity of size and distance	Delegated to local churches by denominational councils; broad in scope

Table 2: Denominations, cooperation and authority[21]

What theological place and practical weight ought to be granted to the denominational organization? It will help to sketch out some of the factors that help us think this through. By necessity, this section is the most technical part of this chapter, as it engages with a range of arguments and counter-arguments; it is a bit like presuming to engage in the comments section on the internet (or walking into a living room covered with Lego at night). Feel free to skip over this section if these issues are not currently of interest to you.

---

21 Note that there is significant variation between each of these rows, and the borders between them are fuzzy. I have not assigned denominational names to each row, since there can be significant differences even between denominations that share the same label. As a result, I have opted for descriptive terms.

1. The New Testament mainly speaks about local congregations

Again and again, God speaks about *churches* (plural) in a particular region, rather than *the church* (Acts 15:41, 16:5; 1 Cor 16:1, 19; 2 Cor 8:1; Gal 1:2, 21-22; 1 Thess 2:14; Rev 1:4). Each and every church, no matter how small or young or socially insignificant, is truly a church of God and should be thought of alongside greater, older and grander churches, rather than subsumed into some larger mass. Each church is a church in its own right, with its own community, leaders and ministry. Moreover, the congregation itself has a role in the disciplinary governance of the local church (Matt 18:15-20; 1 Cor 5:1-5; 2 Cor 2:5-11; 1 Tim 5:19-21)[22] and in the appointment of leaders (Acts 6:1-6, 14:23; 2 Cor 8:19).[23] And to state the important but obvious point: each of these churches actually assemble together as a congregation, and so give physical expression to the heavenly congregation.[24] As Karl Barth says:

> The Church is neither the invisible fellowship, nor the visible community of all those who believe in Christ; nor is it a monarchical, aristocratic, or democratic form of the latter. The Church is the 'event' in which two or

---

22 The first two steps of church discipline laid out by the Lord Jesus in Matthew 18 are to be conducted by regular church members, without reference to the elders. In the light of the Scriptures quoted here, I believe it is difficult to deny that the congregation has a place in the final step of excommunication. For a detailed outline of the various views in the Westminster Assembly, see Powell, *Crisis of British Protestantism*.

23 The Greek word used in Acts 14:23 originally meant 'gesturing with a hand', and so can imply voting; see 'Cheirotoneō', in FW Danker, W Bauer, WF Arndt and FW Gingrich, *A Greek-English Lexicon of the New Testament and Other Early Christian Literature*, 3rd edn, University of Chicago Press, 2000, p 1083. It should be noted that denominations differ as to whether the congregation has the power to ordain, the power to decide on whom should be ordained, or merely the power to give consent to those who will be ordained. At the very least, I believe it is wrong to impose leaders on an unwilling congregation. See Powell, *The Crisis of British Protestantism*.

24 For this reason, I disagree with those in the Westminster Assembly who argued that it is legitimate for a number of congregations to be led by a single presbytery, with no local body of elders at all; see Westminster Assembly, 'The answer of the assembly of divines', p 5. Hunter Powell shows that there was significant diversity on this point among Presbyterians at the Westminster Assembly, with some Scottish Presbyterians agreeing more with the 'dissenting brethren' Congregationalists than with English Presbyterians; see Powell, *The Crisis of British Protestantism*.

three are gathered together in the name of Jesus Christ, i.e. in the power of his calling and commission ...

The primary, normal and visible form of this event is the local congregation, meeting in a 'parish' or 'district' with clearly defined boundaries. Such a local congregation is constituted by the possibility and the actuality of regular public worship, i.e. common worship at which the Atonement made by Jesus is proclaimed, as the ground of our hope ... The Church lives (she actually is) in the form of a local congregation, which is the basis of all other forms of her life.[25]

The danger of a 'Top-Down' denominational structure is that it can impose too much on local churches, so that they lose their distinctiveness and thus become merely an organ or limb of the larger denomination. Another example of this is the description of ministers in some Anglican dioceses as 'vicars'—those simply acting vicariously on behalf of the bishop. This term undermines the integrity of the local church and its leadership by emphasizing the primary leadership of the bishop.

2. There is little explicit instruction about any wider denominational affiliation in the New Testament letters

While the book of Acts gives examples of inter-church relationships and leadership (more on that in a moment), there is little direct, prescriptive teaching about inter-church governance in the Bible. We find no clear mention of routine inter-church councils or ordinary inter-church officials in the apostles' letters.[26] This in itself should make us cautious about any claims around the

---

25 Cited in Robinson, '"The church" revisited: An autobiographical fragment', p 265.
26 The 17th-century *Form of Presbyterial Church-Government* points to 1 Timothy 4:14 as justification for a presbytery having the power of ordination. But since the Greek word for 'presbytery' simply means 'group of elders', this could just as easily be the eldership of a local congregation. The 'dissenting brethren' raised this objection to the Westminster Assembly; see Westminster Assembly, 'Reasons against the third proposition, concerning presbyteriall government, and the principles thereof', in *The Reasons Presented by the Dissenting Brethren*, pp 37-39.

importance and power of such officials, courts and councils.[27] Moreover, the New Testament rarely (if ever) refers to regional and national groups of churches as 'the church'.[28] I suppose you could call a presbytery or general assembly a 'church' in the sense that it is itself a gathering, made up of representatives of local churches.[29] But this would be a derived and extended meaning, which should warn against taking the full weight of the biblical teaching about the church and applying it to the wider inter-church fellowship of a region, state or country.

3. Inter-church fellowship should be organized by godly wisdom, deeply shaped by biblical principles

Some episcopalians (like the Church of England, Lutherans, and arguably the Salvation Army)[30] admit that the structure of dioceses and bishops may not reflect a biblical pattern. But this is irrelevant, they say, because there is no single biblical pattern that God's people must follow; government by bishops is therefore a legitimate structure for governing churches.[31] This perspective has merit, given that there are not clear and specific instructions in the New Testament about the details of inter-church leadership. But even if God's people do have significant freedom, any possible structures we adopt must be carefully evaluated. It is a big deal to adopt a structure that gives significant disciplinary power over multiple churches to an individual bishop. We should take into account key biblical principles: warn-

---

27 R Hooker, *The Works of That Learned and Judicious Divine Mr Richard Hooker* (J Keble, RW Church and F Paget eds), 7th edn, vol 1, Clarendon Press, 1888, Preface IV.4, accessed 15 September 2022 (oll.libertyfund.org/titles/hooker-the-works-of-richard-hooker-vol-1).

28 Acts 9:31 is one possibility, although this may be taken to refer to the recently dispersed members of the Jerusalem church.

29 Assemblies, synods and councils are in principle open to all the members of all their constituent churches to attend. Since such is not practically possible, they send representatives. In practice, only sometimes is absolutely every member present at most weekly church meetings too; cf. Berkhof, *Systematic Theology*, p 591.

30 Taylor, *Like a Mighty Army?*, p 138.

31 JB Lightfoot concedes that the New Testament does not teach episcopacy, but presents a historical case for the development of the threefold ministry of bishops, elders and deacons over time; see JB Lightfoot, *The Christian Ministry*, Macmillan, 1901, pp 8-82.

ings against worldly power; exhortations to servant leadership; recognition of God giving many gifts to the church; the priesthood of all believers; and the emphasis on the local church.[32] It is interesting that Presbyterian pioneer John Calvin himself speaks with approval of the ancient practice of appointing a head elder to facilitate church government. But this is a case where the devil is in the details, for the kind of 'head elder' Calvin describes has a limited role and purpose:

> In each city these presbyters selected one of their number to whom they gave the special title of bishop, lest, as usually happens, from equality dissension should arise. The bishop, however, was not so superior in honour and dignity as to have dominion over his colleagues, but as it belongs to a president in an assembly to bring matters before them; collect their opinions; take precedence of others in consulting, advising, exhorting; guide the whole procedure by his authority; and execute what is decreed by common consent, [so] a bishop held the same office in a meeting of presbyters.[33]

The processes around the appointment of bishops and the description of their peculiar powers need to be thoughtfully examined to see if they reflect biblical priorities in the way bishops are empowered and restrained. It's one thing to delegate administrative responsibility for the practical affairs of a network of churches to an individual bishop; it's another thing to grant hierarchical disciplinary and coercive power over other pastors and churches.[34] For the same reasons, the pastor of an

---

32 See the theological critique of the Salvation Army's military-style leadership structure and its undermining effects on the meek evangelism, servant leadership and the priesthood of all believers in Taylor, *Like a Mighty Army?*, pp 60-66, 73-76, 136-141.

33 Calvin, *Institutes of the Christian Religion*, IV.4.2. See also Lightfoot, *The Christian Ministry*, pp 73-82.

34 This is an ongoing dissonance for advocates of the ecclesiology of Knox and Robinson within the Anglican Church. See Kuhn, *The Ecclesiology of Donald Robinson and D. Broughton Knox*, pp 90-92, 124-126, 174-178, 199-201; and RJW Shiner, *Reading the New Testament in Australia: An historical account of the origins, development, and influence of D.W.B. Robinson's biblical scholarship* [PhD thesis], Macquarie University, 2017, pp 165-176.

individual church ought to recognize the diversity of leadership gifts in the church and the responsibility of the whole congregation. Should 'godly wisdom' bestow a large proportion of power over the congregation on a single pastor?[35]

4. It is unclear that the ministry of Paul and his fellow workers set a pattern of external leaders governing multiple churches

What was the role and power of the apostle Paul and his fellow workers in relation to local churches? Did they operate in a kind of 'bishop' or 'network pastor' role, leaving us a pattern for organizing inter-church fellowship today?[36] Clearly, in writing letters to various churches, Paul assumed an authority over them—an authority that is unique because of his peculiar role as an apostle of Christ (Rom 1:1-5, 15; 1 Cor 7:17; 2 Cor 13:1-10; Gal 1:1; 2 Pet 3:16).

But Paul's fellow workers also have an interesting relationship with local churches. They were mobile, travelling between churches, and they seemed to assume authority wherever they landed. Take, for example, Timothy:

> For this reason I have sent to you Timothy, my son whom I love, who is faithful in the Lord. He will remind you of my way of life in Christ Jesus, which agrees with what I teach everywhere in every church. (1 Cor 4:17; cf. 16:10-11; Phil 2:19-23; 1 Tim 1:3)

Paul also writes this way about Titus: "The reason I left you in Crete was that you might put in order what was left unfinished and appoint elders in every town, as I directed you" (Titus 1:5). Maybe this is because Paul's fellow workers had a unique status, associated with that of the apostles and only necessary for the

---

35 A perplexed presbyterian or congregationalist might ask "If the New Testament doesn't *prescribe* episcopalianism, why on earth would you *choose* it?!"

36 Lightfoot argues that the transient and temporary authority of Paul and his associates set a pattern which the more stable and permanent role of bishops filled in the second century; see Lightfoot, *The Christian Ministry*, pp 27-29.

founding of the church in the New Testament age.[37] In this case, the scope of their power and their activity came from this unique and temporary role, in much the same way that a wider circle—Mark, Luke, James, Jude, and the author of Hebrews—were also able to become authors (and co-authors) of Scripture.[38] In this case, we should not presume to follow their example "*as 'founders'* of the communities and *as translocal overseers*".[39]

Yet even the apostles did not always frame their authority in unique terms. Peter appeals to elders as a "fellow elder" and a fellow heir of the gospel's blessings (1 Pet 5:1), and Paul is careful to say that he and the Roman Christians are able to "mutually encourage" each other (Rom 1:12). Paul sometimes speaks of his relationship to churches and church leaders in more relational terms, which suggests that he also thought of his relationship to these churches as a missionary or church planter who had a historical and relational authority over them, not just an apostolic authority (1 Cor 4:14-16; 2 Cor 10:13-14; Gal 4:12-20). We see this pattern at work in the book of Acts—for example, in chapter 14, where Paul and Barnabas return to the young churches they had evangelized into existence and oversee the appointment of elders in each place (14:21-28). It seems that here is a model that we can follow today: a church planter has a

---

37 When historical Presbyterian documents talk about 'evangelists', they take it to refer to a ministry that was unique to the founding of the church, which is why they say that the gift of 'evangelist' does not endure beyond the New Testament age; see, for example, Calvin, *Institutes of the Christian Religion*, IV.3.4. But I don't think the New Testament uses the term 'evangelist' in this way, and I wonder whether the term 'prophet' is more appropriate, as an office that is explicitly mentioned alongside the apostles as a foundational gift for the New Testament church (see Acts 15:32; Eph 2:20, 3:5, 4:11). Otherwise, the looser extra-biblical expression of 'apostolic associate' could be used.

38 I am hesitant to list those whom Paul mentions as co-authors of his letters (Sosthenes, Silas, Timothy), since it is not clear whether he presents them as cooperative and authoritative co-authors, or merely fellow workers who are present with him at the time of writing. In favour of the former view, note the way Paul uses the plural in 1 Thessalonians 2 ("as apostles of Christ *we* ..."; v 6), only to distinguish himself from this "we" later ("we wanted to come to you—*certainly I, Paul*, did ..."; v 18). But this is not clear cut, since Paul refers to himself with the plural in 3:1 ("left by ourselves in Athens"), which suggests an authorial "we". Further, certainly Galatians 1:1 ("Paul ... and all the brothers ... with me") suggests the latter interpretation. See Allison, *Sojourners and Strangers*, pp 206-207.

39 AC Thiselton, cited in Allison, *Sojourners and Strangers*, p 209, emphasis original.

kind of interim authority over a church until its own leaders are appointed,[40] and subsequently retains a kind of historical, relational influence over them. In fact, it is not clear that even Paul's fellow workers had any kind of external, episcopal (bishop-like) power to assume authority over local churches with an already-established leadership.[41] There is little evidence from Paul and his fellow workers for a stable hierarchy over established local churches.

5. The New Testament describes practices that might justify sharing leadership across multiple churches

Much of the historical discussion on the proper way to think about denominations centres on analyzing the way churches operated in the book of Acts. We need to be very careful not to try to extract too much detail from Acts, since it is not clear that its primary purpose is to lay out detailed principles for church governance. Moreover, we need to realize that this was a very early phase in the development of the church. As the Lausanne occasional paper on church/parachurch relationships quotes Paul Rees as saying: "In Acts the Church is molten—too hot for ecclesiastical engineers to handle."[42] Nevertheless, broad principles can and should still be gleaned with care. As Rees goes on to say, "On the other hand, it is not all ardour devoid of order".[43]

---

40 This is a point of concern for presbyterian theologians. Whereas episcopalians accept that an individual may be entrusted with the power to ordain and the congregationalist might argue that the whole congregation participates in electing its first leaders, the presbyterian insists ordination, at least of teaching elders, is properly the role of the regional presbytery. So, they insist, Paul, Barnabas or Titus practised ordination in their unique role as apostles and evangelists (so argues *The Form of Presbyterial Church-Government*). I think the concern is unfounded and an exception for such pioneer missionary settings does not threaten presbyterian principles: Paul, Barnabas and Titus might have operated as representative elders of the Antioch Presbytery, entrusted with the responsibility to ordain elders on their travels.

41 This leaves the question of to whom such missionaries ought to be accountable. I will save this question for chapter 8 (on cross-cultural missionary teams).

42 Cited in LCWE Commission on Co-operation, *Cooperating in World Evangelization*, p 106.

43 Cited in LCWE Commission on Co-operation, *Cooperating in World Evangelization*, p 106.

In the book of Acts, do we see examples of churches which both meet as separate local house churches and then also operate as a larger city church? See, for example, the church in Jerusalem: "Every day they continued to meet together in the temple courts. They broke bread in their homes and ate together with glad and sincere hearts" (Acts 2:46). Are these 'homes' in fact house churches? If this is the case, then the elders of these house churches shared together a joint oversight over the city church as a whole—it was this larger leadership, for example, that appointed deacons in Acts 6. The Ephesian church appears to be another example.[44] If this is the right way to interpret the evidence, then we have biblical examples of a kind of inter-church authority, similar to that which we find in a presbytery (or a multi-site church; see chapter 12). But these examples are far from conclusive, and theologians interpret the same evidence in quite different ways.[45] There is simply not enough clear evidence to know whether the participants considered these household meetings 'churches', let alone enough evidence to build a theology of church government from these few hints.

The Jerusalem Council in Acts 15 is especially important in thinking about denominations. Here we have leaders from multiple regions meeting together to resolve an important theological issue, and then broadcasting their conclusions not only to the regions they represent but further afield to the

---

44 The Ephesian church is referred to in the singular in Acts 20:17, but 1 Corinthians 16:19 refers to an Ephesian house church hosted by Priscilla and Aquila, which suggests there are in fact several house churches in Ephesus. Paul reminds the Ephesian elders that he taught them "publicly and from house to house" (Acts 20:20), which might refer to the public lectures in the Hall of Tyrannus (Acts 19:9-10) as well as house-church teaching.

45 The house-to-house gatherings in Jerusalem (Acts 2:46) are never called churches. There is significant debate about whether the 'church' in Jerusalem was able to regularly gather as one whole congregation, given the numbers of converts listed in the early chapters of Acts. Some suggest that once you take into account that many of the pilgrims who were converted eventually left Jerusalem with their new-found faith, and that even more were scattered by the persecution mentioned in Acts 8, the numbers that remained in Jerusalem were not so large after all. See Westminster Assembly, 'Reasons against the third proposition'.

churches in Syria and Cilicia as well (v 23).[46] Do we see here a principle of shared, authoritative leadership beyond the local church? Or is this a unique expression of apostolic leadership? If it were a unique event for the early apostolic age, then it is not a model for how churches should structure themselves today. But on close examination, it doesn't seem that this is merely a meeting of the apostles; it is the apostles *and elders* who reach agreement through discussion. It seems, then, that the apostles were acting as fellow elders (1 Pet 5:1) together with the wider body of leaders in this gathering, rather than acting in their unique role as apostles.

Others argue that this council was simply a meeting of the Jerusalem elders, giving advice on the problems in Antioch.[47] But it is difficult to justify the view that the council's decision was mere 'advice'. After all, Paul and Barnabas "delivered the decisions reached by the apostles and elders in Jerusalem for the people to obey" (Acts 16:4). It seems the meeting's conclusions were binding on other churches.[48]

We cannot neatly classify the Jerusalem Council as a routine, representative council like a presbytery or synod. But even if it is seen to be an occasional gathering of leaders from multiple regions, hosted by Jerusalem as the historical 'mother church' of Christianity, we may still be looking at an example of cooper-

---

46 There is no clear mention of representatives being sent from Syria and Cilicia, but this could be a plausible deduction from the evidence. Allison asks whether, perhaps, Barnabas, Judas or Silas made the journey; see *Sojourners and Strangers*, p 270. Perhaps the fact that Paul and Barnabas travelled through Phoenicia and Samaria on the way to Jerusalem (Acts 15:3) might be a hint that these churches sent some of their own leaders as well. On the other hand, since Paul and Barnabas functioned as church planters throughout these regions, they were legitimate delegates for the churches in these whole regions.

47 Westminster Assembly, 'Reasons against the third proposition', pp 28-33.

48 It is good to observe that it was the apostles and elders *of Jerusalem* who were consulted in verse 4, and presumably this same group who met in verse 6 and reached a decision in verse 22 (cf. 16:4, 21:25). Were Paul, Barnabas and the others with them merely guests at this meeting, rather than formal representatives and participants? But referring to the conclusion of this meeting as the decisions of the elders in Jerusalem could simply be a description of the fact that the council was hosted *by* the elders in Jerusalem, or a meeting of the elders (of various churches) *in* Jerusalem, rather than being a meeting of elders *of* Jerusalem alone. See Westminster Assembly, 'The answer of the assembly of divines', p 61.

ative, authoritative leadership, which might serve as a pattern and general principle.[49] It seems that those who are responsible for the leadership of individual churches might combine together to share leadership across the whole group, where needed and appropriate.

The key question is whether groups of local church leaders have the right to delegate authority to an inter-church council and then expect each of their churches to submit to its decisions. Some might consider this to be an abdication of the power and responsibility of local churches. Cooperation may be good when there is agreement and willing compromise, but what about when there is conflict? Can the wider leadership trump local church leaders? When there is a disagreement in a local church, and someone appeals to the wider denominational leadership, is it right for them to overrule the decisions of the local leaders against the will of those local leaders? If the denominational leadership introduces new regulations, is it right for them to impose these even on those churches who strongly disagree with them? If all the leaders and members of a congregation decide to disaffiliate from a denomination, should the local leaders and members be entitled to retain possession of the property it had been using?

The concept of delegating authority to an external group is especially problematic for those who uphold the ultimate authority of the entire local congregation. For if ultimate power for ordination and church discipline rests with the entire local congregation, then it cannot be shared across multiple congregations unless entire congregations gather together in a very large council. Such a view has a strong conviction that the authority of the church must only be exercised by a gathering of

---

49 William Cunningham is cautious when he writes: "The council cannot be shown to correspond fully with the modern idea of a synodical assembly or supreme church court, formally representing, and *simply because representing* a considerable number of particular churches, exercising authority or jurisdiction over them. But notwithstanding this concession, Presbyterians contend, and we think with good reason, that the *general principle or idea* of a representative character or judicial control, is sufficiently indicated" (Cunningham, *Historical Theology*, p 62).

the whole church: the authority rests exclusively with the *gathered* people.

I question whether the power of the local congregation must be seen as quite so restricted, absolute, and non-transferable. It could be legitimate, even for a congregationalist church, to resolve to share some of its responsibilities through delegates or leaders.[50] In this case, a church may also resolve for these leaders to make decisions together with delegates of other churches for mutual benefit. Even a voluntary cooperation between independent churches must decide when the conduct or doctrine of a church requires disaffiliation.[51] How much more is this the case if we conclude that the appointed leaders of the local churches have genuine authority—not merely to enact the decisions of the congregational meeting, to teach and to care for the church, but also to genuinely lead, enforce and direct? Then there is even more reason to say that leaders may resolve to work together on particular matters with leaders from other churches, having a shared oversight of all their congregations.[52]

---

50 "The power of presbyteries, synods, and assemblies, is cumulative, not privative; that is … it consists in the collected power of all the congregations of which it is composed, and in reality adds to the power of each, rather than takes away its proper power from any" (WM Hetherington, *History of the Westminster Assembly of Divines*, Mark H Newman, 1843, p 172). Such sharing of leadership by consent is as between "friends and equals", not "masters and servants" (Westminster Assembly, 'The answer of the assembly of divines', p 3). See also Powell, *The Crisis of British Protestantism*.

51 "When one church gives offense to others, they ought to submit to trial and examination by those offended; and if the offending church should persist in their error, then the others are 'to pronounce that heavy sentence against them, of withdrawing and renouncing all Christian communion with them until they do repent.' This sentence of *non-communion*, as they term it, is what they meant by *excommunication*" (Hetherington, *History of the Westminster Assembly of Divines*, p 161, emphasis original; quoting T Goodwin, P Nye, S Simpson, J Burroughes and W Bridge, *An apologeticall narration, humbly submitted to the Honourable Houses of Parliament*, Robert Dawlman, 1643, p 17, accessed 15 September 2022 [name.umdl.umich.edu/A85427.0001.001]).

52 Cunningham, *Historical Theology*, pp 51-53.

	Biblical justification	Dangers	How power could be corrupted	Strengths
Congrega-tional	NT focus on the local church Whole congregation has authority and responsibility	Isolation Impotent leadership at both local and inter-church level	Mob rule	Liberty
Presby-terian	Elders also have authority and responsibility Sharing leadership between churches is legitimate	Inefficiency, especially at inter-church level Interfere with the integrity of the local congregation	Bureaucracy	Collaboration
Episcopal	No detailed NT teaching about church governance Example of Paul and his associates	Tyranny Impose on the integrity of the local congregation	Oligarchy	Efficiency

Table 3: Comparison of congregational, presbyterian and episcopal views[53]

Ultimately, there will remain points of disagreement between Christians and denominations, and these disagreements will affect the extent to which we can or will submit to a denomina-

---

53 Note that there is significant variation between these three rows, and the borders between them are fuzzy. Here again, the labels for each row are used as descriptive terms, rather than as names of specific denominations.

tion in good conscience (or whether we submit at all). Different denominational structures were established, often at great cost, to honour these differences in conviction and conscience.

But, despite these important differences, I believe there are two principles that we can agree on. Firstly, we should humbly strive to cooperate with fellow Christians across multiple churches for the sake of mutual benefit and fruitful ministry. Secondly, denominational authority should be exercised in a way that gives great dignity and freedom to local churches.

We will now explore these two complementary principles in more depth.

The priority of the denominational association over other parachurch commitments

No matter what your view of church government, *your local church should give an important place to its denominational association*. Other churches might be geographically closer to your church and might be more aligned with your church's philosophy of ministry; you might enjoy greater affection and rapport between the members and leaders of churches outside your denomination. But to be a part of a denomination is to accept a mutually agreed upon commitment to others in that association of churches. Even if you do not consider the denomination to be a divinely ordained or authoritative structure, the denomination still has a special, presumptive place as the 'first parachurch association among many'.[54] How much more is this the case for

54 The simplest qualitative difference between denominations and other parachurches is that, unlike independent parachurches, denominations "at least owe their existence, and are answerable, to assemblies of believers amongst whom may be found the notae [marks] of church reality" (Rees, cited in LCWE Commission on Co-operation, *Cooperating in World Evangelization*, p 105). See also Willmer, Schmidt and Smith: "It is hard to imagine how this definition [i.e. the denomination is just a parachurch] can be seen as a gain. It just muddies the terms … To follow [this solution] … is to lose a useful word and end up with a gray and amorphous word that tries to cover every Christian organization" (Willmer et al., *The Prospering Parachurch*, pp 24-25).

those who are persuaded that there is biblical support, or perhaps even a mandate, for inter-church association and authority.

This doesn't mean the denomination should always demand most of our efforts or the best of our efforts, much less that its leaders can demand loyalty to every denominational organization, initiative and enterprise. A local congregation (or leader, or individual) might well resolve in good conscience to give greater time and energy towards some parachurch ministry opportunity (such as a mission society, theological college or pastors' conference), rather than to the denominational equivalent. There is nothing necessarily disloyal or compromised about this decision. An imperfect analogy might be that of extended family: I give much more of my time to serve friends and colleagues than I do to serve cousins or nephews, and yet there remains family loyalty and privilege. The denominational association has a similarly privileged place. This should also be taken into account by parachurch organizations as they relate to individual Christians, local churches and denominational courts (we will also explore the important limits of denominational allegiance below).

Such a commitment to the denomination has some unique benefits. *It fosters a godly patience and love for fellow Christians who are different from us.* "If you love those who love you, what reward will you get? Are not even the tax collectors doing that?" Jesus warns (Matt 5:46), a principle that holds true in church association. It is easier to love those churches with which we naturally gel; it is more of a challenge to show genuine love for fellow Christians with whom the bond is organizational rather than relational. But by being bound together denominationally, our church can be forced to grow in patience and love.

Denominations can guard against the worst excesses and eccentricities of independent churches. The possibility for church members to appeal to some group beyond the local church, and the implicit permission for church leaders to intervene in another church in their denomination, can be very useful, even in those denominations where there is little or no formal governance authority. Such an appeal may have its limits, perhaps even massive imperfections, as do all human institutions. But even if it only helps sometimes, this can be a great blessing to the people of God and the reputation of the gospel.

Denominational association can provoke a local church to have concern for the kingdom of God beyond its own boundaries. Parachurches also offer this benefit, as we explored in chapter 2. Regular connection with a wider group of churches can help a church make decisions with a broader horizon in view. For example, a church that struggles to reach its community or pay its bills might better serve the kingdom by amalgamating with another church nearby. A large church with a big budget and many staff and facilities could provide support and training to other churches. There are greater things than building up or preserving the interests of our local congregation. Our ultimate agenda is the glory of God in his universal, heavenly church, not our comfort or achievement in the local congregation.

Denominational commitment means investing in some of the most long-term Christian institutions in the world. Of course, there are other parachurches that have a long legacy, and there are many new and fragile denominations. But denominational structures are some of the most stable and well-resourced Christian organizations. The short-term frustration of participating in denominational life is a gift to the long-term wellbeing of churches in your part of the world.

Denominational institutions preserve broad patterns of doctrine, ethics and ministry. Some parachurches have very rigorous doctrinal and ethical foundations, but parachurches are often defined more by their specific vision, mission, values and strategy, rather than by narrow doctrinal concerns. By contrast, a denominational institution is both narrow and broad: it exists to preserve and propagate a precise set of beliefs and practices, but it welcomes *all* who adhere to these beliefs and practices, whatever their emphasis on matters of style, culture, method or politics. Even those denominations that depart from their theological roots and become theologically and morally liberal preserve many of these forms in their heritage, and so ensure the possibility of future reformation and renewal.

Lastly, *some people who aren't Christians will more happily engage with familiar denominational structures.* In this way, the historical forms of our denominations can open opportunities for evangelism and community engagement—through events surrounding Christmas and Easter, invitations to speak in the media, or simply enquirers seeking out churches from their family's heritage. This offers a unique evangelistic opportunity to those churches that are explicit about their denominational identity.

The limits of the denomination in serving the wellbeing of local churches

But even if you believe that a denomination has a necessary divine authority over local churches in certain matters and is practically beneficial in many ways, *it is not right for the denomination to be given priority over local churches.*[55] At most, the denomination has an equal priority but a different function. This different function might include certain kinds of authority over local churches, but these kinds of authority must be limited, and must always be used for the wellbeing of local churches and for the spread of the gospel. As Louis Berkhof writes:

> Every local church is a complete church of Christ, fully equipped with everything that is required for its government. It has absolutely no need of it that any government should be imposed upon it from without. And not only that, but such imposition would be absolutely contrary to its nature …
>
> The authority and prerogatives of the major assemblies are not unlimited … They are not permitted to lord it over a local church or its members … nor to

---

55 For this reason, Louis Berkhof recommends speaking of 'more general' church courts, rather than 'higher' church courts; see Berkhof, *Systematic Theology*, pp 590-591.

meddle with the internal affairs of a local church under any and all circumstances.[56]

Whatever duties we might have to a wider network of churches should not absorb the life and ministry of local churches; whatever power the gathered leaders of churches might have cannot undermine the life and ministry of local churches. In other words, any shared leadership between churches should be more 'democratic' than 'aristocratic'. Whereas 'aristocratic presbyterianism' sees local churches as receiving their existence and authority top-down from the presbytery or assembly,[57] 'democratic presbyterianism' sees the authority as delegated bottom-up to the church courts (see Table 1 above). This bottom-up emphasis much more closely resembles the New Testament's picture of the church.

The most tragic expression of denominationalism is where Christians give such loyalty to their denomination that they maintain Christian fellowship with those who have the same church 'brand', style of liturgy and pattern of church government, but deny fundamentals of the Christian faith—often expressed in the confessional documents of the denomination. It is far better to attend a faithful church that baptizes children, or sings nothing but unaccompanied biblical Psalms, or is governed by a regional presbytery, than to insist on attending the local Baptist church even when it has lost the gospel.

Denominations should primarily function in the service of local churches and the furtherance of the gospel mission. Over time, denominations can launch a range of organizations and initiatives that are no more fundamental to the role of a denomination than they are to the role of a local church (see further discus-

---

56 Berkhof, *Systematic Theology*, pp 589-590. So also Spykman: "A healthy measure of 'fraternal cooperation' is required to strike a happy balance between the rights and responsibilities of local congregations, which are fundamental to all church life, and the organic unity of the church as a whole as that comes to expression in its broader assemblies" (Spykman, *Reformational Theology*, p 467).

57 It is interesting to note that the Westminster Confession doesn't have a separate article about the nature and power of the local church at all.

sion of this in chapter 12). It is not necessarily wrong for a denomination to engage in a range of good activities, or to provide a whole range of helpful supports to gospel ministry. But it is very easy for denominations to become more and more bloated and unfocused, often leading to expensive levies on the local churches. Disciplined and rigorous assessment should be applied to the planning, launching, overseeing and maintenance of denominational programs.

~

In summary, while there is a loose sense in which a denomination might be called a 'church' (such as 'the Reformed Church in America'), this must be very carefully distinguished from the primary biblical meanings of the word: the heavenly assembly and the local church. On the other hand, it is not helpful to describe denominations as nothing more than parachurches. Most denominations have a degree of authority and necessity that no other parachurch has; and most denominations assume a kind of priority that other parachurches do not. I have argued that there is a legitimate place not only for shared fellowship and cooperation, but also for shared oversight of churches. However, such sharing must not undermine the wellbeing, authority and ministry of local churches.

Chapter 4: The kingdom of God and the mission of God

"If your church were to disappear tomorrow, would anyone notice?" asks Robert Lewis in his book *The Church of Irresistible Influence*.[1] How would you answer? A few less people handing out fliers at the train station at Christmas and Easter? A few less awkward religious conversations at the school gate? Easier to find a park near the church building on Sunday? Much of what our churches do is focused on explicitly religious goals, so for those who are not interested in religion, our contribution is often not noticed or valued. But Christianity is about more than Bible reading and prayer and churchgoing and private morals. God's word speaks to every area of our lives, and our worship of God is expressed in every area of our thinking, speaking and doing: in public and in private; in explicitly religious activities and in secular politics; in mundane routines and in creative and recreational pursuits. Devout Christians are also interested in loving their neighbour as themselves—not just those in their church or social groups, but all their neighbours—and even in loving their enemies. "If your church were to disappear tomorrow, would anyone notice?" I would hope so.

1 Cited in E Stetzer, 'Am I my city's keeper?', *Faith Radio*, 22 February 2016, accessed 28 September 2022 (myfaithradio.com/2016/citys-keeper).

And yet the question is framed in a way that seems to invite a particular emphasis: "If *your church* were to disappear tomorrow, would anyone notice?" It is necessary for Christians to live out their faith in love and good deeds. It is good and right that Christians proactively organize themselves to serve God and love their neighbour in all these different spheres of life. But is it necessary for *your church*, as a formal community, to be active in such things? After all, it might be possible for Christians to do all manner of good in their community, but for little of this to be formally initiated by their local church. As discussed in chapter 2, many of these pursuits are not the responsibility of the institutional church herself, and so it is proper that much of this activity takes place beyond the bounds of the local church, and possibly even beyond the denomination (see Diagram I).

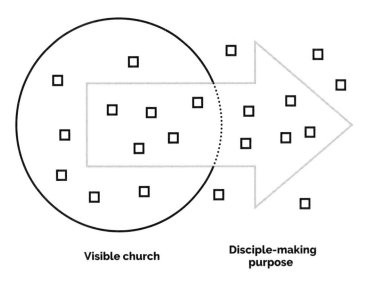

Visible church

Disciple-making purpose

Diagram I: Ministries inside and beyond local church

In this chapter, I will consider in a little more detail the question of how good deeds relate to gospel work, the kingdom of God and the local church. My aim is to help us reach greater clarity on these matters as part of our broader thinking about parachurch ministry, so that we may better understand where the opportunities and responsibilities properly lie.

The gospel and good deeds

We should start by remembering that *the gospel itself is the very practical act of God's gracious love for us.* The greatest personal, physical and spiritual need we have is to be forgiven of our sins, rescued from the eternal wrath of God, reconciled to our Creator, and given the sure hope of the resurrection of the dead. The gospel cannot be separated from good deeds, because the gospel itself is a supreme good deed.

The necessary response to the gospel includes wholehearted worship of God and love of our neighbour. Genuine conversion results in a Spirit-led life of love and good deeds. We are saved *from* sin and death and saved *to* a holy life. The God who saved us is worthy of all glory, honour and praise. And our Saviour God is also the Creator of all things, and so he commands us to serve him as a part of his creation. The more we dwell upon the truths and implications of the gospel, the more motivation we have for spiritual adoration and humble service. Furthermore, this love and worship is never purely individualistic; we also express this in the network of relationships established by marriage, family, friendship, neighbourhood, and the church.

Worship of God and love for our neighbour includes the proclamation of the gospel. The Great Commission is not an entirely separate thing from the greatest commandments. We rightly worship God by believing his gospel, praising him for his gospel, and proclaiming his gospel. And we proactively love our neighbour by holding out to them the word of life. As John Piper said at the Lausanne Congress of World Evangelization in 2010: "Christians care about all suffering, especially eternal suffering".[2]

The gospel should be proclaimed in a just, loving and truthful manner. We must not leave concerns about godliness to one side when we turn to evangelism, as if the ends justify the

---

2 Cited in J Taylor, 'We care about all suffering in this age—especially eternal suffering', *Between Two Worlds*, 19 November 2010, accessed 17 September 2022 (thegospel coalition.org/blogs/justin-taylor/we-care-about-all-suffering-in-this-age-especially-eternal-suffering).

means. Honesty and kindness should characterize the conduct of the preacher, and the gospel must be offered free from any favouritism, discrimination or coercion.

Good deeds are not only a necessary response to the gospel. *Good deeds also commend the gospel.* They give credibility to both the sincerity of our personal profession of faith and to the claim that our message is about the righteous and merciful God (see Titus 2:5, 8, 10; 1 Pet 2:11-17; 3:1, 15-16). This is true not only of personal holiness, but also of the loving community life of the church, as Jesus promised: "By this everyone will know that you are my disciples, if you love one another" (John 13:35). The church is, in a sense, a "hermeneutic for the gospel".[3] Or consider the opposite: where professing Christians live hypocritically, "God's name is blasphemed among the Gentiles because of you" (Rom 2:24). Good deeds become a "bridge to evangelism".[4]

Good deeds also provide opportunities for gospel proclamation. Being attentive to the troubles and needs of others, not to mention being active in helping to meet those needs and alleviate those troubles, brings us into relationship with wider circles of people—not only those we naturally like and those we hope to partner with, but perhaps also those whom we seek to persuade, and even those we oppose. In our loving engagement with others, we end up reaching people we would never have contact with if we focused solely on doorknocking outreach and friendship evangelism.

In these and many other ways, the gospel is necessarily related to our whole lives of love and worship.

Nevertheless, *gospel preaching can be separated from other good deeds.* This is perhaps seen most clearly in gospel publishing and broadcasting. It is possible to communicate the gospel to someone through a website, a radio show, a tract, or Bible distribution

---

3   MW Goheen, *"As the Father Has Sent Me, I Am Sending You": J.E. Lesslie Newbigin's missionary ecclesiology*, Boekencentrum, 2000, pp 175-176.

4   Lausanne Committee for World Evangelization and World Evangelical Fellowship, *Evangelism and Social Responsibility: An Evangelical Commitment*, Lausanne Occasional Paper 21, The Lausanne Movement website, 25 June 1982, p 17, accessed 17 September 2022 (lausanne.org/content/lop/lop-21).

without any direct personal relationship or accompanying loving action. This doesn't make these forms of evangelism somehow suspicious or deficient; they may ordinarily be less effective than more holistic forms of evangelism, but this doesn't make them bad. Such ministries remind us that gospel preaching is narrow and specific, something which can be distinguished from all the other good and true things Christians can think, say or do.

Christian thinkers have sought to make this distinction in a variety of ways: John Dickson talks about "proclaiming the gospel" as a narrower thing than "promoting the gospel";[5] Lesslie Newbigin says that 'missions' is narrower than 'mission';[6] Abraham Kuyper talks about 'the church as institution' and 'the church as organism';[7] Kevin DeYoung and Greg Gilbert talk about the 'disciple-making mission of the church' and 'good deeds'.[8] In the Bible, the apostle Peter distinguishes between "prayer and the ministry of the word" and the ministry of "wait[ing] on tables" (Acts 6:2-4).

Whatever language is used, drawing this distinction does not necessarily create a 'dualism' between the sacred and the secular, nor does it necessarily introduce a 'clericalism' between ordained Christian leaders and everyone else.[9] It is a distinction within the larger holistic reality: the larger reality of Christians serving God in everything they do.

Evangelism and good deeds are no more in conflict or com-

---

5   JP Dickson, *Promoting the Gospel: A practical guide to the biblical art of sharing your faith*, Blue Bottle Books, 2005, p 15.

6   Goheen, *"As the Father Has Sent Me"*, p 275.

7   Spykman, *Reformational Theology*, pp 430-433. I'm not convinced these are good terms to use. We shouldn't remove any concept of 'organism' from the local church institution, as if somehow the local congregation is marked only by formal structure. Likewise, 'church as organism' might associate in its own formal 'institutions'. See Tuit, *A Study and Comparison*, p 133. See also Kuiper, who writes "such language does not excel at precision" (*The Glorious Body of Christ*, p 115). See also D Strange, 'Rooted and Grounded? The legitimacy of Abraham Kuyper's distinction between church as institute and church as organism, and its usefulness in constructing an evangelical public theology', *Themelios*, 2015, 40(3):429-444.

8   K DeYoung and G Gilbert, *What is the Mission of the Church? Making sense of social justice, shalom, and the Great Commission*, Crossway, 2011.

9   Contrary to Stuart Heath, 'Discouraging words: Ministry', *The Gospel Coalition Australia Edition*, 4 August 2016, accessed 17 September 2022 (au.thegospelcoalition.org/article/discouraging-words-ministry).

petition than evangelism and holiness.[10] Godly Christians ought to be committed to doing good to their neighbours in a whole range of ways on a whole range of levels. Faithful preaching and discipleship will challenge and inspire Christians in this, both individually and cooperatively—and, in some cases, perhaps even encouraging cooperation with non-Christians. For many reasons, there have been ebbs and flows throughout history as Christians have sought to hold together evangelism and good deeds.[11] But neither element has ever been entirely absent.

So what place do each of these things have in the organizational life of the church?

The kingdom of God and the church

There is more to God's sovereign rule than the salvation and corporate life of the church—whether local or universal. The Almighty rules over all creation, and his ultimate purpose is to renew all creation. In that sense, all things are in 'the kingdom of God'. Therefore, beyond our submission to the rule of God in the specific activities and responsibilities of church life, we ought to also serve our divine king in any number of other activities and responsibilities (as family members, rulers over his created world, citizens of our nation, and so on).[12] In fact, beyond everything we do as Christians, God continues to work out his sovereign purposes in the lives of non-Christians and over the non-human world.[13]

In the New Testament, 'the kingdom of God' usually refers to something a bit more specific than this: it is something we can

---

10 Williams, *Relocating Holism*, pp 48-55.

11 For a description and analysis of these ebbs and flows over the past few hundred years in British evangelicalism, see Bebbington, *Evangelicalism in Modern Britain*. For a similar look at Australian evangelicalism, see S Piggin, *Spirit, Word and World: Evangelical Christianity in Australia*, Rainbow Book Agencies, 2012.

12 Tuit, *A Study and Comparison*, pp 157-159, 164-165, 186-195; "Everything does not have to be loaded on the mission mandate given to the church because there is already the cultural mandate" (p 193).

13 Berkhof, *Systematic Theology*, p 406; and Bavinck, *Reformed Dogmatics*, p 618.

'enter' or 'receive' or 'seek'. This could be called 'the saving kingdom of God'—a kingdom in which we are reconciled to the Almighty King and now live in conscious obedience to his rule. The kingdom 'comes' or 'draws near' as God's saving rule is extended through the life, death and resurrection of Christ and the subsequent preaching of his gospel. And it will come to fullness when every enemy, including death, is defeated (1 Cor 15:24-28).[14] But even in this sense, 'the saving kingdom of God' is not identical to 'the church', for Christ's saving rule is at work beyond not only local churches, but in fact beyond everything that we Christians do. The church is a visible expression of the saving kingdom of God, but not entirely identical with it (see Diagram J).[15]

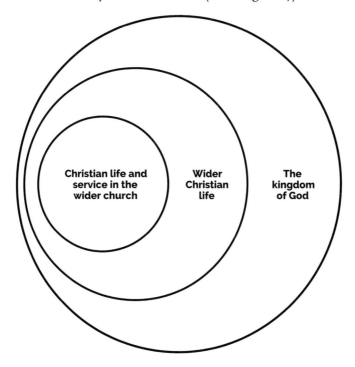

Diagram J: Kingdom of God and the church

14 Contrary to some 'missional church' authors for whom, according to Pieter Tuit, "little or no distinction is made between God's providential rule over all creation and his saving rule in Christ. Everything seems to be included in God's reign which then is his saving reign" (Tuit, *A Study and Comparison*, p 152).
15 "It is closely related to the Church, though not altogether identical with it" (Berkhof, *Systematic Theology*, p 409). See also LCWE and WEF, *Evangelism and Social Responsibility*, p 24.

All of this helps us to think about 'the mission of the church'. As God's image bearers, as citizens of the kingdom of God, and as members of the universal church, Christians are to obey all the commands of God and fulfil all the responsibilities entrusted to us.[16] In that sense, we could say that 'the mission of God's people' is to worship God, love our neighbour and obey everything God has commanded us, including the preaching of the gospel and the building of the church, but also ruling over creation, nurturing of families and communities, the alleviation of physical suffering, and opposition to injustice.[17]

But as local church communities, we are entrusted with the responsibility of prayerfully making disciples of all the nations and building up holy, pure and faithful churches.[18] Not everything we do as God's people needs to be done formally and communally *as the church*. As Peter De Jong explains:

> Not everything may be undertaken by the church in this world. This needs emphasis today. Often we find the church expected to build schools, maintain nurseries, introduce recreational programs for the youth, plan programs in good citizenship and directly influence the course of politics. Whatever seems to go wrong in society is charged against Christ's church. In consequence, many church leaders find themselves over-

16 We cannot and should not presume to figure out how God is sovereignly ruling the universe, so that we seek social progress in cooperation with God's universal kingdom work. Rather, we are simply to serve our universal King in faithful obedience, submitting to his sovereign purposes for the nations of the world, whatever they might be.

17 However, I agree with Keith Ferdinando that this easily creates confusion: "Thinking of mission in such terms tends towards a collapse of categories traditionally distinguished from one another ... if all that God does in the world is indeed mission, a new terminology is required to categorize his specifically redemptive activity" (K Ferdinando, 'Mission: A problem of definition', *Themelios*, 2008, 33(1):46-59. Pieter Tuit likewise warns that if the *missio Dei* (the mission of God) is used to describe all that God does, then "creation collapses in redemption" (Tuit, *A Study and Comparison*, p 140). Tuit also quotes Stephen Neill as saying, "if everything is mission, nothing is mission", and Walter Freytag as warning about "the spectre of panmissionism" (p 168, fn 20).

18 In this I disagree with the even narrower vision of the church's purpose described by Donald Robinson and Broughton Knox: the church gathers for the purpose of fellowship, but has no mission; the church is the result of mission, not a vehicle for mission. See Williams, *Relocating Holism*; and also discussion of these issues in chapter 1.

burdened with so many responsibilities in and for the community, that the proper calling of the church is forgotten.[19]

This is not to say that church communities should never engage in some of these other projects—but these are not necessary, primary, and essential duties for local churches and denominations.[20]

This clarity will also ensure that charitable, cultural and political groups respect the distinct mission and responsibility of the visible church. Passion for a particular cause, if not restrained, can lead to unjustified expectations of the church. Also tempting is the potential leverage that could be gained by mobilizing the church community and church institution: what a captive audience! What a recruiting ground! What a broad base! This is where we should remember that parachurch organizations exist, at least in part, to fulfil other valuable Christian goals that are not the primary responsibility of the church, and that it is good for them to be convinced of and content with that role.

'Baptizing' or 'spiritualizing' good deeds

In pursuing good deeds that are outside the church's primary responsibility, and then in seeking to dignify our efforts or per-

19 De Jong, *The Church's Witness to the World*, pp 296-297. See also DeYoung and Gilbert, *What Is the Mission of the Church?*; and DA McGavran, 'What is Mission?', in AF Glasser and DA McGavran (eds), *Contemporary Theologies of Mission*, Baker Book House, 1983, pp 15-29.

20 In this I disagree with the Lausanne occasional paper on evangelism and social responsibility: "Just as each local church has an inescapable responsibility before God to bring the gospel to all the people ... in its neighbourhood, so the social needs of the neighbourhood should be a special concern of the local church" (LCWE and WEF, *Evangelism and Social Responsibility*, p 37). This paper contains many helpful clarifications around the relationship between evangelism and good deeds. However, it undermines this clarity when it says, "Social activity not only follows evangelism as its consequence and aim, and precedes it as its bridge, but also accompanies it as its partner. They are like the two blades of a pair of scissors or the two wings of a bird ... Both also issue from the lordship of Jesus, for he sends us out into the world both to preach and to serve" (pp 17-18).

suade others of their value, we can be tempted to say too much. Powerful, biblical, spiritual words like 'kingdom' and 'ministry' and 'redeeming' and 'renewing' and 'gospel-centred' can be used to demonstrate the great value of our project. A charitable organization is one thing; a charitable *ministry* sounds much better. A studio for Christian artists is not quite as spiritual as a *fellowship* of Christian artists. A seminar series around some basics of godly parenting might better be rebranded as a *gospel-centred* parenting course. Investing in inner-city infrastructure becomes urban *renewal*, film reviews become *redeeming* the arts, and financial planning becomes *kingdom* stewardship.

These descriptions might help us to appreciate that everything we do is an expression of our worship of God and should be an outworking of our faithful obedience to the Lord Jesus. But in most or all of these cases, the simple adjective 'Christian' might do just as well. Sometimes, it seems that the implicit (or explicit!) claim is that painting a picture, running a school, feeding the hungry, managing your finances, lobbying the government or reviewing a film is somehow equivalent to the saving work of the Lord carried out in prayerful proclamation of the gospel. And this is not true. These things can all be spiritually significant and morally valuable without needing to be reframed in churchly and salvific terms.

Parachurches should present themselves and their activities clearly, showing what kind of 'ministry' they are undertaking—whether word ministry or practical ministry—and how directly they serve God's saving work in the world. Denominations, churches and individual Christians should also take into account these different types of parachurches in the way they promote and support their activities. While it is great for a church to send a Christian doctor to do a 'medical ministry' in a developing country, it is not as directly related to Jesus' Great Commission as sending a theologian to teach at a newly established theological college, and we should not obscure the difference. An event where the meaning of the gospel is explained and people are urged to respond in repentance and faith is different from an event where

Christians speak broadly about how aspects of their faith inform their values and actions in some practical area of life.

Things aren't cut and dried. Sometimes, missionaries travel overseas with clear evangelistic intent, but use their professional work to gain access to certain countries or to fund their missionary work. Such 'tent-making' missionary work is different than 'marketplace missionaries', who might hope and pray to contribute to local churches and take opportunities when they arise, but who are not primarily going with an evangelistic intent. Or again, an organization might host a disciple-making ministry within a larger structure, such as chaplaincy and religious education within a Christian school, or Bible study and discussion groups hosted by a Christian hostel. In doing so, these groups mark themselves out as a different quality of thing than general education or accommodation services. The more transparency and specificity that parachurches can provide on such things, the better.

This is where it is also helpful to *consider whether the charitable, cultural or political activities of the church should be constituted as a separate parachurch organization.* As we have seen, one of the benefits of the parachurch is that it protects the church from mission drift. Such a separation does not necessarily cut off these organizations from Christian identity and witness.[21] When the charitable, cultural or political ministries become very large, they might create an imbalance in the life of the local church or the economy of the wider denomination. As these organizations become larger and more self-sufficient, and as the employees and participants become less directly tied to the life

---

21 Contrary to Newbigin's view as described in Goheen, *"As the Father Has Sent Me"*, pp 302-305. However, note that in another place Newbigin says, "When men say 'The Church should go into educational work', they mean that the Church as an organized body should employ paid teachers. But if thousands of Church members are teaching in the schools of the nation that is not regarded as 'Church work', we have largely lost the great Biblical conception of the Church as the Body of Christ through whose entire membership the Lord wills to do His will in the world" (Goheen, *"As the Father Has Sent Me"*, p 306). I agree with this sentiment (although I wouldn't use the term 'church' in this context), and so agree with Goheen's assessment (pp 306-308) that Newbigin is equivocal when he speaks about the duties of 'the Church'.

of the church, it becomes less and less obvious that the church or denomination ought to be directly owning and managing them. Some parachurch work might also provide more accessible benefits to a wider circle of people if not tied to a church. Additionally, as will be discussed below, such work might involve making commitments to certain courses of social and political action from which it is helpful to keep the church separate.

~

Good deeds are central to the Christian life and connected to the evangelistic mission of God in a range of very important ways. But not every good thing that Christians can and should do is therefore equally or directly part of the mission of God, nor is it necessarily part of bringing the kingdom of God—at least not in the same direct way that preaching and prayer are. There are substantial theological reasons for mobilizing and sustaining Christians in their godly activity without needing to identify these activities directly with the kingdom of God or the mission of God. Furthermore, not every good thing that Christians can and should do is necessarily something that the local church must formally organize and facilitate. One of the great reasons for establishing parachurches is that they enable Christians to band together to pursue a whole range of good deeds that are not the primary focus of the local church.

Summary of part 1

In these first four chapters, we have laid down complex but important theological foundations:

- The church is, first and foremost, the universal, heavenly gathering of all those who are in Christ.
- The local church is a faithful, formal community of Christians who gather for the purpose of meeting God in his word, praying to him, praising him, building up each other in the faith, building unbelievers into the faith, loving one another, and managing the affairs of the church.
- The parachurch is organized Christian activity that is distinct from the visible, institutional church.
- A denomination is an association of churches that recognizes commonality between churches, facilitates loving cooperation, and makes possible the shared exercise of leadership.

From these theological foundations, we have drawn out a series of important principles, which must be reflected in the way we establish and run churches, parachurches and denominations:

- The primary identity and loyalty for the Christian is to Christ and his heavenly church, rather than any earthly, human community or institution.

- The local church has a priority in God's purposes.
- The denomination has a certain privilege and importance for local churches.
- The denomination must serve the wellbeing of local churches and the ministry of the gospel.

With these theological foundations and principles in place, the rest of this book will explore various types of parachurch activity, considering additional biblical principles, commands and prohibitions, learning from historical examples, and proposing practical guidelines. But first, we will consider some more general issues around how churches, denominations and parachurches should work together for the cause of Christ.

PART 2 //
PRACTICAL
RECOMMENDATIONS[1]

1   The material in part 2 was originally presented in seminar format at the Challenge
    Conference, Hobart, in 2019.

Chapter 5: How are we serving the Lord's mission?

The diverse ecosystem of churches, denominations and parachurches is a wonderful thing. But the sad reality is that we might at times find ourselves with efficient organizations, vibrant events, sophisticated publications and all sorts of wonderful good deeds, but little in the way of saved souls or godly Christians. So before I ask *how* churches and parachurches might work together for the cause of Christ (chapters 6 and 7), I want to ask a more fundamental question: *Are* we working together for the cause of Christ? Could our local church, parachurch, denomination or regional Christian ecosystem be described in Macbeth's words: "a tale told by an idiot, full of sound and fury, signifying nothing"? I hope and pray that, for many readers, this chapter is not urgently needed—that it is primarily a good reminder to stay faithfully on course. But for some of us, it may well be a wake-up call. How are we serving the Lord's mission?

Who's preaching the gospel?

The gospel of the Lord Jesus Christ is the power of God for the salvation of everyone who believes (Rom 1:16). It is through the revelation of Christ Jesus and his saving death that he builds his church, which the gates of Hades won't overcome (Matt 16:18). This gospel is revealed to us in the Scriptures, which are God-breathed and able to thoroughly equip us for every good work (2 Tim 3:16-17). Without God's revelation, God's people become deaf to God's love, blind to God's will, and powerless to participate in God's saving work in the world. God's word in all its richness ought to be treasured, as it speaks to us in all sorts of ways about God, ourselves and the world. And central to that revelation is God's grand saving purpose—his reconciling purpose, which is fulfilled in the new creation.[1]

The Scripture readings and sermon in the Sunday gathering, the devotion at the start of a Christian charity's board meeting, the chapel service in the Christian school, the morning devotion in the Christian household, the Scripture references in a Christian book, and the personal quiet time for the Christian individual are not mere token gestures or liturgical habits. They are expressions of a supernatural reality: the Lord God who spoke the world into being is now doing a work of new creation through his word (2 Cor 4:6). At this point, we are accessing extraordinary power.

What place does God's word have in our lives, our work, and our ministry? Is it shrinking or peripheral? Or is it central and vibrant? How seriously do our ministries treat our confessional statements? Does sincere adherence to a shared confession determine our fellowship? Or is a vague Christian commitment —perhaps a denominational affiliation, or a general spirituality invoking the words 'Holy Spirit' and 'Jesus'—sufficient? Do we

---

1 For a great summary of the overarching story of Scripture and its relevance to Christian life and ministry today, see Marshall and Payne, 'What in the world is God doing?' in *The Trellis and the Vine*, pp 29-39, and Marshall and Payne, 'Conviction 1: Why make disciples?' in *The Vine Project*, pp 47-60.

humbly submit to God's word in reverent awe? Or is it used in a light, proof-texting manner, nothing more than a collection of illustrative material and isolated 'thoughts for the day' along with a few practical tips?

Not every parachurch ministry exists primarily to preach the gospel. And not every Christian committee meeting or blog post must be formally marked by the explicit quoting of a Bible text. Such practice could, ironically, reduce the Bible to a mere formal artefact. But all Christian spirituality and activity should be ruled by and richly soaked in the word of God. And all our efforts, whether formal or informal, ought to be alert to God's great purposes. As Colin Marshall and Tony Payne write:

> This is what God is doing in the world: Spirit-backed gospel preaching leading to the salvation of souls. It's his program, his agenda, his priority, his focus, his project, or whatever business-related metaphor you'd like to use. And by it, he is gathering a new Christ-centred people as his very own; a quiet, steadily-growing profusion of leaves on the great vine of his kingdom ...
>
> If this is really what God is doing in our world then it is time to say goodbye to our small and self-oriented ambitions, and to abandon ourselves to the cause of Christ and his gospel.[2]

Even if we are not all cross-cultural missionaries, this remains the big picture of which we are a part. Even if the parachurch organization we lead is not primarily about evangelism or Christian discipleship, we are still implementing our mission in the context of this larger flow of salvation history. It is terribly short sighted—and, sooner or later, unhealthy—for any Christian to lose sight of this. Yes, there's more to Christian life and ministry than making disciples. To fixate on a narrow definition of Christian life and ministry would not do justice to the whole counsel of God, and would ultimately distort our gospel in subtle ways. And yet making disciples holds a central place in

2 Marshall and Payne, *The Trellis and the Vine*, pp 35, 38.

Christian life and ministry. Every Christian and every Christian organization should stop and reflect on what part we play in this great work. Every Christian and every Christian organization ought to ask if we might do things differently to best serve this work (depending, of course, on our situation and our gifts).

More still, what if we look around our local area and see that little is being done in preaching the gospel, saving the lost, and maturing and equipping believers? Where have we gone wrong? In such circumstances, surely leaders of churches and parachurches must pray and ponder with great seriousness how to remedy this situation. Why persist in a specialized parachurch ministry when there is a dire need for church pastors or Bible translators? Why publish superficial devotional literature when there is so little substantial Christian publishing? Why pour hours into refining our doctrinal standards and ecclesiastical polity if we are neglecting to do almost anything for the rescuing of souls from hell?

Who's doing evangelism?

The central work of making disciples can be represented in a simple diagram like this:[3]

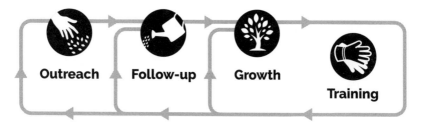

Diagram K: The gospel growth process

---

3   Diagram used with permission from Marshall and Payne, *The Trellis and the Vine*, p 85.

This is helpful for thinking about personal ministry: where does Vithusha currently stand, and what would be most helpful to move her further along to the right in this diagram? Or, once she has been trained, how do we mobilize her back to the left so that she can minister to others? It is also a helpful diagnostic tool for thinking about a whole church or parachurch ministry: where are the gaps? Are we great at outreach but lacklustre in follow-up, or vice versa?

So who is doing the outreach? Who's actually finding meaningful ways to bring the saving message of Jesus Christ to those living in darkness? Sadly, even missionary societies and evangelistic parachurch groups often end up spending more and more of their time in maturing and training the believers, rather than making a significant impact in the work of evangelism. Or worse, they abandon gospel ministry almost entirely in favour of other charitable purposes. Other so-called outreach ministries devote enormous amounts of time and money to building bridges with people who aren't Christian, whether through discussion forums or building meaningful friendships, but the gospel is never actually preached and therefore no one is ever actually converted.

The solution is not necessarily simple. Sure, we can 'do more evangelism' by handing out more gospel tracts, posting John 3:16 on our Facebook profiles, or hosting evangelistic rallies. And, to a certain extent, that's a whole lot better than nothing. All these things have a pure and direct simplicity about them. They broadcast the central gospel message to a whole lot of people. So if you are at a loss for what else you might do, hand out some tracts at the local train station.

But since our goal is not merely to preach the gospel but also to persuade our hearers, we need to consider not only how to be faithful, but also how we may effectively win an audience and then engage that audience; to communicate meaningfully and persuasively; to bring someone on what might be a drawn-out journey from first contact to saving faith. This complexity means that, in our focus on evangelism, there will be a place for cultural engagement, charitable activity and building friendships. And we need the discernment and intentionality to make sure that all these things work effectively towards an evangelistic goal.

Who is actually doing evangelism? Are we leading our churches and evangelistic parachurches with a proper, faithful focus on this most important work? Does it occupy our thoughts and populate our prayers? Does it disturb us when we are thriving in all sorts of ways but bearing little fruit in evangelism? For those of us involved in non-evangelistic parachurches, are we keeping an eye out for ways that our other parachurches might indirectly contribute to evangelistic efforts? Do we find ways to partner with more explicitly evangelistic works? Do we ask whether we can release some of our leaders who are better suited to evangelistic work? Do the prayers prayed throughout our organizational life ever dwell upon missionary concerns?

Who's maturing believers?

It's possible to be extremely active as a Christian while remaining desperately immature in your faith. Churches and parachurches are wonderful places for social support, and the basic truths of the Christian faith are, in and of themselves, wonderfully inspiring and comforting. For this reason, it is possible to be happily engaged in Christian life for decades without deepening significantly in spiritual disciplines, theological knowledge or godly living.

So who's maturing believers?

There is more to Christian maturity than just attending more Christian events or doing more Bible study. The Gospel Growth Process (see Diagram K earlier in this chapter) is fuelled by prayerful teaching and reading of the word of God, but is also facilitated and reinforced by example, community life, emotional engagement, habits and practices, and perseverance through suffering. Without these things, a vibrant Bible-teaching ministry often penetrates less deeply into the lives of individual Christians.

On the other hand, without a rich ministry of the word all these other things become much less powerful and much less effective in genuinely maturing believers. And maturity is not a simplistic linear process, as if there is always a program or piece of Bible content that will move someone the next step along in their faith. Consider the pile of metaphors Paul uses in Colossians 2: 'rooted', 'built up', 'strengthened', and 'overflowing' (2:6-7). Our roots may grow deep through suffering, even as we are less regular at church. We may be strengthened through a season of diligent theological education, but be filled to overflowing through a season of investing more attention in prayer, praise and meditation. For some, the expression of maturity will be dogged perseverance through life-long battles with physical or mental hardships that may look like they will never improve. Yet in most circumstances, maturity does involve a significant linear component of deepening in the knowledge and adoration of God, progressing in repentance and godly living, and stepping up in Christian service. And whatever this maturing process may look like, it all happens best under the prayerful speaking and hearing of the word of God in the midst of loving Christian relationships and active Christian ministry.

Many parachurch ministries, even those that may not primarily exist for the purpose of maturing believers, can still contribute to the spiritual life of their staff, volunteers and members. Team meetings, training programs and informal interactions can all bring rich components of the word and prayer, encouragement, and challenge, and so can bring wonderful spiritual benefit to everyone involved.

It's worth pausing to seriously consider this. How could our parachurch meaningfully help Christians to grow up in their faith? It would be a pity if participants in our parachurches became experts in the core competencies or concepts of our work, yet remained fairly unaffected in the deep things of God—diligent drug and alcohol counsellors, perhaps, or technically skilled musicians, or sophisticated apologists, but baby Christians.

Worst of all is the church or parachurch ministry whose climate of spiritual immaturity is corrosive on the godliness and faithfulness of those who are drawn into its orbit—a ministry with leaders or core members who are flippant with their words or are living blatantly immoral lives; who know little of the Scriptures and entertain eccentric theological ideas; who delight in the glamour of worldly success and prestige; who are bullies or cowards. Sadly, ministry cultures can become rotten or toxic, and the same dynamics that can facilitate deeper maturity can be twisted to facilitate immaturity, heresy and immorality.

Who's maturing believers?

Who's equipping Christians for ministry?

Lastly, consider the place of training in the gospel-growth process pictured above. It's very easy for churches and parachurches to treat their participants as a mere 'crowd' or as 'clients', or to treat their teams as mere 'volunteers' or 'employees'. Many budgets are bloated because the first thought is always to employ staff, rather than to delegate, train and empower. Do we foster ministry cultures where people are called to move from 'audience members' to fellow workers? From disciples to disciple-making-disciples? Do we employ staff merely to do the work, or to train and mobilize others to share in the work with them? Do we create environments where we seek to identify and fan into flame the various gifts that God gives to his people?

Who's equipping Christians for ministry?[4]

More challenging still, as the rest of this book will explore, is that our concern needs to extend beyond our ministry (or ministries) to the growth of the word of God in the whole world. We should also fill our members and fellow workers with this same vision. This will sometimes mean we end up releasing them to

4   See Marshall and Payne, 'The heart of training' and 'Training and gospel growth' in *The Trellis and the Vine*, pp 69-91.

go further afield for the sake of the kingdom. Are we merely recruiting and retaining staff and volunteers? Or are we raising up fellow workers for the global vine? This is a significant mind-shift for many of us.

Marshall and Payne tease out this different way of thinking in a chapter of *The Trellis and the Vine* called 'ministry mind-shifts'. Among the eleven key points raised in this chapter, the mind-shifts most relevant to ministry training are:

2. From running events to training people
If we want our strategy to be people-focused, we should concentrate on *training*, which increases the number and effectiveness of gospel communicators … But please note: this is a chaotic strategy—an inconvenient strategy … It will mean we have to relinquish control of our programs for, as the gospel is preached, Christ will gather his people into all kinds of fellowships that may not fit into our neat structures …

3. From using people to growing people
The danger of having such willing volunteers is that we use them, exploit them and forget to train them. Then they burn out, their ministry is curtailed, and we find that we have failed to develop their Christian life and ministry potential …

4. From filling gaps to training new workers
If we just focus on gap filling, we'll never move out of maintenance mode: we're just keeping existing ministries afloat instead of branching out into new ones.

We should start with the people God has given us, not our programs … So instead of thinking, "Who can fill this gap in our personnel?", perhaps the question we need to consider is "What ministry could this member exercise?" …

11. From seeking church growth to desiring gospel growth

> Once we've spent time and resources training our leaders, we soon fear losing them. However, one of our goals in training people should be to encourage some of them into ... denominational or missionary ministry. We must be exporters of trained people instead of hoarders of trained people ... Our view of gospel work must be global as well as local: the goal isn't church growth ... but gospel growth.[5]

Of course, we do need to maintain a critical mass of people in our churches and parachurches to ensure that the good work they are already doing is sustained and the effectiveness of existing good work is preserved.[6] Sometimes, this will mean urging a potential church planter to stay with our existing ministry to help strengthen what is already thriving, or putting a hold on a great new initiative until we have the capacity to pursue it. But we need to check our motives to ensure that we do not become fixated on only growing our local work. We need to trust God and embrace a certain degree of risk for the sake of the wider growth of the gospel. Part of this will be identifying, equipping and sending out appropriately gifted people.

So who is equipping Christians for ministry? How can our ministries play their part in raising up the next generation?[7]

---

5   Marshall and Payne, 'The heart of training' and 'Training and gospel growth' in *The Trellis and the Vine*, pp 17-26, emphasis original.

6   A warning of going to the opposite extreme is found in KJ Smith, *The Origins, Nature, and Significance of the Jesus Movement as a Revitalization Movement*, Asbury Theological Seminary Series in World Christian Revitalization Movements in Intercultural Studies, no 5, Emeth Press, 2011. Smith tells the story of a movement that grew out of Redeemer Episcopal Church, Houston: "The demise of this charismatic movement may have resulted from giving too much ... The weakness to this pattern was that too many of the cream of leadership were taken out of the basic group, thus weakening the foundations and eventually leading to the breakdown ... The principle of 'skimming the cream from the top for mission' ... becomes the law of diminishing returns, if new cream is not brought to the vat at a commensurate rate" (p 290).

7   For more on training future Christian leaders, see Marshall and Payne, 'Multiplying gospel growth through training co-workers', 'People worth watching', and 'Ministry apprenticeship' in *The Trellis and the Vine*, pp 109-150.

The trellis takes over

Who's doing evangelism? Who's maturing believers? Who's equipping Christians for ministry?

And if we're not doing it, why not?

There are many possible reasons, from thoughtlessness to laziness. Sadly, one simple reason is that we are too busy running the organization itself. We are maintaining the 'trellis' to the almost complete neglect of the 'vine'. As bizarre and embarrassing as it sounds, many of us are engaged in an extraordinary amount of work for churches or parachurches often for no real or lasting reason at all—but we feel we have achieved a great deal because the church property is well kept, the database is up to date, the staff retreat was great fun, the website looks fantastic, the fundraiser exceeded its target, and 70% of members are in small groups. As we continue to think about how best to build a wide variety of trellises for the global vine, we need to ensure there are indeed healthy vines—rather than dead branches or toxic weeds—growing on these trellises.

Chapter 6: Local church partnership with parachurches

Leading a local church can be overwhelming. Just when you have the rosters to fill, yet another key family announces they will be on an overseas holiday for six weeks. There is a wedding to officiate, a member to visit in hospital, and child safety training to coordinate. The treasurer tells you that giving is a month behind budget, and the building committee has just highlighted additional repairs that are urgently needed. A young professional tells you that you need a website, a podcast, and social media presence. You want to run that evangelism course next term, ensure those young people are discipled, and give some time to training a few potential elders—but you will be away much of next week at your denomination's state general assembly. On top of all this, you still haven't prepared the sermon on 1 Samuel 4 for this coming Sunday.

While pastors struggle to stay afloat in this sea of pressures and demands, parachurch organizations can start to seem intimidating, like circling sharks just waiting to devour more of your members' time, energy, enthusiasm and financial resources. Not only do these ministries seem quick to kill what little momentum you manage to generate and constantly bombard you with promotional emails inviting you to their prayer breakfasts and vision dinners; their leaders can also seem annoyingly eager to further deflate you with (probably well-intentioned) words of smugly constructive criticism about how you could conduct your own ministry better.

While there have always been various parachurch activities in the life of God's people (as we will survey in part 3), the past century has seen a massive increase in the number of these activities. As Willmer, Schmidt and Smith report, "it is estimated that parachurch organizations [grew] more than a hundredfold" in the 20th century, and that "almost half of the giving to religions is going to parachurch organizations, not to the traditional local churches or denominations".[1] And Jerry White claims: "The proliferation of para-local church movements and organizations will be one of the distinguishing hallmarks of the last half of the twentieth century."[2] No wonder church leaders feel threatened! Hurt feelings, suspicion, frustration and competition are all too common, and sadly are often justified by the poor behaviour of some of those involved in parachurches.

Yet these parachurches were started for a reason—often a very good reason. They provide so many exciting opportunities for Christians, and even for whole local churches, to work together for the glory of God and the salvation of the world. If they didn't exist, sooner or later we would probably start them all over again. Far from being bloodthirsty sharks, at their best parachurches can be life rafts, radios, pontoons, lighthouses, transport ships, cruise liners, aircraft carriers, ice breakers, sea planes and fishing boats. They can support, enhance and extend local church ministry in wonderfully positive ways. And churches are not without fault in this complex relationship, either—sometimes undermining the legitimate work of parachurch organizations, as we will explore at various points in this chapter.

It is very difficult to wrap our heads around the various theological and strategic issues involved in all these diverse Christian

---

1   Willmer et al., *The Prospering Parachurch*, pp xi-xii.
2   White, *The Church and the Parachurch*, p 35.

ministries. Because there is a spiritual and personal work taking place, it is impossible to fully contain and control—gospel work is wonderfully messy and unpredictable. Where churches and parachurches overlap with each other, this fuzziness can produce a great deal of tension and suspicion. Each one can fail to listen to, learn from and respect the unique strengths and insights of the other. That's why it's so important to take the time to think through these issues carefully and to put plans in place that will help us to consistently act in line with our convictions.

In part 1, I have proposed some theological definitions to help us think about the tricky issue of church and parachurch. In this chapter, I want to think from the point of view of local church members and leaders. In particular, I want to explore the important principles and practices they should consider in their relationship with parachurches.

The primacy of the universal church

The universal church has primary importance in Christian identity, life and ministry. We must not govern our local churches or denominations in a way that undermines or obscures our spiritual union in the heavenly church under the leadership of the Lord Jesus. As I have already said, parachurches manifest this reality by showing us that God is at work in the world beyond church structures and inviting us to share in this larger work.

Because Christ is the supreme ruler of the church by his word, over any human authority, *the earthly church and parachurch should allow Christians to exercise appropriate freedom of conscience and conduct.* As the apostle Paul says:

> For none of us lives for ourselves alone, and none of us dies for ourselves alone. If we live, we live for the Lord; and if we die, we die for the Lord. So, whether we live or die, we belong to the Lord. For this very reason,

Christ died and returned to life so that he might be the Lord of both the dead and the living.

You, then, why do you judge your brother or sister? Or why do you treat them with contempt? For we will all stand before God's judgement seat. It is written:

> "'As surely as I live,' says the Lord,
> 'every knee will bow before me;
>   every tongue will acknowledge God.'"

So then, each of us will give an account of ourselves to God. (Rom 14:7-12)

Both the church and the parachurch over-reach when they presume to have direct and total authority over every aspect of a person's belief, behaviour and ministry.[3] Sincerity of belief is smothered by narrow dogmatism, and fear of discipline can start to matter more than genuine conviction. Joy in the grace of God in Christ provides greater fuel for missionary zeal than mere duty. It is right for churches to leave room for individual Christians to serve the Lord and his gospel according to their godly desires—"not because you must, but because you are willing, as God wants you to be" (1 Pet 5:2).

Moreover, *the local church and denominational association must continually reaffirm that their ultimate goal is to build Christ's universal church.* So while we will each have our own ministries and programs and assessments of priorities for strategic effort, these are secondary and provisional compared with the greater goal. Even if we might not fully support certain methods or teachings, or even if we suspect the motives of others aren't as pure as they might be, we ought to still pray that the Spirit will lead us to join with Paul in saying, "But what does it matter? The important thing is that in every way, whether from false motives

---

3   "We feel that leaders would be going beyond their God-given mandate to impose on others their own preferences in secondary matters. Some, in their zeal, deny their flocks the freedom of inter-denominational contact, out of fear of doctrinal contamination" (LCWE Commission on Co-operation, *Cooperating in World Evangelization*, p 29).

or true, Christ is preached. And because of this I rejoice" (Phil 1:18). We should be able to say, with the Lord Jesus, "whoever is not against us is for us" (Mark 9:40). This doesn't mean there is no room for discernment or critique—or even, in the worst-case scenario, for separating ourselves from those who deny Jesus. After all, in another context Jesus himself said, "Whoever is not with me is against me" (Matt 12:30). But it does mean that we must beware of functionally shrinking the true church to the boundaries of *our* church or denomination.[4]

We must admit that ultimately it is Christ—not us or our human efforts—who builds his church by his Spirit through his word. Jesus says, "I will build my church, and the gates of Hades will not overcome it" (Matt 16:18). He reassures us: "I shall lose none of all those [God] has given me, but raise them up at the last day" (John 6:39). While it is true that we are God's fellow workers, entrusted with his gospel (Rom 15:17-19; 1 Cor 3:5-11; 2 Cor 2:14- 4:18; 6:1), we are very much the minor party:

> "Night and day, whether he sleeps or gets up, the seed sprouts and grows, though he does not know how. All by itself the soil produces grain—first the stalk, then the head, then the full kernel in the head." (Mark 4:27-28)

> The wind blows wherever it pleases. You hear its sound, but you cannot tell where it comes from or where it is going. So it is with everyone born of the Spirit. (John 3:8)

> I planted the seed, Apollos watered it, but God has been making it grow. So neither the one who plants nor the one who waters is anything, but only God, who makes things grow. (1 Cor 3:6-7)

No earthly church court can know our Father's mysterious will and purposes for the church. We seek to obey his commission

---

4 "Denominationalism is therefore a heresy. No church may absolutize its own existence. Catholicity [universality] banishes all parochialism and sectarian tendencies" (Spykman, *Reformational Theology*, p 447).

wisely, prayerfully and faithfully while praying: "Yet not as I will, but as you will" (Matt 26:39). Such a humble recognition will help us a great deal in the complicated world of overlapping and competing ministry activities and agendas.

Remember, too, *growing gospel ministry is not about fighting over who gets the biggest piece of pie; it's about baking more pies.* Pastors can be fearful and protective of their church members' time, energy and money. They worry that parachurches will divert desperately needed resources into their ministries, which may seem more exciting than the boring old church budget and Sunday rosters. While this is a concern that parachurches must take seriously, it is often unfounded. The healthiest para-churches don't merely swallow up existing Christians; they contribute to the spiritual birth of new Christians who go on to become members of local churches—often the churches which are more supportive than suspicious of the parachurch. More than this, parachurches often help to mature, equip and ener-gize Christians, so that they serve their churches more skilfully and zealously than before. Likewise, it seems that people tend to give from "different pockets"[5]—that is, when a new kind of ministry need arises, they 'find' money to give. As they grow in the joy of giving and in the sense of responsibility to partner in gospel ministry through prayer and finances, they end up giving more than they had before, rather than giving less to the local church. The end result is that more resources are poured into gospel ministry. Gospel generosity is not a zero-sum game.

Plug into the wider gospel ecosystem

Because the ultimate reality is our heavenly Father's universal church, which he is building for his glory, we are wicked and foolish if we set our ambitions exclusively on building up our

---

5   I first heard this clever way of expressing things in personal conversation with Andrew Heard.

local church. Ministry can so easily become about our convenience, our tribal identity, or our ego. But even if our motives are purer than this, simple carelessness can lead to a very narrow scope of concern, which fails to delight in or contribute to God's work in the world. A healthy local church will have its eyes fixed on the eternal hope of "a great multitude that no one could count, from every nation, tribe, people and language, standing before the throne and before the Lamb" (Rev 7:9).

So a local church ought to be driven by Christ's global vision: "All authority in heaven and on earth has been given to me. Therefore go and make disciples of all nations" (Matt 28:18-19). It is not only fitting to be invested in the growth of the kingdom of God; it is also strategic. We will not reach our suburb, town, region or country by a single church, nor even by church planting alone. This is all part of the "ministry mind-shift" about which Colin Marshall and Tony Payne write: "our view of gospel work must be global as well as local: the goal isn't church growth ... but gospel growth."[6] Building trellises for this larger vine work helps increase the overall impact of gospel ministry.

How does a local church play a part in that? We can't give equally to every possible parachurch ministry out there. There is no absolute requirement for which ministries a church might support, or for how many ministries to support. This is a case of recognizing "who you are, where you are and when you are".[7]

However, here are several principles to keep in mind.

First, invest deeply in a few parachurch ministries. No single local church can or should contribute equally to every parachurch in their region, let alone to all the mission societies serving around the globe. Churches need to embrace their finitude rather than resent it, and to be content to support a few

---

6   Marshall and Payne, *The Trellis and the Vine*, p 26.

7   Lynch, *The Good Life in the Last Days*, p 58. Some further factors under these headings might include: 'who you are'—denominational affiliation, demographic makeup of congregation, or expertise of congregation; 'where you are'—needs of neighbourhood, nation and region, or political and historical connections; and 'when you are'—history of parachurch support, or the unique freedom a church plant might bring.

ministries well. By deliberately investing in a few parachurch ministries, your engagement with them can be richer and more holistic. Congregation members will be able to remember the details of the ministry and keep up with the various people and projects. A deeper investment in a few ministries will likely mean you are able to contribute to a larger proportion of the practical needs of the parachurch, which both relieves its leaders from having to seek more support elsewhere and enables them to meaningfully concentrate their communication and connection on a smaller number of supporters. This results in a greater degree of affection and accountability between the church and the parachurch.[8]

Second, invest in a mix of ministries. While each church does not need to (and could not possibly) have a perfect balance of local and global, evangelistic outreach and theological education, physical relief and political advocacy, a certain degree of diversity will both reflect the reality of our various concerns as God's people and represent the range of interests among the church members. Is your church entirely committed to development work overseas? Could you explore which Bible teaching ministries you might support? Or are you not currently contributing to any charitable work? Why not take on something in this area, alongside your primary focus supporting evangelists and pastors? Are you praying for and giving to global outreach, but doing nothing locally or regionally?

Third, look for partnerships that fit with your doctrinal convictions and ministry philosophy. There will be a much richer and happier connection with a parachurch where you agree on core matters of doctrine and on their practical approach to ministry. It pays to take the time to get to know parachurch ministries well and to ask searching questions. In this process, be careful to listen generously (as discussed under 'The importance of humble, honest and loving communication' below), because

---

8   As discussed in J Leeman, *J Leeman interviews Mark Dever: On Missions* [interview audio file], Pastors' Talk episode 21, 9 Marks, 3 October 2017, accessed 21 September 2022 (9marks.org/conversations/episode-21-on-missions).

leaders of some parachurches might express themselves in a way that is unfamiliar to you.

Fourth, follow the ministries with which your church members are already engaged. It is very likely that members of your church have all sorts of ties to local and global parachurch ministries. For example, the church might have sent some of its members to work in overseas mission; others might be staff, volunteers or board members for local parachurch groups. Church members might have been greatly blessed in all sorts of spiritual and material ways by particular ministries. Why not further invest in the ministries with which your people are already engaged? This is another application of 1 Corinthians 12:18: "God has placed the parts in the body, every one of them, just as he wanted them to be." Of course, church leaders might perceive some blind spots in the congregation's pre-existing connections, and so work to introduce them to other parachurches. But it will be a lot harder to engage and enthuse your congregation with a set of ministries where they have no acquaintance. It is even appropriate at times for the church leadership to revise its inherited parachurch connections and adjust them to better reflect the reality of its congregation in the present.

Fifth, link with existing parachurches rather than launching a new ministry. There is a particular temptation here for mega-churches (I will return to it again in chapter 7), but even smaller churches are not immune. It can be tempting to see a ministry opportunity or identify a need, and so move to establish a new church ministry. It might even make organizational sense to do so—strategic plans require this new venture, and vocal board members are pushing for it. But often there are existing para-church ministries already at work. Even if nothing is currently operating in your area, it may be worth inviting a parachurch that specializes in this work to come and partner with your local church in starting a new work; this may be a healthier way for-ward than starting something in-house. Such combined ventures can usually still be included in reports to parish councils, bish-ops or grant bodies—it can be a strategic activity of your church to proactively partner with an existing parachurch organization, and the fruit of this partnership can achieve strategic outcomes for which your church has been praying and planning. It is short-sighted to think that the only way your church can fulfil its mission is through ministries that carry your church's branding.

The importance of humble, honest and loving communication

It is so easy to become wary of parachurches and their possible agendas. We can be protective of our financial resources and our ministry volunteers, and defensive about the limitations of our local church programs. Parachurches, because of their specialization and broad support base, can offer a quality of program and an excitement of opportunity with which some local churches struggle to compete. Suspicion and defensiveness are magnified if a parachurch is not connected with trusted denominational or relational networks. A local church can become very negative towards a parachurch if they have a negative experience of a staff member or participant in the organization.[9] Soon, every snippet of formal communication, every choice of conference topic or every innocent request can be interpreted critically. This wariness could be totally justified. But, sadly, an intensity of ungodly suspicion can flourish out of all proportion to reality. Charles Spurgeon vividly warns against such suspicion:

> Suspicion makes a man a torment to himself and a spy towards others. Once begin to suspect, and causes for

---

9 "When I was on the faculty of the Air Force academy, we occasionally had overly zealous young Christians offend a chaplain because he did not meet their set of expectations in preaching or teaching. Then the chaplain might fix the blame on the Navigators or whichever group the young men were involved with. I remember telling one chaplain, 'Please remember that these men are only eighteen or nineteen years old—and that they often act their age. Please don't blame the Navigators for all their actions. If there is a problem call me and let's work it out.' It's a bit like a speech a first grade teacher gave the parents at the beginning of each year. She said, 'I'll promise not to believe everything they tell me about you, if you'll promise not to believe everything they tell you about me!'" (White, *The Church and the Parachurch*, pp 131-132).

distrust will multiply around you, and your very suspiciousness will create the major part of them. Many a friend has been transformed into an enemy by being suspected ...

It would be better to be deceived a hundred times than to live a life of suspicion. It is intolerable ... Nor is suspicion merely a source of disquietude, it is a moral evil, and injures the character of the man who harbours it. Suspicion in kings creates tyranny, in husbands jealousy, and in ministers bitterness; such bitterness as in spirit dissolves all the ties of the pastoral relation, eating like a corrosive acid into the very soul of the office and making it a curse rather than a blessing. When once this terrible evil has curdled all the milk of human kindness in a man's bosom, he becomes more fit for the detective police force than for the ministry; like a spider, he begins to cast out his lines, and fashions a web of tremulous threads, all of which lead up to himself and warn him of the least touch of even the tiniest midge. There he sits in the centre, a mass of sensation, all nerves and raw wounds, excitable and excited, a self-immolated martyr drawing the blazing faggots about him, and apparently anxious to be burned. The most faithful friend is unsafe under such conditions.[10]

This kind of toxic suspicion feeds on our human frailty—the mess of insecurities and fears that cloud our hearts and minds from a young age. We need the power of the Spirit, often working through the wisdom of close friends (and in some cases trusted professionals, too), to untangle many of these underlying issues. And even then, we will not be fully free from our flaws and hang-ups until the Last Day.

But there are also some good habits we can foster that will prevent suspicion getting a foothold. A simple way to flee suspicion

10 CH Spurgeon, *Lectures to My Students: 28 Lectures on Preaching in One Volume*, Monergism Books, 2018, pp 417-420, accessed 20 September 2022 (monergism.com/thethreshold/sdg/spurgeon/LecturestoMyStudentsCHSpurgeon.pdf). Please note that the word 'faggots' in this quote refers to a bundle of sticks used for fuel.

and foster loving relationships is to take the time to communicate clearly, honestly and humbly, and to make the effort to listen carefully, openly and generously. The authors of the Lausanne occasional paper on church/parachurch relationships write:

> As we began to wrestle with possible answers to these problems, it quickly became obvious to us that, in most of them, the urgent need was dialogue. It actually reached the point of embarrassment to us that we were not showing enough creativity and variety in coming up with different kinds of solutions. But we had to be honest in our recommendations. For dialogue is most certainly, in our opinion, the primary need. If only we were really open to it![11]

Communicating with humility means we ought to be more concerned with truth, godliness, love and effectiveness in the mission than with our reputation and our point of view. A humble spirit will be open to the fact that we don't see the full picture, that we might have done something foolish or wrong, that we may not be conducting our ministry in the most effective way possible. The humble person is eager to listen and learn. The humble person will not be distracted by the different appearance and vocabulary of others, but will strive to perceive who they really are and hear what they really mean.[12] We can be

---

11 LCWE Commission on Co-operation, *Cooperating in World Evangelization*, p 15.

12 Some parachurch leaders may seem to church leaders to be worldly and proud of their overly professional attire and promotional materials, or to be juvenile and flippant in their overly casual attire and manner. Moreover, every tribe, including Christian groups, has its own key buzzwords and shibboleths. We must be careful not to react too strongly when someone uses Christian words differently than us, but should seek to discern whether or not they believe fundamentally different things. "Words can build bridges or erect insurmountable barriers. Depending on the hearer, a word can be soothing ointment or a caustic acid. Some use words with intention to shock, while others, without due care or forethought, create unnecessary walls. Even biblically derived words such as 'evangelical', 'ecumenical', 'charismatic', or 'eucharist' can make the blood of some biblically strong Christians boil, simply because of current usage or exclusive adoption of the word by suspect groups. While we may not be walking dictionaries, we should at least use our mine detectors when passing through a battle zone. We must also exercise Christian love before branding fellow Christians with unfair labels, and show extra caution before judging between Christians and non-Christians or between evangelical and liberal" (LCWE Commission on Co-operation, *Cooperating in World Evangelization*, pp 25-26).

very attuned to feeling disrespected; a good working relationship becomes much harder when we draw the conclusion that the other person does not take us seriously.

At the same time, *communicating with honesty* means we are courageous enough to say what we really think in matters of doctrine, ministry practice and strategic priority. While it is right to be considerate and not say everything you are thinking, church leaders often avoid speaking truthfully with one another in the name of love and unity, only to end up in relationships filled with resentment and confusion, which spills over to others in their ministries. It is often more loving to be honest with parachurch leaders about your level of agreement with their doctrine and practice and your level of alignment with their cause.[13] You are often much freer to love and pray for fellow Christians in peace when you are not entangled in formal ministry partnerships that keep bringing up points of tension and disagreement.

Communicating with love means that we want the best for the other person, not merely ourselves—"we want them to do well", as the pastor of my church often says of those with whom he is in conflict. The apostle Paul urges us:

> Do nothing out of selfish ambition or vain conceit. Rather, in humility value others above yourselves, not looking to your own interests but each of you to the interests of the others. In your relationships with one another, have the same mindset as Christ Jesus … (Phil 2:3-5; cf. 1 Cor 13:4-7)

There is no substitute for Christian maturity. When we are growing in the grace of Christ Jesus, we will be able to navigate with much more skill and kindness the messy world of many trellises all playing a part in the global vine.

---

13 This is made much easier when parachurch ministries are themselves honest about their doctrinal position and ministry philosophy. When ministries claim to be broader than they are in practice, this can deepen distrust. See the next chapter for further discussion.

Proactive approach to prayer, promotion and planning

A lot of the irritation churches feel towards parachurch organizations comes from being almost entirely reactive in planning.[14] Without a thought-out approach to parachurch partnerships and missionary support, the requests to give an announcement or update on Sunday, the appeals for support and the promotional correspondence can seem relentless. Secular productivity guru David Allen talks about this as "potential meaning overload". The amount of information is not the problem; if that were the case, our heads would explode whenever we walked around in information-rich places like a library, or perhaps even somewhere like a forest. But, in fact, these are some of the most soothing places to spend time, because we know what to do with all the potential meaning, including which parts we are free to ignore.[15]

In the same way, when we have made some clear decisions about missionary partnership and promotion, it is much easier to filter out those requests and invitations that don't fit. This all comes from approaching missionary support and parachurch connection as a more integrated part of your local church ministry. Rather than being stray vine tendrils or random weeds, they can be approached as extensions of the main vine—and trellises can be built to best accommodate them.

Plan a pattern for prayer and mission updates. Church leadership should not be reactive to the many requests to distribute mission updates and prayer newsletters. It's far better to be proactive in praying for the wider work of gospel ministry. One approach could be to appoint a mission support overseer, who is responsible to write and administer a plan for mission updates, answering questions like:

---

14 "Cooperation between [parachurches] and congregations must be planned. It will not happen on an ad hoc basis even with real good will. Such cooperation must become a feature of the planned structure of both participants" (P Adam, 'The church and ECU', *Salt*, Spring 1986, p 6).

15 D Allen, *Making it All Work*, Piatkus, 2008, p 22.

- How frequently will these updates take place?
- Which groups get priority?
- What is the time limit on a mission update in church?
- What processes are required for PowerPoint or video content, to avoid last-minute technology troubles?
- What do you allow in terms of handing out promotional material or setting up expo tables after the formal church meeting?
- How do you deal with requests from different workers from the same organization (local staff, regional and national representatives, etc)?

The mission support overseer should also write and administer a plan for ensuring that prayer updates are effectively integrated into the church's ongoing prayer ministry. He or she can receive and digest prayer updates, then make sure these are included regularly in Sunday prayers, raised at congregational prayer meetings, emailed to the church prayer list, and passed on to leaders of small groups, youth groups and children's ministries as appropriate. Such plans do not merely provide a framework for fielding requests and filling prayer newsletters; they promote the fact that prayer is a ministry of the whole congregation, to be given the same attention as any other ministry.

Establish a communication and promotional plan. A prayer support plan can form the basis for a larger plan about how to receive and communicate other kinds of information from parachurch ministries. Drafting such a plan will bring benefit to the church's whole ministry on many levels. After all, a communication plan is simply a tool to help a church decide what to communicate and when to communicate it.[16]

With a communications plan in place, some parachurch events will be considered 'Level 1'—ministries of highest importance: a

---

16 For more in-depth thoughts and practical steps on setting up a church-wide communications plan, see S Kryger, 'Avoiding church calendar overload', *Communicate Jesus*, August 2010, accessed 21 September 2022 (communicatejesus.com/post/avoiding-church-calendar-overload).

Christian Union Mid-Year Conference (for a church with many university students), or the annual fundraiser for a major world mission partner, for example. But other parachurch ministries will receive minimal formal promotion from the church, or even none at all. This is not to say that these ministries don't matter, but simply that one church does not have the bandwidth to cope with every possible good work. To promote everything ends up promoting nothing but chaos and confusion.

Factor parachurch people, events and programs into local church plans. A similar proactive approach can and should be applied to all church planning. Consider asking these kinds of questions:

- What events should we reschedule to avoid clashes?
- What are the busy times for our members who are also involved in parachurch ministries?
- Which events can be programmed to work together with parachurch ministries—such as an evangelism course starting soon after a city-wide evangelistic rally?

All this is helped if churches and parachurches communicate with one another regularly and start their planning early. The result can be not just less competition and confusion, but also some happy synergy.

Commissioning, support and accountability

One of the great strengths of parachurch ministries, as discussed in chapter 2, is their capacity to release for ministry people who might not get the opportunity in the local church or through denominational structures. While this flexibility is a strength, it can also lead to a careless approach to recruitment, support and accountability. Sometimes, people are not given roles in church life for very good reasons, and parachurch leaders ought to take this into account. At other times, people may be entrusted with a massive spiritual responsibility in parachurches, but with no framework of encouragement and supervision. If the church works together with parachurch leaders, a much better outcome can be achieved for both ministries, ensuring that leaders receive the support and encouragement they need.

Commissioning leaders. We will discuss this in more detail in the next chapter (see 'Recruitment, support and discipline'), but a brief comment here will be helpful. In most cases, it is good for church leaders to provide a recommendation (or discouragement) for those people under their care who are taking a role in a parachurch organization. In many cases, some kind of commissioning for that ministry is appropriate. It is best when parachurch activities are carried out with the knowledge and support of the individual's home church, and perhaps even with some degree of oversight from the home church. Local churches can encourage the parachurch leaders to develop better practices on these matters. Even where the processes of parachurches are not as thorough as they should be, the local church can still establish a helpful pattern for its own members and commend this pattern to parachurches as they have opportunity.

Supporting church members in parachurch ministry. There are many ways in which the local church can support those involved in parachurch ministries, both locally and globally. This can range from informal questions and contact, to passing mentions and acknowledgement in sermons, right through to more formal actions. Each parachurch will have its own needs, but support might include:

- providing administrative help
- offering facilities or equipment[17]

---

17 "Property upkeep and staff salaries often consume 50% or more of the income of a church. Yet a [parachurch] Christian organisation is strongly criticised when its total administrative overhead exceeds even half of that. It seems that while a church has freedom to police the organisations (even publicising its findings), the reverse is not considered ethical. While para-church leaders are frequently asked about 'responsible stewardship,' many church buildings lie deserted for 165 out of 168 hours of each week. Furthermore, requests by various ministry groups for rented space in these buildings is more often turned down than approved. At a time when the Christian public is becoming increasingly aware of the administrative overhead of para-church ministries, church boards could do much to further the cause of world evangelization by making facilities available at cost to groups doing the kind of work the church approves" (LCWE Commission on Co-operation, *Cooperating in World Evangelization*, pp 69-70).

- sending visitors for personal support and connection (don't underestimate how encouraging this can be, even for local parachurch workers)
- sending short-term mission teams to provide practical help (this can be helpful both for local and global parachurches).

Minister to the staff of parachurches and their families. All the logistical and political complications can mean that local church leaders forget about caring for the staff (and heavily committed volunteers) of parachurches as fellow Christians involved in very demanding work in the service of the Lord Jesus. Parachurch workers can really benefit from the care of a local church family. As Jerry White writes:

> Para-local church staff need the fellowship of the body of Christ like anyone else. Often they are geographically separated from other co-workers and family, and lack real caring fellowship. Normally their ministry specialization does not meet the needs of their children. Draw them into your fellowship and minister to their family needs. Your church can be a place of refuge for them. Remember, too, that they could well have had negative experiences in other congregations. Some need to be encouraged to value the local church's ministry to their family.[18]

Accountability. While the leaders of the local church generally do not have governance power over the conduct of parachurch ministries, they can still exercise several very important roles in ensuring that these organizations are held to account.

First, the members and leaders of parachurch ministries are under the pastoral oversight of their local church leadership, just like any other member, and so should be corrected and disciplined for serious matters of doctrinal error or immoral conduct, just like any other member. Some matters might be difficult for

---

18 White, *The Church and the Parachurch*, p 133.

the local church to oversee, and in such cases they need to work in partnership with the leaders of the parachurch itself.

Second, leaders of the local church should be empowered to give counsel and critique to the leaders of the parachurches with which they have a relationship.

Third, leaders of the local church can also hold parachurch ministries to account by withdrawing support from ministries that they believe have strayed from a good and true path. The collective influence of local churches and individual Christians can be a very powerful force of restraint for parachurches.

Fourth, local churches or denominations can give a more formal rebuke if they are sufficiently concerned about the conduct or doctrine of a particular parachurch. This kind of stern and difficult step might be the wisest and most loving course of action for the long-term health of the gospel ecosystem.

Listen, learn and leverage

The wonderful opportunity of being in close connection with parachurch ministries is that local churches can draw from their specialist insight and expertise. It is a great tragedy if defensiveness or thoughtlessness means that a local church misses out on the wonderful blessings that parachurches can offer to them. Jerry White encourages church leaders to consider how they might draw on the expertise of parachurch staff who attend their church and to benefit from their unique knowledge, without expecting that they will be foundational to your church structure.[19] As a result, local churches can be blessed with cutting-edge insights into ministry, theology, mission, contextualization, community care and more. Moreover, sometimes parachurch groups pioneer excellent approaches to other ministry skills like financial support raising, marketing and teamwork, which the local church can also learn from.

19 White, *The Church and the Parachurch*, pp 133-135.

Financial support[20]

There are two broad ways in which the local church can support parachurch ministry, each with a clear rationale and various pros and cons. Church leaders should take the time to clarify their philosophy of financially supporting parachurches, and should also find ways to maximize the strengths of their approach while minimizing the weaknesses. Clear communication with parachurch leaders about the church's particular approach will help them know what to expect.

The first approach is to pledge a line item in the church budget. Just as the church plans how much it will spend on Sunday school resources, so also it decides how much to give to its mission partners. As I began to read more widely about the parachurch in preparation for this book, I came across a lot of interaction with the idea of 'storehouse giving' in the older American books. I don't know whether this idea used to be popular in Australia, but I had never encountered it before. The expression comes from the Old Testament prophet Malachi:

> "Bring the whole tithe into the storehouse, that there may be food in my house. Test me in this," says the Lord Almighty, "and see if I will not throw open the floodgates of heaven and pour out so much blessing that there will be not room enough to store it." (Mal 3:10)

The idea, then, is that the church budget is the New Testament 'storehouse', and all Christian giving should go there; church leaders will then make decisions about how these funds should be distributed to meet the needs of the church and of mission partners and charity work. In some cases, there will be several denominational layers to this, where each congregation pays a contribution to the running costs of the denomination, but then money is given out of this regional or national denominational budget to parachurch ministries, including the denomination's

---

20 An earlier version of this material was published in the newsletter of The Vision 100 Network in July 2019.

own organizations—for example, to subsidize the running of their theological college.

One advantage of this approach is that it means members can be united in their support of the same organizations. Such united engagement can overflow into more than just giving and praying; it can also include short-term mission trips, for example. A second advantage is that it aims to prevent the neglect of the local church in favour of high-profile fundraising appeals from parachurch groups. A third advantage is that giving to the best parachurch ministries—and to a good mix of ministries—will require the careful reflection of the church's leadership.

This approach also has certain advantages for the parachurch. It provides some certainty about their support-raising for the coming year and simplifies the number of individuals with whom they need to communicate. Further, because the communal giving feels like something they didn't choose, church members might be happy to give twice to a single parachurch: not only the portion of their giving which goes towards the church's contribution, but also a separate personal contribution. This latter benefit is not the intention of the church that adopts this approach, but will sometimes be the end result—and a welcome one, from the parachurch's point of view.

But this approach is not without its weaknesses, especially in its strictly idealized form ('all giving *must* go to the church'). First, if not communicated carefully, it can disconnect individual church members from the parachurch ministries they support. The portion which goes towards external ministries functions more like a tax than a deliberate, generous offering. Second, because it can end up feeling like a tax, it can lead to the same kind of wastefulness that often characterizes government spending: local congregations can be taxed by a denomination to keep ineffective ministries on the field and keep afloat outdated denominational organizations. Third, on a more pragmatic level, if the church (and denomination) managed all Christian giving, much less ministry would end up being funded. It is most likely that the local church would just not generate the same amount of giving, nor would it distribute that giving in the same diverse fashion.[21] There is also a disadvantage for parachurches in this approach: they can become dependent on the local church to mediate their relationship to its members.

A second approach is to select certain recipients of a second collection. The traditional pattern of 'tithes and offerings' in church liturgies reflects this approach, in which there is one collection for the general budget of the church itself and a second collection for an external recipient. An advantage of this approach is that, while still providing the church leadership with some degree of authority through choosing the mission partners, individual members have the freedom to choose how much they will give (or abstain from giving) in any given week. A disadvantage of this approach, if it is not communicated carefully, is that a disproportionate amount of giving may go to missionary groups for poor reasons: church members with a sentimental connection, a parachurch leader with greater up-front panache, or an offering being taken on a long weekend when many members are away. A second disadvantage is that the offerings might be spread across far too many organizations, so that the congregation takes little ownership of the various ministries and no ministry is helped to any great extent.

To counteract some of these weaknesses, a variation of this approach includes a giving target set by the leaders. In setting a clear goal, the leaders indicate what they think is a realistic and wise amount of giving. This approach maintains a balance between leadership and freedom.

A third approach is for individuals to choose which parachurches to support (and how much), independently of the local church. This is rarely the sole stated policy of a church, but it is an approach that many church members adopt in practice and that most

---

21 As Jerry White writes, "The bare fact remains that if para-local church groups were dependent on churches for their total support, there would be no para-local church groups! The majority of para-local church support comes from individuals not churches" (White, *The Church and the Parachurch*, p 32).

church leaders recognize as a reality. The strictest policy of 'all giving should go to the church', described above, is unworkable in practice; how likely is it that the majority of church members will comply with that? Perhaps this is partly why there is little talk about 'storehouse giving' today. In practice, most people will give to the church, happy in the knowledge that some of this will go towards certain mission projects, and then give additional support to parachurches of their choice.

It is not appropriate for church leaders to try to ensure that all giving by members of their congregation complies with their policies. As explored in the first section of this chapter ('The primacy of the universal church'), there remains a degree of Christian freedom in how and where Christians exercise their virtue of generosity.

Whichever policy is adopted, the weaknesses can be counteracted by wise leadership which seeks to disciple the church in generosity, community life and holistic gospel partnership, and which seeks to build meaningful two-way relationships, especially with their key mission partners.

~

I hope this chapter does not feel merely like a list of 'Dos and Don'ts' or a suffocating cloud of considerations. Rather, I want to provide a way forward for local churches to be as useful as they possibly can—not only in tending the 'vine' of God's work in their congregation, but also in helping the local, regional and global vine work to prosper.

Chapter 7: The primacy of local church and parachurch involvement

Can I let you in on a little secret? Many parachurch leaders find themselves thinking: "If only *I* were in charge of all the churches, then I'd do things right." We daydream about how we'd steer things in the right direction, tidy up the inefficiencies, improve the quality across the board, and address all those blind spots. What's more, if we had the power, we'd be so much better at fostering healthy relationships with all the people we left behind to run the parachurch. It all seems so easy and obvious to us as we look in. Why can't they get their act together?

In our worst moments, we take these fancies too seriously. But, as we shake ourselves and return to the reality, the wisest of us know that it wouldn't be that easy. As the proverbial saying goes: "Don't criticize someone until you've walked a mile in their shoes."

A far more godly and constructive thought experiment would be: "If I were leading a church, how would I like the leaders of parachurches to treat me?"

In this chapter, I will give some advice on how leaders and participants in parachurch ministries can best conduct themselves, especially in relationship with the local church. Many issues that are unique to certain kinds of parachurch organizations will be covered in part 3. In this section, I have tried to focus on general principles that are relevant to most parachurches in some way or other.

The importance and responsibility of the local church

As we have seen, the local church has great importance in Christian identity, life and ministry—an importance that, in the purposes of God, places it ahead of other forms of organized Christian activity. The universal church is the end goal of salvation history; the local church, which God orders through the teaching of Scripture, is an expression of this spiritual reality. The local church should understand its wonderful dignity, and the individual Christian and the parachurch ministry should also hold the local church in very high regard.

More than this, the local church has responsibilities to its members. The leaders of the local church are charged with keeping watch over those in the church, and they will have to give an account for how they fulfil this responsibility (Acts 20:28; Heb 13:17). Likewise, church members have responsibilities toward their leaders—to honour them, submit to their godly authority, and so make their work a joy and not a burden (Heb 13:17; 1 Tim 5:17-18). Church members also have duties towards one another: to love and care for each other; to provide for each other (Gal 6:2, 10; 1 Tim 5:16); and to exhort and encourage each other (Heb 3:7-15). Indeed, Paul can say that "each member belongs to all the others" (Rom 12:5). In this sense, we might talk about the office of the individual Christian, for all Christians are members of the "royal priesthood" (1 Pet 2:9) and exercise this ministry in the first place in the local church.[1]

These truths have many implications for those who are heavily involved in parachurch ministries. John Hammett rightly advocates for a "servant-partnership" model of church-parachurch relationships:

> Parachurch groups are seen as partners, or helpers, raised up by God to aid the church, but possessing a status subordinate to that of the church. Thus, the parachurch group should defer to the church, honor the church, accept its ministry under the authority of the church, and "find justification for its existence only in the mission of the church" (Jason 1986:200-201). Still, the relationship is a partnership in which each has something to offer the other: "the local church should offer the para-church its priority, structure, polity and security ... while the para-church should bring to the local church the power of deep dedication, specialist knowledge and adaptability" (Jason 1986:202).[2]

With this in mind, *parachurch ministries should ensure that they do not functionally take the place of the local church.* The temptation to take over can come from very good motives, when leaders identify spiritual needs and missionary opportunities being neglected. A strength of parachurches is that it can be easy for them to swiftly and effectively step in to compensate for the perceived inadequacies of local churches and denominations. The problem is that in doing so parachurches can drift from their specific mission, while also leaving local churches

---

1   Bavinck, *Reformed Dogmatics*, pp 619-20. Avery Dulles describes the church as a "polycentric community" (cited in M Volf, *After Our Likeness*, p 224). (I don't share Volf's strong commitment to remove as much hierarchy as possible from church life. He claims, "within a community of perfect love ... hierarchy and subordination is inconceivable" [p 217].) Timothy George helpfully corrects against an overly individualistic view of the 'priesthood of the believer' rather than the 'priesthood of all believers', cited in Hammett, 'How church and parachurch should relate', p 204.

2   Hammett, 'How church and parachurch should relate', p 200. While much of Hammett's article appears to argue in favour of all parachurches being governed by church or denominational leadership, his conclusion provides a range of other ways that a servant-partnership model can manifest itself, similar to those discussed throughout this chapter.

and denominations further weakened. As Carl Trueman says, "it is not a clear line between the para and the quasi-church".[3] In addition to getting on with the work of Christian ministry, mature Christians must also persist in the work of helping churches to become healthier and more effective. We will come back to this under 'Programming and support raising restraint' below.

Find a spiritual and social home in the local church. This should be a requirement for the staff and other volunteer leaders in a parachurch organization. It is inappropriate to presume to minister to others if one is not living out a basic aspect of the Christian life: involvement in a local church. Parachurch staff cannot always be expected to have a heavy ministry load in their local church; in fact, they may be less involved than an 'ordinary' active member.[4] But they still ought to express the importance of the local church in the way they live and in serving in their church as they are able.

It can be helpful for the leaders of parachurch organizations to help set expectations of local church involvement for staff, volunteer leaders and board members. Beyond this, parachurch ministries also need to plan how they will encourage a culture of local church involvement among their converts and active members.[5] In the AFES ministry I lead, all our staff and student leaders must have an endorsement from their local church; for students, this must be a local church in Hobart, not their home church from somewhere else in the world. We also talk regularly about the importance of the local church in our teaching program.

The local church can present a unique challenge for the person converted through a parachurch ministry. Because of the contextualized, hothouse environment of an evangelistic parachurch

---

3 CR Trueman, 'Parachurch groups and the issues of influence and accountability', *Foundations*, 2014, 66:25-37, accessed 21 September 2022 (affinity.org.uk/foundations/issue-66/issue-66-article-2-parachurch-groups-and-the-issues-of-influence-and-accountability).

4 While it is noble and often possible for the parachurch leader to seek to be the model of an actively involved church member, this is sometimes not possible or desirable. For example, large amounts of travel associated with their work can prevent service on regular church teams and rosters, and intense involvement in another Christian fellowship might make immersion in a church small group more draining than supportive.

5 White, *The Church and the Parachurch*, pp 141-142.

ministry, it is often able to provide things that the church cannot (and sometimes should not) emulate. Jerry White writes to the parachurch convert:

> *Do not expect the same relationship and help from the local church.* The local church cannot be a duplicate of the group you came from. Both its purpose and structure are different ... In a sense you were in an incubator where input was geared to your specific needs. Now you have grown and been equipped to relate in the larger world of believers ... *Give the church a fair opportunity to prove itself.*[6]

He also helpfully reminds the local church leader of the unique experience of someone converted from an unchurched background. They may have spent months in a parachurch ministry as a young Christian, but they are still unfamiliar with regular Sunday church:

> It may take a year or more to guide people into a church relationship if they come from non-evangelical backgrounds, or if a church setting is totally foreign to them.
>
> Non-church people feel very uncomfortable in the normal worship service of a church. They become confused, wondering what the purpose is for all the ritual. They experience a frustration similar to one who sees a soccer game for the first time, and tries to follow the play and understand the rules. We need to bridge the new believers into the fellowship, not drag them in and hope they will survive.
>
> Attending a Sunday worship service regularly does not ensure growth. It makes some members of a local church feel better, but it may not help the new believer significantly.[7]

---

6   White, *The Church and the Parachurch*, pp 153-156, emphasis original. White also gives the handy hint to look at more than the Sunday morning service to get an accurate picture of what a church is really like. Sunday evening services and mid-week meetings often give a fuller picture (p 154).

7   White, *The Church and the Parachurch*, p 121.

Parachurch leaders should be aware of this dynamic, and should therefore support their members and collaborate with local churches during this transition. They should beware of giving in to conceit when their members sing the praises of the parachurch in comparison to the church. Local churches also need to be aware of this dynamic and should be proactive and patient, not giving room for resentment or impatience.

Consultation and transparency

Often we get involved with a parachurch because we are eager to get on with some area of ministry, and the parachurch offers a quicker way to do so. The perks of a focused and driven parachurch culture can make us reluctant to collaborate with churches that, by comparison, seem so slow and distracted. Some of us have personality types and tendencies that gravitate towards parachurch ministry, so we struggle with this even more. But this ought to be a simple case of setting aside our own preferences and our own convenience for the sake of loving others. Moreover, it is about setting aside expediency and efficiency for the sake of a more robust, long-term effectiveness. More still, it is about having the principled integrity to honour a God-ordained institution: the church.

It is right for parachurch leaders to take the time to communicate openly with church leaders, and to make the effort to incorporate their feedback wherever possible. Consultation is not just about courtesy. Regular consultation reminds the parachurch of ways in which the nature and purpose of the local church are different from their own, but also of ways in which they share the same heart and the same goals. Without this reminder, parachurch leaders can lose balance and begin to think churches just need to be more like parachurches. Diligent consultation is also needed for national (or international) parachurch organizations looking to establish a new work. This helps them to recognize whether there are already ministries doing equivalent work in a given area, which would mean they are not really needed. It also helps these larger organizations to appreciate any cultural and contextual factors that should influence their approach. Boards of larger parachurches can help to develop this culture of consultation by having flexible strategic measures for their staff on the field. If the strategic plan says, 'start a new branch in x city', it may then pressure field staff to launch something whether it is needed or not. But a goal to 'start a new branch OR identify and work with an equivalent ministry in x city' more explicitly encourages partnership.

It is also important to be clear and up-front about your mission statement, strategies, doctrine and plans.[8] Genuine consultation needs space in the planning timeline. Purporting to consult with others when your plans are already in motion is really nothing more than a public relations exercise. What if the fruit of your consultation is a consensus from the locals that 'this is a terrible idea'? Would you really listen? A thin veneer of consultation ultimately has a negative effect on goodwill.

Serve but don't judge

It's understandable that those who are passionate about a particular cause will want this cause to be championed. But parachurch supporters should balance this good desire with an appropriate humility. This is particularly true where the parachurch was formed because it was not appropriate for the local church to pursue the cause—either at all, or at least with the same degree of intensity. Kevin DeYoung corrects what he calls 'the terror of total obligation':

> The Bible is a big book, and there's a lot in there. So the Bible says a lot about the poor, about marriage, about prayer, about evangelism, about missions, about justice; it says a lot about a lot. Almost any Christian

---

8 White, *The Church and the Parachurch*, pp 142-143.

can make a case that their thing should be the main thing or at least one of the most important things ... *Care is not the same as do* ... [We] can't do something about everything. But we can care. This means when we hear about grinding poverty or legal abortion or biblical illiteracy, we are not indifferent. We think and feel that these things ought not to be so. We won't all care about every issue in the same way, but there are some issues we should all care about, some issues that should at least prick our hearts and prompt us to pray. Not giving a rip about sex slaves is not an option for the Christian. Not doing something *directly* to combat this particular evil *is* an option.[9]

Rather than expecting the church to be the parachurch, we should rejoice that each has their part to play—the parachurch is being the parachurch so the church doesn't have to! Mack Stiles writes:

> **A healthy parachurch ministry does not pressure the church to act like a parachurch.**
> With some frequency, parachurch leaders will tell "the Church" what "the Church" needs to do. They will advise it to partner with Catholics, to patch holes in the gospel by caring for the poor, to adopt new leadership structures, to become more relevant, to just about anything you might imagine ...
>
> It's not just the leaders of parachurch organizations who pressure the church to act like a parachurch, either. Church members do, too ... Church members who have benefited from them can naturally want these programs to be reproduced by their church ...
>
> Too many people view the church through parachurch lenses. Perhaps that explains why so many churches today look like the campus group or high school ministry of yesteryear?[10]

9   Kevin DeYoung, *Crazy Busy: A (mercifully) short book about a (really) big problem*, Crossway, 2013, pp 47, 49, emphasis original.
10 Stiles, 'Nine marks of a healthy parachurch ministry'.

The parachurch exists to serve the local church and the wider Christian community. The service can be offered, but it can't be imposed on local churches. Parachurch participants are involved in the parachurch because they are convinced it really is valuable. But they mustn't assume that everyone else is equally convinced. All too often, a parachurch ministry such as a training conference is established because of the vision of a few, but with no wider consultation. And yet once the ministry is in place, the founders are hurt and offended if local churches don't support them. But we are not justified in our offence if people didn't ask for our help in the first place.

> You say you are serving the churches, but who gave you that mandate? I do not feel you are, in fact, always sensitive to what the church is, or where we are in terms of our needs, even in terms of assistance with evangelization. Should not true service to us involve setting this right?[11]

A true servant heart will also be generous and positive to churches wherever possible. A parachurch movement with prophetic zeal can become destructive and critical of local churches, poisoning its participants rather than preparing them to graciously serve their churches, warts and all.

There's a lovely scene towards the end of the film *Mary Poppins* where the One-Man-Band/Chalk artist/Chimney Sweep Bert, played by Dick Van Dyke, gives a reality check to the two runaway Banks children who are disillusioned with their distant and stern father:

> You know, begging your pardon, but the one my heart goes out to is your father. There he is, in that cold, heartless bank day after day, hemmed in by mounds of cold, heartless money. I don't like to see any living thing caged up.

---

11 Anonymous survey respondent quoted in LCWE Commission on Co-operation, *Cooperating in World Evangelization*, p 18.

Look at it this way. You've got your mother to look after you and Mary Poppins and Constable Jones and me. Who looks after your father? Tell me that. When something terrible happens, what does he do? Fends for himself, he does. Who does he tell about it? No one. Don't blab his troubles at home. He just pushes on at his job, uncomplaining and alone and silent.

Parachurch leaders can advocate for church leaders like this, too. Rather than being a negative and critical voice, they can be a force for good: fellow Christian leaders who know something of what it's like to lead God's people and who speak up to advocate for the leaders of local churches. Aware of the peculiar strengths of their ministries (as discussed in chapter 2), they can explain to their members and fellow leaders that many of these strengths exist precisely because they are parachurches. Far from feeling superior to church leaders, the humble parachurch leader recognizes that we would struggle with the same challenges if we were primarily working with the local church.

Recruitment, support and discipline

No Christian 'belongs' to any earthly organization, whether parachurch ministry or local church. But we can slip into thinking this way if we are not careful. This sense of 'ownership'— together with the ever-present need for new staff, volunteer leaders and helpers—can mean a parachurch recruits people to the task with little thought of involving the local church. They're 'our people', aren't they? But parachurches should take the time to consider how they recruit people to their ministry, and then figure out the proper place for the local churches in this process.

Many parachurches are so informal (e.g. a neighbourhood Bible study) or so tangentially connected with Christian fellowship (e.g. a Christian social soccer league) that any formal appointment process is not feasible. But then again, even these types of parachurches can benefit from at least a self-assessment framework of some kind to ensure participants hold basic shared convictions about life, doctrine and purpose. As a parachurch becomes more formal, more care needs to be given to membership and leadership appointment processes. At a bare minimum, parachurches should require that all potential leaders provide a letter of support from their church. It is utterly inappropriate for someone to be appointed to a formal Bible teaching role in a parachurch without any church contact or reference check whatsoever.[12]

The more significant the role, the more substantial the support needed from the local church or denomination. Indeed, the more the leaders and teachers of parachurches function like elders of a local church, the more we should explore with their home churches whether they might be ordained as elders or deacons or missionaries and then commissioned for this external ministry. Historically, the general assumption was that any public, formal ministry of the word should only be conducted by properly ordained leaders. So for example, chaplains and missionaries were simply ordained ministers operating in a different capacity; members of authorized religious orders would be recognized as 'regular priests' (that is, priests 'regulated' by the vows of the order) alongside 'secular priests' (serving in the wider world).[13] While I believe a strict insistence on this rule of ordination is neither biblically necessary nor practically enforceable, it is a good general principle.[14]

When it comes to the ongoing support of parachurch staff, leaders and helpers, it makes a lot of sense to work in cooperation with local churches, which should be well positioned to

---

12 There is at least one exception to this general rule: new converts might take quite a while to be meaningfully connected with a local church (as discussed in chapter 6), and yet already be suitable for some degree of responsibility in the parachurch in which they were converted.

13 G Peters, *The Story of Monasticism: Retrieving an ancient tradition for contemporary spirituality*, Baker Academic, 2015, pp 155-156.

14 "I am concerned that the realization that the missionary is at heart one who holds the office of the minister of the Word is beginning to disappear also in Reformed circles. More and more, missionaries are beginning to be seen as employees of the mission agency of the church" (Tuit, *A Study and Comparison*, p 176, fn 40).

provide for all sorts of their spiritual, personal, relational and practical needs. If the parachurch is too quick to meet all these needs internally, it can squeeze the church out of a role it would love to play. By contrast, a collaborative approach will take pressure off the parachurch, allowing it to focus on its mission.

While some matters of discipline are narrowly workplace-related or must be handled with privacy, discipline is another area for proper and fruitful cooperation between churches and parachurches. In every step—from investigation to coaching, confrontation, consequences, and restoration or dismissal—there might be a part for the local church to play, whether it is participating in the process or simply being informed. On the other hand, parachurches must also heed the disciplinary activity of the local church or denomination (and other parachurches, secular employers and civil authorities) without presuming to re-prosecute the matter.[15]

This is a complex area where it is hard to make simple rules. And there are further considerations, such as:

- Are the accusations directly related to the activities of the parachurch, or do they go beyond it?
- How is 'membership' conceived—are churches or denominations affiliate 'members' of the parachurch, or mere beneficiaries?
- Who is responsible for formal investigation of the accusation in question—the parachurch, the church, or the civil authorities?
- How serious are the accusations?

---

15 This is made more difficult because the disciplinary process carried out by a church or denomination might appear to have been woefully inadequate. In some cases, a parachurch's leadership may go so far as to choose to urge a church (or one of the parties in an accusation) to undertake a more thorough process. In extreme cases, a parachurch's leadership may go so far as to undertake an additional investigation of their own. It is important to investigate accusations with sufficient care to neither disown someone simply on the basis of an accusation nor dismiss an accusation too lightly. Parachurches are not bound to adhere to the absolute legal standard of 'innocent until proven guilty', nor are we bound to refuse to "entertain an accusation … unless it is brought by two or three witnesses" (1 Tim 5:19). We should follow a broad principle of 'good evidence' rather than a strict requirement for multiple witnesses for any discreet wrongdoing.

This fraught but important area of integrity deserves careful attention from parachurch leaders, both to establish clear policies and to maintain those policies over time.

All Christian activity should pay attention to God's pattern for church life

The apostle Paul reminds Timothy:

> All Scripture is God-breathed and is useful for teaching, rebuking, correcting and training in righteousness, so that the servant of God may be thoroughly equipped for every good work. (2 Tim 3:16-17)

The sufficiency of Scripture is equally true for church and parachurch ministry, and all forms of organized Christian activity must pay close attention to their patterns of life and ministry in light of the biblical revelation. This includes God's instructions about how ministry and leadership ought to be exercised. Sometimes, parachurches talk and act as if all the biblical instructions given to the local church—about the roles of women, the need for interpreted tongues, the 'Regulative Principle' and so on—do not apply to them "because we're not a church".[16]

There is a truth here, for we have seen that the local church is a distinct type of entity, so there might be unique elements in the ordering of this unique entity. But we must not make a sharp break between the local church and every other type of Christian ministry. The ministry of the word and prayer is not

---

16 The Regulative Principle is expressed in the Westminster Confession in these words: "the acceptable way of worshipping the true God is instituted by himself, and so limited to his own revealed will, that he may not be worshipped according to the imaginations and devices of men, or the suggestions of Satan, under any visible representations or any other way not prescribed in the Holy Scripture" (XXI.1). This principle can be applied with a great degree of inflexibility, with a strong emphasis on the uniqueness of 'public worship' as parallel to Old Testament temple worship, and with an insistence on explicit biblical texts. I commend broader application of the principle, which seeks to be deeply biblical in all Christian ministry but works from principles more than from proof texts.

fundamentally different when conducted outside the church, and so we must not expect it to be governed by entirely different rules. The way in which Christian teaching should be conducted in a parachurch ministry ought to reflect similar teaching ministries within the life of a local church. Just as in a local church there are some kinds of teaching that are informal, egalitarian, private or interactive, and others which are formal, authoritative, public and declarative, so also in a parachurch. I propose that *the more a ministry aligns with the latter description, the more the biblical commands about the authoritative teaching of the church should be applied.*[17]

As for the structure of governance, not everything about the church's unique character—one that allows it to be described as a 'household' or family (1 Tim 3:15)—necessarily applies to every type of parachurch organization.[18] General ethical concerns ought to apply to the structure of all parachurches, as they should to businesses or clubs of any kind. But *the more closely a parachurch resembles a church community, the more the leadership structure should reflect a biblical pattern, and the more diligently the biblical standards for leadership should be applied.*[19]

Likewise in the ordering of a parachurch's communal gatherings—not every Christian meeting needs to closely mirror a

---

17 In 2018, an interesting discussion took place over whether it was appropriate for female faculty members to lecture in theology and biblical studies in mixed seminary settings. John Piper began the discussion with a negative answer: J Piper, *Is There a Place for Female Professors at Seminary?* [interview audio and transcript], Desiring God, 22 January 2018, accessed 21 September 2022 (desiringgod.org/interviews/is-there-a-place-for-female-professors-at-seminary). Among the many responses to Piper, Mark Thompson and Jonathan Leeman were both very helpful. See M Thompson, 'Is there a place for women on a theological college faculty?', *Moore Theological College*, 7 February 2018, accessed 21 September 2022 (moore.edu.au/resources/is-there-a-place-for-women-on-a-theological-college-faculty-2); and J Leeman, 'A word of empathy, warning, and counsel for "narrow" complementarians', *9 Marks*, 8 February 2018, accessed 21 September 2022 (9marks.org/article/a-word-of-empathy-warning-and-counsel-for-narrow-complementarians).

18 For more on the relationship between local churches and 'families' or 'households', see chapter 13.

19 Perez highlights the problems with parachurch leadership models being largely drawn from private enterprise or the military, rather than from the church; see P Perez, 'The relationship between church and para-church: Theological reflection', in Nicholls (ed), *The Church: God's agent for change*, pp 206-209. See Taylor, *Like a Mighty Army?*

Sunday church gathering. Conference plenary sessions, theological lectures, evangelistic rallies or youth events all have a specific purpose and audience which makes them different from each other. There are broader ethical and spiritual principles which should always be enforced, but depending on context and purpose there is space for flexibility. This could be, for example, in the use of drama or other performance components, in untranslated foreign-language elements, or in the degree of (in)formality.[20] But as with the previous case studies, *the closer the parachurch event is to a regular public gathering of the church, the more closely it should reflect the biblical teaching on the church meeting.*

Co-exist, compare, contrast and complement without ruthlessly competing

This point is important not only for how parachurch organizations relate to local churches, but also for how they relate to one another. There will be unavoidable points of tension and overlap between various groups, and this needs to be handled with integrity and discernment. We don't want to smother ministry or stop it from growing and developing, nor do we want to fracture Christian relationships. The risk in having a gospel ecosystem of many diverse churches and parachurches is that it can spark proud tribalism that boasts in distinctives, looking down on some and condemning others. Paul addresses this kind of party spirit (albeit operating within a single church) several times in 1 Corinthians:

> My brothers and sisters, some from Chloe's household
> have informed me that there are quarrels among you.
> What I mean is this: One of you says, "I follow Paul";

---

20 Even so, influential parachurch ministries, such as youth and campus ministries, need to be aware of their role in setting expectations for Christian gatherings, which their members might wish to extend beyond the parachurch setting.

another, "I follow Apollos"; another, "I follow Cephas"; still another, "I follow Christ." (1 Cor 1:11-12)

Brothers and sisters, I could not address you as people who live by the Spirit but as people who are still worldly—mere infants in Christ. I gave you milk, not solid food, for you were not yet ready for it. Indeed, you are still not ready. You are still worldly. For since there is jealousy and quarrelling among you, are you not worldly? Are you not acting like mere humans? For when one says, "I follow Paul," and another, "I follow Apollos," are you not mere human beings? (1 Cor 3:1-4)

When this same attitude works itself out beyond the local church, it can have tragic and shameful results. Christian leaders can be tempted to ruthlessness, wasteful duplication of ministry activity, and dubious marketing practices. The legacy can be resentment and suspicion.[21] Such worldly competitiveness and boasting fails to see clearly that it is concerned with pathetic matters of human status and group identity. It refuses to glory in what God has graciously done for us:

Is Christ divided? Was Paul crucified for you? Were you baptized in the name of Paul? (1 Cor 1:13)

What, after all, is Apollos? And what is Paul? Only servants, through whom you came to believe—as the Lord has assigned to each his task. I planted the seed, Apollos watered it, but God has been making it grow. So neither the one who plants nor the one who waters is anything, but only God, who makes things grow. (1 Cor 3:5-7)

So then, no more boasting about human leaders! All things are yours, whether Paul or Apollos or Cephas or the world or life or death or the present or the future— all are yours, and you are of Christ, and Christ is of God. (1 Cor 3:21-23)

---

21 See 'The importance of humble, honest and loving communication' in chapter 6.

When a parachurch feels the pinch of its fundraising targets, or a local church notices members of its youth group migrating to a larger and more exciting group in the next suburb, it can be so easy to feel things, think things and say things that are more about preserving our human 'trellis' than about seeking the advance of the kingdom of God. On the other hand, when a movement is gaining momentum and seems to have the Midas Touch, it can be easy to believe in a kind of manifest destiny: that it is ultimately God's will for your movement to expand even at the cost of smaller churches and ministries. But a generous heavenly perspective will not allow us to be motivated by our own church's or ministry's current circumstances. Rather, such a perspective will allow us to echo the sentiment of Jesus: "whoever is not against us is for us" (Mark 9:40). It's the same attitude expressed by his apostle: "What does it matter? The important thing is that in every way, whether from false motives or true, Christ is preached. And because of this I rejoice" (Phil 1:18).

John Stott powerfully argues the case against ruthless competitiveness:

> It is sometimes argued that competition in Christian work is healthy, on the ground that it stimulates and challenges people, and brings the best out of them. This may be true, as an observed fact. In evangelism, as in athletics and commerce, competition can be a spur to success. But an empirical fact is not necessarily a theological truth. Can the competitive spirit in Christian service be defended biblically? ...We can certainly defend from the Bible the principle that human beings made in God's image should be free to develop their creative gifts. But it can also be argued from the Bible that they should not use these in such a way as to harm others, especially those who go under in the struggle to survive. Moreover, sometimes the attempt to glorify the spirit of competition among us thinly disguises a sinful evangelical power-struggle of which we need to repent in dust and ashes ...

> Certainly, the biblical emphasis is rather on co-operation than on competition.[22]

Even on the level of seeking better outcomes, cooperation achieves a better outcome in the long term: a richer and more robust ecosystem. Ruthless competition, on the other hand, produces a cheaper, sicker and thinner end result.

The temptations and pitfalls are not only in the area of competition, however. Perhaps John Stott betrays his cultural bias in how little space he allows for healthy, godly competition. He writes: "[human beings] should not [compete] ... in such a way as to harm others, especially those who go under in the struggle to survive." However, if a 'free market' approach to Christian ministry can lead to the problems of capitalism, a 'mutual support' approach to Christian ministry can lead to the problems of protectionism.[23] Lethargic, comfortable or stubborn ministries can refuse to change, secure in their denominational protection zone. They might even appeal to principles of mutual concern as they demand that healthy ministries keep them afloat with finances, leadership and even members.

The Bible does not command that every single local church must be kept distinct and independent for as long as possible; much less do biblical ethics require the preservation of every parachurch program. Sometimes, the realities of the changing context suggest that ministries should shut down, merge, or go through a radical process of rebirth or revitalization. Co-existing in an environment of thriving ministries can help us to acknowledge these hard truths.

22 LCWE Commission on Co-operation, *Cooperating in World Evangelization*, pp 7-8. See also Vinay Samuel and Chris Sugden, who describe how multinational parachurches can behave a lot like multinational corporations, using (or bypassing) local churches more like 'distribution centres' and recruiting all the best local 'talent', perhaps attracting them with higher salaries (cited in Perez, 'The relationship between church and para-church', p 205).

23 This is arguably one of the reasons that religion has historically thrived in the USA, even while it has declined in Europe: there was no established or de facto state church. Rather than hindering religion, this 'free market' allowed diverse expressions of Christianity to thrive, develop, compete and improve. By contrast, state churches can easily become complacent in their position of privilege. See also Noll, *The Rise of Evangelicalism*, pp 201-202, 206.

In a recent Facebook discussion, a church planter helpfully observed: "[When I hear the word 'competition'] I usually think of 'survival of the fittest' competition. Sporting competition is the better analogy and there's something healthy about vying for the same prize/goal."[24] But 'competition' is not the best word to describe this dynamic, because it carries with it the idea of winning against others in the process, rather than acknowledging that, in the end, we are all on the very same team.

The heading for this section offers a better alternative: 'Co-exist, compare, contrast and complement without ruthlessly competing'. That is, we should freely allow co-existing ministries that overlap with one another, we should learn honestly from one another, and we should even be stirred by one another's success. But we should do it in a way that complements one another in striving for a common goal. John Stott is reaching for something similar when he writes:

> At the same time, it is perfectly true that, in general, Christians are exhorted to "consider how to stir up one another to love and good works" (Heb. 10:24); and that, in particular, Paul used the example of Macedonian generosity to stir up the Corinthians to contribute sacrificially to his collection (2 Cor. 8:1-7), just as he had previously used the zeal of the Corinthians to stir up the people of Macedonia (2 Cor. 9:1-5). Nevertheless, we need to observe that the "provocative" nature of Christian example is here only within a common Christian life and work ... These important examples may be said, therefore, to encourage mutual stimulus to co-operation, not rivalry of competition.[25]

If these things can be held together, we can make sure that saving souls—not sentimentality, ego or convenience—is our concern, while also ensuring that loving individuals and honouring God shapes the execution of our mission.

---

24 Thanks to Russell Williams for permission to use this comment.
25 LCWE Commission on Co-operation, *Cooperating in World Evangelization*, pp 7-8.

Programming and support-raising restraint

Parachurch organizations need to exercise restraint so that they do not overstep their bounds and to ensure that they leave room for other parachurch ministries and, more importantly still, for the local church.[26] A healthy, holistic view of Christian life and ministry will always drag parachurch ministries—particularly those whose purpose is evangelism and discipleship—toward more integrated and holistic ministry. There's something appropriate about this tug, but it needs to be kept in check by remembering that there is life and ministry beyond the parachurch. Otherwise, the parachurch may slowly adopt the presumption that it can provide every form of support and growth that its members need, while beginning to functionally operate as a home church for its members. Indeed, as we will see in part 3, some parachurch ministries end up becoming churches or denominations. This is where a clear, precise mission statement is very useful.[27] Jerry White urges that:

> *Para-local church organizations should clearly define their purposes and goals, and be willing to be evaluated.* Organizations become ineffective as they compromise their vision. Para-local church societies need to know why they exist, and be able to clearly communicate their goals. They also need to demonstrate their effectiveness in some measurable way.[28]

---

26 This is actually possible, contrary to the pessimism of an anonymous Christian leader quoted by Michael Reeves: "I hope that folk at UCCF [the Universities and Colleges Christian Fellowship (UK)] would see that while most would agree in principle with the Priority of the local church the present structure and activities of a CU as set out by UCCF make that practically impossible to achieve. Pragmatically the message given is, be involved in everything at CU, and Oh yes do go to church on Sunday to meet some old people. (Slight parody perhaps!)" (Reeves, 'What is a church? What is a CU?', p 2).

27 "There are parachurch organisations which are truly para-church, in that they exist to serve, and be subservient to, actual churches, and which fulfill such a narrow function that they cannot be confused with churches" (Trueman, 'Parachurch groups and the issues of influence and accountability', p 26).

28 White, *The Church and the Parachurch*, p 120, emphasis original; cf. pp 140-143. In their book *The Prospering Parachurch*, Willmer, Schmidt and Smith provide lots of very practical guidance in the whole area of strategic planning and financial management.

It needs to be clear what role each parachurch trellis plays in the larger vine work, and how each interacts with the trellises of local churches, denominations and other parachurches. What is true for non-denominational parachurches is also true for denominational parachurches: neither has a free pass to multiply the number and size of their auxiliary organizations without restraint.[29] Such clarity in principle will, of course, only be helpful if the ministry's leaders exercise self-discipline in practice.

This is not an issue only for those more holistic parachurches. Enthusiasm for your cause or program can become all-consuming if you are not careful. Alongside passionately casting a vision for your organization, you need to recognize the place for the many other important ministries with which Christians might be concerned or involved. Creative leaders can also tend to add programs and try out ideas without carefully asking whether they are really leading to 'mission creep' where their group starts to fill almost all the discretionary time of their members.[30] Enthusiasm can be hijacked by a sinful, ambitious spirit, or by a desperate attempt to raise more funds or justify your existence.

It is vital, then, that parachurches regularly and honestly assess their motives. Parachurches are established to bless the church and the Christian community, and they should only exist while they continue to be needed. Unlike the church, the parachurch does not *need* to exist; it must always justify its existence. Willmer, Schmidt and Smith write:

---

29 Bruce Ballantine-Jones speaks about the need for a Diocese to have clarity about its purpose. Reflecting on the Anglican Diocese of Sydney, he writes: "What this examination shows is that apart from looking after parishes, there never has been a clear and consistent idea about what the purpose of the Diocese should be, nor how those in charge of the central administration should use their instruments of power to accomplish whatever it was thought they should do. This lack of clarity often led to decisions being made on intuitive or political grounds" (B Ballantine-Jones, *Inside Sydney: An Insider's view of the changes and politics in the Anglican Diocese of Sydney, 1966-2013*, p 268).

30 Willmer et al. write: "A parachurch organization tends to act like a snowball rolling down a hill, always picking up new ministries and new responsibilities" (*The Prospering Parachurch*, p 136). TS Rainer and E Geiger's book *Simple Church: Returning to God's process for making disciples* (B&H, 2011) is a very helpful book in assisting churches, and by extension parachurches, to stay focused and aligned with their mission.

This is a painful possibility, but parachurch leaders must have the honesty to consider the possibility that the need their organization set out to meet no longer exists. And if that is the case, then the parachurch organization is better off either shifting to another ministry or folding altogether.[31]

Because parachurches can draw on an external financial support base, they can maintain their existence even without local support and success. This can lead to parachurches continuing well beyond their point of usefulness, or to the unnecessary duplication of parachurches with more or less the same purpose.[32]

Both church leaders and parachurch leaders need to take responsibility for the entire gospel ecosystem in their area of oversight. While it can be more trouble than it's worth to agree on every event and every decision, it is right to weigh up what other ministries, programs, events and conferences are taking place in your area, and to assess whether you ought to change your plans. Giving some time to consultation will often improve overall results and can also free up a lot of the local Christian community's time, energy and money. This could have several other positive effects:

- Parachurches could share staff across organizations, or churches could deploy their staff to work part-time with a parachurch.

---

31 Willmer et al., *The Prospering Parachurch*, p 137.

32 "Constant births of new para-local church organizations along with few deaths is one factor producing the great explosion of organizations. 'In the not-for-profit world of such agencies, almost no organization ever goes out of existence. … No forces seem to operate to eliminate the unproductive and ineffective group, or the group that has exhausted its usefulness or fully accomplished its purpose. This is in sharp contrast to the for-profit world in which the weak yield what they have to the strong and then succumb, purging the system as they themselves are purged.' Though this may be an overstatement, the fact still persists that groups do not die easily even if they are not now, or ever were, effective. If donors keep giving, the group keeps going. Para-local church organizations need to periodically review their reasons for being. Some groups need to join forces with others. Some need to close down. One person's vision is not sufficient reason to keep functioning; there also needs to be the obvious hand of God upon the work" (White, *The Church and the Parachurch*, p 93).

- The dates may change for some events or programs so as not to conflict with other events for a similar target audience. For example, conferences and other events could move to running on a biannual or triennial basis, to avoid cluttering up the calendar every year.
- National parachurch organizations may decide to roll out only some of their programs in a new region, because other organizations are already doing similar work.
- Those hosting a visiting speaker could consult with others well in advance so that costs can be shared and the speaker's unique gifts used to the full by arranging multiple preaching and teaching opportunities.
- Parachurches working in a similar field could form a consortium to provide administrative support and office space or to hold support-raising events together.
- Churches and parachurches in a region could create a platform and a process for advertising ministry staff positions nationally or to coordinate ministry apprentice training.

The shift to a gospel ecosystem mindset means that the co-existence of churches and parachurches need not be seen as a problem to be tolerated and managed. On the contrary, it can and should become an opportunity to be seized and delighted in for the sake of the gospel.

PART 3 //
CASE STUDIES

Introduction to part 3

P art 3 is the longest and strangest part of this book. A brief introduction might help you to navigate through it.

Whereas part 1 was primarily theological in nature, establishing biblical and theological principles for thinking about church and other Christian activity, part 2 was much more practical, as is part 3. This doesn't mean that parts 1 and 2 are no longer biblical or theological—there are numerous quotes from the Bible and much reflection on theological principles throughout every part of the book. Moreover, everything builds on the basic concepts laid down in part 1. If you have been tempted to skip ahead to the more practical sections of this book, I recommend that, sooner or later, you take the time to return and read through part 1.

Perhaps it will help to think of parts 2 and 3 as biblical ethics applied to church, parachurch and mission. In part 3, a significant amount of church history is thrown in, as we examine various issues and historical precedents. This means that much of what is discussed here is not 'black and white'. We are applying theological and biblical principles to concrete circumstances, often going beyond the clear commands of Scripture and drawing out possible implications. You almost certainly won't agree with everything I say in this final section; in fact, you shouldn't go along with everything I say without your own careful reflection. The purpose here is to lay out many of the big questions that we need to think about in various kinds of parachurch ministry, and to give some historical perspective on how these questions have been answered in the past. As I seek to analyze all this information and give my own assessment and recommendations, I hope I can be a model (albeit an imperfect one) of how to go about this process. You don't have to reach the conclusions I have reached to benefit from this section; these chapters are intended to be much more a starting point on each topic than the final word.

Indeed, at various points I often don't have strong opinions on the matters being discussed; sometimes I think there are important insights on all sides of a debate. If I seem to tread on your toes with respect to your personal convictions or ministry activity, it's unlikely that I'm taking aim at you or your ministry in particular; I may not necessarily be as critical as I first appear. Take the time to follow the thread of my argument as I try my best to provide a balanced perspective. Highlighting a potential danger is different from offering a devastating critique; our ministry practice is safer and smarter when we are fully conscious of the various risks we are taking.

This final section of the book doesn't need to be read from beginning to end. Each chapter stands alone as an exploration of one area of mission and ministry. You might prefer to jump ahead to read about the kinds of parachurch ministry that are most relevant to you. Regardless of how you use this section of the book, I hope that it will serve as a helpful resource, assist you in considering how to minister with effectiveness and integrity, and inspire you to persevere zealously in your work.

Basic timeline of parachurch ministry

3rd century
Hermits (an early form of the monastic movement)

4th century
Proliferation of monasteries
The Christianization of the Roman Empire and the first ecumenical council (Nicaea)

11th century
The Crusades begin
First universities begin to form

13th century
Establishment of mendicant religious orders (friars)

16th century
The Protestant Reformation(s)

17th century
English Puritans, German Pietists and Dutch Nadere Reformatie
English Civil War and the Westminster Assembly

18th century
The Great Awakening
Modern Protestant missionary movement

19th century
Faith missions: a new approach to non-denominational cross-cultural mission
Revivalism: a growing set of practices for effective evangelism and spiritual renewal
Proliferation of volunteer societies, including university ministries
Hospital and army chaplaincy formalized
Secularization of universities and establishment of Bible colleges and seminaries

20th century
Pentecostalism
Ecumenicalism
The Jesus Movement
Proliferation of modern parachurches
Proliferation of megachurches

Chapter 8: Local churches, cross-cultural missionary organizations, and cross-cultural missionary teams[1]

C entral to God's purposes in the world is the proclamation of the gospel to all nations. To be a faithful Christian and a faithful church is to be committed to world mission. This is now God's agenda for the world (cf. Luke 24:44-47; Acts 1:6-8). Commitment to Christ's mission stretches us: to reach out to our neighbour, or our workmate, or our fellow parents at the school gate; to look to the stranger, the migrant, or the people we don't already know; to look to the next suburb, the next town, the next region, or the next state. Ultimately it compels us to also look to neighbouring islands and nations and people groups across the world. This means that the faithful Christian life is willing to be flexible, sacrificial, outward looking, generous and mobile.

But also central to God's saving purpose is building the church. We are not charged with converting individual, independent disciples, nor are we to pursue an endlessly fluid sea of

---

1 Earlier versions of this material were delivered in sermon form in 2019 at Crossroads Presbyterian Church, Hobart, and at the Camp Clayton Easter Festival, Ulverstone.

Christian movement. Our heavenly Father's intention is to gather his people into his one, holy, universal, apostolic church, from where they may glorify and enjoy him forever. And, as we saw in the first part of this book, in this age it is God's will that we express this purpose in local gathered fellowships, expressing truth, love, order and justice in our lives together. This means that things like church gatherings, church leadership, church membership, church discipline, church doctrine, church governance and church order are not merely human, institutional concerns; they are genuine spiritual priorities. They reflect the concerns of God himself.

The church must be a missionary church, and the mission must be a church-planting mission. These two things go together. As Lesslie Newbigin says, "an unchurchly mission is as much a monstrosity as an unmissionary church".[2] But it's easier said than done. It's a real challenge to work out these two priorities in practice, especially when we consider the challenges of long-distance and cross-cultural mission. Of course, there is no fundamental difference between local mission in our neighbourhood and global mission in another country. It's wrong to think of 'mission' as something that only happens somewhere else. Yet it is still useful to separate out those types of mission that require us to cross larger cultural and geographical distances. The greater the distance we must cross to preach the gospel, the greater the challenges we face.

---

2   Cited in Goheen, *"As the Father Has Sent Me"*, p 174. However, I don't think it's quite true to say with Lesslie Newbigin that "the church is mission" (cited in Goheen, p 165) or with Michael Frost and Alan Hirsch that "our Christology informs our missiology, which in turn determines our ecclesiology" (M Frost and A Hirsch, *The Shaping of Things to Come: Innovation and mission for the 21st-century church*, Hendrickson Publishers, 2003, p 209). Rather, the church has an identity that comes from Christ's person and his saving work, which leads to us sharing in his work in the world: Christology (who Jesus is) achieves soteriology (how Jesus saves), which creates ecclesiology (what the church is) and leads to missiology (sharing in Jesus' mission). John Bolt and Richard Muller say, "The marks of the church indicate her fundamental identity, and her identity is the basis for the performance of her task … the expression 'mission-shaped church' is vacuous. A church cannot remain church unless it is shaped by a mission that is itself shaped by the church's essential identity" (cited in Tuit, *A Study and Comparison*, p 129).

These challenges are not just practical, but also theoretical and theological. When we identify, train, ordain and commission people to go and preach the gospel, plant churches and train leaders far from home, many questions arise:

- In what sense are they still members of our church?
- In what sense are they now members of the church in the new country?
- How do we think about all the overlapping groups (such as multiple sending churches, mission societies, prayer and financial supporters, and denominational leadership) who have an interest in this work?
- Where do the children of missionaries fit in?

In this chapter, we will turn our attention to thinking about cross-cultural missionary work and the various church-parachurch relationships involved in such work. I will begin by making some observations about the missionary work of the apostle Paul, before providing some principles for how missionaries should relate to both their sending church(es) and the churches in their destination countries.

Paul's missionary journeys

Before we begin, I need to give a warning about method. There's a risk in the approach summarized in the title of the famous book *Missionary Methods: St Paul's or Ours?*[3] The book of Acts was not written to give detailed guidelines for ecclesiology or missiology, and it is easy to read our own traditions or personal ideals into the book (or to draw dogmatic conclusions where Acts is silent). Furthermore, the missionary work in Acts is unique in several important ways. Firstly, it describes the unique apostles of Christ, not the everyday Christian leader.

3   R Allen, *Missionary Methods: St Paul's or Ours? A study of the church in the four provinces,* Robert Scott, 1912.

Secondly, it focuses on describing the founding of churches from nothing rather than the ongoing mission of churches or the growth and expansion of churches. Thirdly, this work takes place within the comparatively small area of the Roman Empire —there is not the same massive geographical distance or dramatic difference in language, culture and technology that today's missionaries can face.[4]

Still, Acts is useful in helping us to think about how we approach missionary work. How dare we absolutely outlaw something that Paul and his fellow workers did? How dare we be strict in our governance where Paul and his fellow workers enjoyed freedom? We should be hesitant and reflective as we adopt methods that differ dramatically from what we see in Scripture. There may be reasons to do so, but the scenarios described in Scripture should at least give us pause.

So with that in mind, here are four observations from the book of Acts:

1. Missionary planning is a combination of direct divine intervention, human planning, and providential opportunity

Jesus Christ himself is the one who gave the church its mission (Acts 1:6-8), made possible by his atoning death, resurrection and ascension to universal authority, and by the gift of the Spirit (Luke 24:44-49). Likewise, he is directly involved in the conversion and commissioning of the apostle Paul as his apostle to the Gentiles (Acts 9:10-16; 22:6-16; 26:15-23). Acts shows Christ's divine intervention (often through the Spirit) throughout the story, demonstrating that it is ultimately his work (11:27-30; 13:1-3; 16:6-10; 18:9-11; 21:4, 10-14). While Christians should not expect that Christ will be active in precisely this way beyond that first age of the apostles, we cannot rule out this type of involvement. More than this, whether he intervenes through direct revelation

---

4   K Caruthers, *Church in the Dead Zone: Practical church for missionaries in pioneer church planting contexts*, CreateSpace Independent Publishing Platform, 2017, pp 47-51.

or he providentially works 'behind the scenes' and through the spiritual empowering of his gospel word, it is important to acknowledge that he is always the Lord of the mission.

At the same time, Acts also shows Paul's missionary activity being directed by human decisions and in response to circumstantial opportunities (9:23-24; 11:19-21; 17:16-21). Judging from his longer stays in Corinth (eighteen months, 18:11) and Ephesus (twenty-seven months, 19:8-10), it seems likely that Paul was deliberately establishing new missionary centres in certain large cities. A great example of human planning and secret providence working together is seen in Paul's desire to go to Rome: he tells the Romans he was planning to travel there after his visit to Jerusalem (Rom 15:23-29), but he didn't know that this would happen through persecution from Jewish leaders in Jerusalem, which led to his arrest by the Romans and his appeal to Caesar (Acts 22-28).

We will see more examples of human deliberation and providential circumstances working together in the next few sections of this chapter, but the point is this: truly spiritual leaders do not passively depend upon divine guidance; they also make plans and decisions in the light of God's word and because of the situations in which they find themselves. Such decision-making is not worldly and presumptuous, but a faithful response to the Great Commission with which we have been entrusted.[5]

2. Missionaries enjoyed freedom of movement and recruitment

As Paul says in Galatians 1, he did not wait for permission to begin his missionary work, but rather:

> When God, who set me apart from my mother's womb and called me by his grace, was pleased to reveal his

---

5   Allen points out how often Paul's plans had to change because of circumstances, or due to direct divine guidance, but also argues that there were clearly some underlying principles guiding him (*Missionary Methods: St Paul's or Ours?*, pp 6-13). We return to this under 'Missionaries established local churches and appointed local leaders', below.

Son in me so that I might preach him among the Gentiles, my immediate response was not to consult any human being. I did not go up to Jerusalem to see those who were apostles before I was, but I went into Arabia. Later I returned to Damascus. Then after three years, I went up to Jerusalem to get acquainted with Cephas and stayed with him fifteen days ... Then I went to Syria and Cilicia. (Gal 1:15-18, 21)

This degree of freedom—to begin preaching without human ordination—was because of the special calling he received directly from Christ Jesus himself. But at the risk of making an argument from silence, a significant degree of freedom appears to mark the ongoing work of Paul, his fellow workers (Acts 15:36-41; 18:24-28),[6] and even the wider Christian movement (8:4, 11:19-21), in a way that might helpfully warn us against trying to tightly control the progress of missionary work. This freedom appears to mark not only their travels, but also their recruitment and deployment of leaders. Barnabas seeks out Paul (or Saul, as he is called until 13:9) to join him in Antioch (11:25-26); Paul and Barnabas choose Silas and Mark respectively to join them in their work (15:39-40); Paul recruits Timothy in Lystra (16:1-3); and it seems that Luke, the author of Acts, also joins him in 16:11. Timothy and Silas do not travel exclusively with Paul, but begin to work separately from him at times, supplementing his work (17:14-15; 18:5; 19:22).

Acts 18 recounts two cases of a more reactive, opportunistic kind of partnership: when Paul met Priscilla and Aquila in Corinth, they began to live, work, minister and later travel together (18:1-3, 18-19).[7] Later, when Priscilla and Aquila met Apollos in Ephesus, "they invited him to their home and explained to

---

6   Interestingly, the sad occasion of Paul and Barnabas' "sharp disagreement" did not lead to the smothering of either Paul's or Barnabas' mission works. In this case it was possible for the painful parting of ways to lead to the creation of two mission teams: Barnabas and Mark to Cyprus, and Paul and Silas to Syria and Cilicia.

7   Priscilla and Aquila are an extraordinary couple: wherever they go, they seem to host a house church (cf. 1 Cor 16:19; Rom 16:3).

him the way of God more adequately" (18:24-26). Subsequently, Apollos himself expressed a desire to go to Corinth and was supported in this by the church in Ephesus (18:27). That's an amazing string of events worth getting clear:

- Apollos, from Alexandria, comes to Ephesus.
- He becomes the student of Priscilla and Aquila, from Rome.
- They were the co-workers of Paul, whom they met while in Corinth.
- Apollos now wants to leave Ephesus and go to Corinth ...
- whither he goes to strengthen the ministry of Paul!

So as Paul says in 1 Corinthians: "I planted the seed, Apollos watered it, but God has been making it grow" (3:6). Acts 20:4 surprises us with a picture of just how large Paul's network of fellow workers might have been, with a list of seven names from various places where he had worked—a picture which is greatly expanded by the many names mentioned in his letters (especially at the end of these letters).[8] The early decades of the Christian movement were marked by a significant amount of mobility.

It is, of course, theoretically possible that in between the details recorded in Acts various church leaders gave much more detailed and prescriptive instructions and permissions to Paul and his fellow workers. But the narrative itself doesn't point in that direction. This emphasis on freedom for the early missionaries is reinforced by theological truths such as Christ's supremacy over his mission, and the authority that comes with the gospel word and the presence of the Holy Spirit. How directly this applies to local church leaders and modern missionaries is another question—one to which we will return below.

---

8   Later church tradition claims that many of these were originally disciples of Jesus himself, part of the 70 (or 72) disciples mentioned in Luke 10; see Hippolytus, 'Appendix to the works of Hippolytus' in AR Roberts, J Donaldson and AC Coxe (eds), *Ante-Nicene Fathers: The Writings of the Fathers Down to A.D. 325*, vol 5, *Hippolytus, Cyprian, Caius, Novatian, Appendix*, Hendrickson, 1996, pp 254-256, accessed 22 September 2022 (ccel. org/ccel/schaff/anf05/anf05/page_254.html).

3. Churches endorsed and supported missionary work and missionary deployment

While they enjoyed a large amount of freedom, Paul and his fellow workers did not operate in total independence from local churches. Not only did they respond to churches' requests from time to time, but they also worked and recruited with the explicit endorsement of local churches (11:22; 13:1-4 and 14:26; 15:2-3, 23-34, 40; 16:2; 18:27) and proactively returned to communicate with these churches—both in Antioch (14:26-28, 18:20-23) and Jerusalem (15:3-4, 12; 21:17-29)—about their work. We do not have enough detail to confidently declare whether this was merely wise and courteous fellowship, or a kind of accountability with more governance power attached to it; we will return to consider this issue under the heading 'Missionaries sent and accountable but free and flexible' below.

Before Paul began his second missionary journey, he went to Jerusalem to seek a decision about whether Gentile converts needed to be circumcised and obey the entire law of Moses (15:1-35). This important, cooperative meeting of home church, sending church and secondary sending church proved crucial for the ongoing health and unity of the missionary work. Church and mission were working together: a commitment to world mission, from Jerusalem to Antioch, to Lystra, Iconium and Derbe; and a commitment to Christian unity and doctrinal agreement from Lystra to Antioch to Jerusalem.[9] What could have been seen as a distraction from mission actually ended up laying important foundations to establish and strengthen the churches and the mission for the long term. Likewise, even though he had open doors in Ephesus, Paul was willing to delay forward-looking evangelistic work to reconnect with a sending church and strengthen existing churches (18:20-23).

9 The financial support of the Judean churches (11:29-30, and a later and more ambitious relief effort described in Paul's letters to Rome and Corinth) are other practical expressions of this commitment to Christian unity.

4. Missionaries established local churches and appointed local leaders

The work Paul was doing was not simply an evangelistic work, but also a church planting work. He proactively gathered new believers together and sought to establish them in the faith (14:21-22; 15:36, 41; 16:4, 18:23; 20:1-3), and when the time was right he appointed leaders from among their own number (14:23). Acts 20 stands at the end of the story of Paul's three missionary journeys and provides a useful summary of his ministry, as he passes the work on to local leaders in preparation for his visit to Jerusalem and in light of his plans to visit Rome. In both Troas (20:7-12) and Miletus (20:17-38), Paul devotes time to intensive instruction.[10] In Miletus, he gives targeted teaching for the elders of the church in Ephesus. His prolific correspondence, which makes up a large proportion of our New Testament, is perhaps the most powerful and enduring demonstration of his concern for the maturity of his disciples. The ultimate success of his ministry is marked not simply by the raw number of responses to his message, but by ongoing healthy churches.

The establishment of strong churches is not only the right and noble goal of missionary work, but also an effective strategy for future mission. As has been noted, Paul spent extended periods of time in the large cities of Corinth and Ephesus, as well as continuing to return to Antioch. Roland Allen comments on Paul's strategy:

> St. Paul's theory of evangelizing a province was not to preach in every place in it himself, but to establish centres of Christian life in two or three important places from which the knowledge might spread into the country round ... Thus the centres at which St. Paul established his Churches were centres indeed; they were not centres which were self-centred; and they were not centres

---

10 Acts 20:7-12 is not about being so boring that people go to sleep, but about being so eager to maximize time for the sake of a last opportunity for discipleship and training that it pushes the limits of human endurance.

which absorbed and restrained. They were not centres at which St. Paul must stop, but centres from which he might begin ... He seized strategic points because he had a strategy. The foundation of Churches in them was part of a campaign. In his hands they became the sources of rivers, mints from which the new coin of the Gospel was spread in every direction. They were centres from which he could start new work with new power.[11]

Acts 19:10 describes the effects of having Ephesus as a mission centre: "This went on for two years, so that all the Jews and Greeks who lived in the province of Asia heard the word of the Lord." Perhaps one of the specific results of the word ringing out from Ephesus was the establishment of the church of Colossae, founded not by the apostle Paul but by Epaphras, who was perhaps converted and equipped in Ephesus (Col 1:7). In the establishment of any church, the evangelistic mission can extend even further—in the case of the early church, extending beyond the direct capacity (or control) of the apostle Paul, let alone the leaders in Antioch or Jerusalem.

So from our study of Acts we have observed the freedom and flexibility of missionary teams that still worked in partnership with and submission to the leadership of local churches. We also noticed that the goal of the apostle's missionary work was establishing new local churches with their own local leadership.

In the remainder of this chapter, I want to explore these biblical observations still further by applying them to the practical challenges faced in missionary work around the world. I will first address the relationship of the missionary to their sending church, before addressing the relationship of the mission to the people and churches they have travelled to serve.

---

11 Allen, *Missionary Methods: St Paul's or Ours?*, pp 9, 13. Allen also observes that Paul seems to confine his work primarily to areas of Roman administration (providing both peace and a mentality of common citizenship), Greek culture (providing a medium of communication and baseline of education), Jewish influence (with their shared beliefs, shared values, and recognized place in the Roman empire) and economic power (and so wider influence and greater transience of population); see pp 7-13.

Missionaries and the sending church

1. Missionaries are sent from a church and accountable to that church

Even Christ-appointed, Spirit-selected apostles worked in ongoing partnership with the local church from which they were sent. True, there's little detail about the nature of the relationship between Paul's missionary team and the church in Antioch, or about the relationship between the churches in Antioch and Jerusalem. So we can't be too insistent about basing our own approach on these examples. Besides, whenever drawing inferences from the conduct of Paul and his fellow workers we need to recognize that they were not only missionaries; this was the work of a divinely appointed apostle and his companions.

Therefore, our thinking about missionaries and sending churches should also be shaped by our conclusions about the nature of denominations. The same principles that I explored in chapter 3 directly apply here:

- Churches ought to commit to working in loving fellowship with one another.
- Membership, ordination and discipline should be recognized beyond the scope of a single local church.
- Churches and church leaders legitimately work together in ongoing primary associations (denominations), but these associations should respect the integrity of the local church.
- Missionaries and church planters have a temporary authority over the churches they help establish, along with a subsequent relational influence.

But an important question has so far been left unanswered: to whom is the missionary rightly accountable?

It is helpful to begin by clarifying what role such people hold. To do this, we need to think about the traditional Protestant view of church leadership alongside the more recent 'five-fold' view of ministry, together with some other biblical reflections. As will quickly become apparent, it is not easy to find clear and simple answers, which means we need to emphasize some important underlying principles for the accountability of missionaries.

With some variation, Protestant theologians have insisted that the only enduring formal offices in the church are elder and deacon.[12] If this is right, then the missionary must be seen as either an elder or deacon with a peculiar assignment or as an unordained Christian exercising their spiritual gifts. Their status as 'missionaries' does not bestow any proper authority that is separate from God's word, their local church and their denomination.[13] Within this framework, then, they ultimately have a responsibility to give an account of their ministry to the local church and denomination to whom they belong and by whom they were ordained and commissioned as a leader.

More recently, missiologists have argued from Ephesians 4:11 that we should recognize and empower *five* distinct roles in the church: apostles, prophets, evangelists, pastors, and teachers.[14] The church and its mission suffers, they say, when we have only pastors running stable institutional churches. But when all five roles are identified and released, the church will reach her full potential.

This framework does not provide clarity on how these roles work together in formal decision-making in local churches, denominations or church-planting situations. This is generally because the advocates of this framework do not believe it necessary to be overly concerned about lawful church authority—aside

12 There is some variety in how these offices are further explained. For example, as four offices (pastor/minister, teacher/doctor, ruling elder, and deacon), as three offices (teaching elder/pastor/minister, ruling elder, and deacon), or even just two offices (elder, whether teaching or ruling, and deacon). Evangelical Episcopalians ordinarily hold to three offices—bishop/overseer, priest/elder, and deacon—but often argue that the role of bishop is permissible rather than divinely ordained (see, for example, Lightfoot, *The Christian Ministry*).

13 The Special Committee on Elders and Deacons, *Shepherds and Servants: The two offices Christ ordained for his church*, Presbyterian Church of NSW, 2016, accessed 4 October 2022 (eldersanddeacons.weebly.com).

14 Metcalf, *Beyond the Local Church*, pp 71-72, 103-111; and Frost and Hirsch, *The Shaping of Things to Come*, pp 165-181.

from arguing that such authorities should grant more freedom and flexibility to modern-day apostles, prophets and evangelists. Many advocates of this approach might also argue that modern apostolic teams are parallel structures to the local church, in no more need of authorization than the local church itself.[15]

This framework is practically useful in recognizing the diversity of spiritual gifts, even among those who are leaders.[16] But ultimately this approach lacks any strong scriptural basis. For example, whatever merit there is to using the word 'apostle' to describe other kinds of 'sent ones' (the literal meaning of the word 'apostle'), the context of Ephesians 4 makes clear that the 'apostle' is explicitly a foundational role for the church, entrusted with divine revelation (cf. Eph 2:20; 3:5).[17] I fear that this view also undermines the importance of the local church and the ownership of missionary work by the local church and denomination.

I am inclined to consider the 'evangelist' of Ephesians 4:11 as a modern-day missionary.[18] It could be that, just as both apos-

---

15 This is the argument of Metcalf in *Beyond the Local Church* (discussed in chapter 2 of this book). While it is self-evident that missionary work requires flexible organizational structures beyond the local church (as argued by Winter in 'The two structures of God's redemptive mission', pp 121-139), I do not accept that to be effective such structures must be recognized as another expression of 'church', nor that they must be granted freedom and flexibility on that basis. Although Christian missionaries are ministers of the gospel and always operate within the sphere of the expansion of the universal church (in its militant mode), they are not called 'churches', and Scripture never gives them the charge to function as a parallel alternative to the local church. Ken Caruthers in *Church in the Dead Zone* proposes a better model, where the church planting team might temporarily establish itself as a church until a local church is established.

16 In personal correspondence, Arthur Davies summarized this approach as "Harvard Business School equivalent for missiology". That is, a strong emphasis on pragmatic ideas and frameworks, as opposed to careful biblical and theological argumentation.

17 There are several other problems with basing this practical framework on Ephesians 4:11. In addition to the point made about the 'apostles', something very similar is true of the 'prophet'—although I must add that there is no biblical justification for describing someone with mere strategic visionary capacity as a 'prophet'. What's more, the Greek grammar suggests that, rather than being two separate gifts, the pastor and teacher is a single role: 'pastor-teacher'.

18 It is also legitimate to use the word 'apostle', for in Scripture it has a range of meanings beyond the authorized twelve apostles and Paul. It is sometimes used this way of members of Paul's apostolic band, or of others who are 'sent' from churches for a particular purpose. See Calvin, *Institutes*, IV.3.5. I personally agree with Allison in *Sojourners and Strangers* that it is not clear or helpful to use 'apostle' in a secondary sense.

tles and prophets served as founding gifts to the church, so also the evangelists and pastor-teachers fulfil the ongoing work of building the church until Christ returns. It is often argued that the office of 'evangelist' is not a perpetual office in the New Testament age because we have no instructions about the continuation of this office (compared to the elder/overseer and deacon roles, mentioned in 1 Timothy and Titus).[19] But by the strict application of this rationale, we should therefore also say that the office of pastor-teacher has also ceased, for 1 Timothy and Titus don't explicitly mention this as an ongoing role. But if, as is rightly argued, some elders are also pastor-teachers, then it is equally true that some might be evangelists.[20]

From the perspective of a weak and divided Europe, somewhat surrounded by the Islamic empires for 800 years, it might have seemed that there was little ordinary need for evangelists or that the Great Commission was not an enduring, ordinary priority for Christian churches.[21] But in more recent times, an increased awareness of the need for global missionary activity has brought with it an increased awareness of the ongoing need for this kind of Christian leader, along with a forced reassessment of the church's ordinary and ongoing responsibility for world mission. As Gordon Spykman helpfully observes about the universality ("catholicity") of the church:

> Catholicity therefore implies mission ... [it] conjures up a big picture of the church's worldwide embrace, its international scope, its ecumenical outreach—in short, its universality. It crosses the fixed boundaries between peoples. It breaks through barriers of resistance. The

19 The Special Committee on Elders and Deacons, *Shepherds and Servants.*

20 In correspondence with Scottish Presbyterians, George Whitefield called himself "a Presbyter at large" (cited in Noll, *The Rise of Evangelicalism*, p 103).

21 Goheen, *"As the Father Has Sent Me"*, p 314. See also S Neill, *A History of Christian Missions*, Pelican History of the Church (O Chadwick gen ed), vol 6, Penguin Books, 1964, pp 244-245. Calvin acknowledged that God sometimes raises up evangelists. Alluding to Martin Luther he writes: "although I deny not, that afterward God occasionally raised up Apostles, or at least Evangelists, in their stead, as has been done in our time" (Calvin, *Institutes*, IV.3.4).

church must seek a presence, lift its voice, and share
its witness in every domain claimed by its Lord.[22]

But no matter how the role of missionaries is understood and
described, they are rightly accountable to some extent to the
churches and denominations that send them.[23] Even with their
unique apostolic role, Paul and his fellow workers were not lone
rangers: they maintained regular contact with other churches,
regularly returned to the church that sent them, and sought to
consult with and submit themselves to the wider Christian community and its judgements.[24] Once we take into account the
explicit teaching of the rest of the New Testament, with the special place it gives to the local church and its leaders, how can we
possibly support almost totally independent mission teams?
Maintaining good communication with the sending church is
not a distraction from the work of mission, but is a vital part of
the overall work, just as it was for the apostle Paul.

This does not mean that ideally all mission agencies should
be denominational departments. But it does mean that, except
in exceptional circumstances, missionaries and mission agencies should not operate in total independence from local churches
or denominations.[25] William Carey, often called the 'father of
modern missions', argued that one of the significant means that
Christians should use for the "conversion of the heathens" was
the establishment of mission societies to facilitate the work—

22 Spykman, *Reformational Theology*, pp 446-447.
23 Contrary to De Jong: "All mission work ought to be ecclesiastical" (*The Church's Witness to
     the World*, p 298); and Newbigin: "The New Testament knows of only one missionary society
     —the Church" (cited in Goheen, *"As the Father Has Sent Me"*, p 199).
24 "What we can see, however, is that while local churches may have blessed, and even
     regulated, such sodalities, the actual administration of the sodality (including the
     appointment of new members) was left to itself. The result of this cooperation between
     the churches and the sodalities as seen in Acts was evidently a symbiotic relationship of
     mutual encouragement and edification between the two: just as the missionary bands
     were blessed and supported by the churches, so the churches were strengthened and
     equipped through the work of the bands" (Reeves, 'What is a church? What is a CU?', p 13).
25 See Kuiper, *The Glorious Body of Christ*, p 241; Missions Interlink, *The Croydon Declaration:
     Mission leaders express regret* [unpublished conference statement], Australian Evangelical
     Alliance, Croydon NSW, 2005; and Hammett, 'How church and parachurch should relate',
     pp 199-207.

societies associated with but distinct from denominations. Carey thought these societies should be inter-denominational efforts, but realized that they may need to remain denominationally distinct because of the difficulties in overcoming differences.[26]

If missionaries are accountable to their sending church, it follows that the sending church is also responsible for the missionaries whom they send. We don't just send the missionary to the mission agency, put their picture on a noticeboard, and give them some money. They came from us; they belong to us in some ongoing sense. The mission agency should work to help us both send them and support them, and should not accept applicants who come to them with no endorsement from their local church at all.[27]

Taking seriously the responsibility to the local church can be a great blessing to cross-cultural missionaries. They can sometimes be under a great deal of strain and feel desperately alone. There may even be pressures and pains that come from relational difficulties with other Christians serving alongside them, leaders of their mission agency, or local Christians. These pressures can then make missionaries vulnerable to the temptation of sinful behaviours and habits, whether lashing out at others or seeking to comfort themselves in ungodly ways. In the face of such pressures, it can be a great help to know that their local

---

26 W Carey, *An Enquiry into the Obligations of Christians, to Use Means for the Conversion of the Heathens: In which the religious state of the different nations of the world, the success of former undertakings, and the practicability of further undertakings, are considered*, sec V, Ann Ireland, 1792, pp 77-87, accessed 22 September 2022 (https://www.wmcarey.edu/carey/enquiry/anenquiry.pdf).

27 I am aware that most, if not all, of what I say in this chapter applies to the local church where a missionary has been a member—which then becomes *the* sending church—but I have said little about other local churches that choose to 'adopt' missionaries as partners by praying, giving money, and welcoming them as guests during home assignment. These types of links are wonderful, genuine expressions of gospel partnership, and should be encouraged and celebrated. Nevertheless, there remains a unique role for the missionary's own local church—the body of Christ that has nurtured them, trained them, encouraged them and commissioned them for their new field of ministry. We would not expect missionaries to be accountable to other partnering churches in the same way. However, as relationships develop over time, a natural level of mutual accountability and responsibility will develop. There is no need for *the* sending church to feel threatened by the involvement of many sending churches; on the contrary, they should welcome the partnership and support offered to the gospel workers who have gone out from them.

church and sending denomination still count the missionaries as 'one of us'.[28]

We also need to be considerate of the human limitations of cross-cultural missionaries. It's not as simple as saying, "You have gone overseas, so you are now a member of the local church in the new country; join the culture and settle down there". The idealism of total identification is difficult for many to fully embrace. Both the missionaries themselves and their fellow Christians where they are ministering are often very aware that they are not exactly the same as each other. The missionaries are not fully at home in the new country, nor are they likely to see it as their permanent home—and there may be many cultural factors that keep drawing attention to these differences.

Likewise, the children of missionaries are not necessarily children of the country where their parents are ministering. Knowing that the family may not stay long-term, is it better to bind the children to the health care and education of the country their parents are ministering in? Or might it be more loving for them to share in the health care and educational benefits of their home country? There is no single, simple answer to these and other similar questions, but they remind us that local churches should consider not only how to support missionaries in their gospel proclamation, but also how to support families—especially those with young children—as they make sacrifices for the sake of Christ.

Such sensitivity can be instructive even for thinking about pastors and other employees much closer to home who still have to move to serve in a new ministry setting. Even relocating to the next city or suburb can bring a lot of upheaval. Somewhat like overseas missionaries, paid church staff are aware of being 'outsiders' to some extent, and should be shown some consideration because of this unusual situation.[29]

---

28 A useful handbook is B Dipple, *Becoming Global*, SMBC Press, 2011.

29 The denomination serves a useful function for formally trained and paid ministry staff, who might move from church to church. As with cross-cultural missionaries, this denominational accountability and support is often supplemented by informal networks of fellowship.

2. Missionaries need to be empowered to be flexible in their work

The simple reality of distance means that the missionary team cannot be *closely* accountable to the sending church or denomination. Even in the 2020s, with affordable air travel and communications technology, no sending church can be on the ground, watching the details, understanding the full picture. Global mission forces us to see the limitations of the earthly, institutional church. Living in the light of the universal lordship of Christ and the work of the Spirit in advancing and protecting his mission, we go beyond the reach of institutional church, even of the non-denominational mission society.

Henry Venn, the honorary secretary of the Church Missionary Society in the mid-19th century, wrote: "[Missionary] work is so varied, and its emergencies so sudden, that the evangelist must be left to act mainly on his own responsibility and judgement."[30] We don't have to systematically monitor and control missionaries, as if this is the only way to safeguard sound doctrine and conduct. We can be confident that the Lord Jesus is ultimately the head of the church, which he rules by his Spirit through his word. Ralph Winter captures this point by saying that missionaries are 'regulated' by denominations and churches, but not 'dominated' or 'administered' by them. He describes the devolution of missionary oversight:

> On the one hand, there were men like Henry Venn ... who championed the semi-autonomous mission sodality, and they voiced an attitude which was not at first contradicted by any significant part of the leaders of the ecclesiastical structures. On the other hand, there was the centralizing perspective of denominational leaders ...

---

30 H Venn, *The Missionary Life and Labours of Francis Xavier Taken from his own Correspondence: With a sketch of the general results of Roman Catholic missions among the heathen*, Longman, Roberts and Green, 1862, p 146. Stephen Neill says that the increase in denominational control over missionary work could also be explained by telecommunications: "The invention of the electric telegraph spoiled all" (Neill, *A History of Christian Missions*, pp 510-511).

which gained ground almost without reversal throughout the latter two-thirds of the nineteenth century, so
that by the early part of the 20th century, the once-
independent structures which had been merely related
to the denominations gradually became dominated by
the churches, that is administered, not merely regulated.
Partially as a result, toward the end of the nineteenth
century, there was a new burst of totally separate
mission sodalities called the Faith Missions ... It is not
widely recognized that this pattern was mainly a recru-
descence of the pattern established earlier in the century,
prior to the trend toward denominational boards.[31]

Because sending churches, denominations and mission agencies can become overbearing, missionaries need discernment to
consider how best to work in partnership with them—to be
shrewdly pragmatic while also preserving honesty and integrity.
For the sake of genuine accountability and fellowship, missionaries must accept that often they will be slowed down or
frustrated, and yet there remains some wiggle room for them to
discreetly carry on unhindered if they are strategically tactful in
how they manage this relationship.

We now turn to the relationship between missionaries and
the local church in the country where they are working.

Missionaries and the local church

1. Missionaries are equal partners with local churches

The missionary may have expertise, insight and spiritual maturity, but they always come to a new country as a fellow human
being—both a divine image bearer and a guilty, forgiven sinner.
When people are converted, these new converts are equally
humble and repentant; equally adopted sons and daughters of
God; equally gifted by the Spirit to build the church.

31 Winter, 'The two structures of God's redemptive mission', p 133.

The wonderfully named Lancelot Threlkeld was a missionary in early 19th-century Australia who was outspoken in decrying violence against Australian aborigines. He famously wrote:

> Human nature is just the same, whether cloaked with the most delicate alabaster skin, or comely but black exterior of the image of God. Accidental circumstances may make individual differences but it is 'of one blood God hath made all nations of men for to dwell on all the face of the earth'. The mind of man is the same, whether of saint, or savage, or of sage, darkness itself until the divine light shines within the soul and opens the eyes of the understanding to see the glory of God in the face of the Lord Jesus Christ.[32]

When missionaries appoint new leaders, whether in local churches or parachurches, these leaders are truly fellow workers in the ministry, empowered and ordained by the Holy Spirit. Missionaries should have the same attitude towards local ministry colleagues when they arrive to work with already-established churches.

Cross-cultural missionaries need to beware of clericalism, professionalism and paternalism: seeing themselves as different than and superior to their fellow Christians, and so conducting themselves in a way that is aloof from them or standing over them. A particularly problematic expression of this is the failure to truly hand over leadership to their converts. The goal of missions must not be to establish new churches in such a way that they exist in long-term dependence upon the external missionary leaders. Rather, the goal must be to raise up local leaders and hand over to them both the local ministry and the responsibility for further missionary work. A healthy local Christian movement will have not only churches and denominations with indigenous leaders, but also local parachurches and mission societies with indigenous leaders. This is what the concept of

---

32 Cited in JW Harris, *One Blood: 200 years of Aboriginal encounter with Christianity: A story of hope*, Albatross Books, 1990, p 35.

the 'three selves' of missionary work is all about.[33] The goal of mission work is to establish local churches that are *self-governing*, *self-funding* and *self-extending*.[34] Henry Venn says:

> Regarding the ultimate object of a mission, viewed under its ecclesiastical aspect, to be the settlement of a native Church, under native pastors, upon a self-supporting system, it should be borne in mind that the progress of a mission mainly depends upon the training up and the location of native pastors; and that, as it has been happily expressed, 'the euthanasia of a mission' takes place when a missionary, surrounded by well-trained native congregations, under native pastors, is able to resign all pastoral work into their hands, and gradually to relax his superintendence over the pastors themselves, till it insensibly ceases; and so the mission passes into a settled Christian community. Then the missionary and all missionary agency should be transferred to the 'regions beyond'.[35]

To be committed to this requires the missionary to begin with that end in mind and let it shape all that they do. Roland Allen has argued that mission work must be established in such a way that it can be easily passed on to local leadership. This requires the fostering of relationships not just between the local leaders and the missionary, but also between local leaders of other young churches and parachurches.[36] The complexity and the financial demands of the church structures need to be adjusted

---

33 Neill, *A History of Christian Missions*, pp 259-260. By contrast, Lesslie Newbigin bemoaned how, instead of being empowered to be the vanguard of mission, young churches were seen as "a sort of bowl into which the fish that were caught could be put for storage" (cited in Goheen, *"As the Father Has Sent Me"*, p 199).

34 David Bosch has argued that there needs to be a fourth 'self': 'self-theologizing'; see DJ Bosch, *Transforming Mission: Paradigm shifts in theology of mission*, American Society of Missiology Series, no 16, Orbis Books, 1991, pp 451-452.

35 Cited in WR Shenk, 'The origins and evolution of the three-selfs in relation to China', *International Bulletin of Missionary Research*, 1990, 14(1):29. See also Goheen, *"As the Father Has Sent Me"*, pp 316-317, 322-323.

36 An interdependence that Newbigin also advocated for strongly; see Goheen, *"As the Father Has Sent Me"*, pp 325-326.

so that they can realistically be sustained by the local church without external funding and administrative support.

Allen emphasized that missionaries should be willing to face the problems and challenges that would come with this approach for the sake of the long-term outcome.[37] This requires great patience, skill and care. It requires a keen self-awareness to identify the many cultural assumptions that a missionary brings—assumptions that are often bundled up with their understanding of God's word—and to be alert to the subtle ways in which racism seeps out of our sinful hearts, presuming to judge those from other cultures while counting our own culture as normal and good.[38] Missionaries arriving to work with churches that have been established for decades, or even centuries, may still encounter the legacy of these attitudes, and need to discover how they might contribute to the local Christian movement heading in a healthy direction.

2. Missionaries are transient experts

Yet it remains true that missionaries, just like everyone else, are not the property of any local community or any earthly church—either the sending church or the receiving church. They are free to be sent, free to arrive, and free to leave again. In their role, they are sent from a church and remain in fellowship with and accountable to this church. Even though it is right for them to also have a secondary fellowship with and accountability to the church where they are ministering, this often doesn't transfer entirely. The reality is usually quite complex. There are likely to be several overlapping circles of community, belonging, loyalty, responsibility and accountability: the local community of believers; the local denomination; the mission team; the local mission agency; the sending mission agency; the sending denomination;

---

37 Allen, *Missionary Methods: St Paul's or Ours?*, pp 203-204.

38 Stephen Neill recounts the great difficulty cross-cultural missionaries often had in changing their attitudes and behaviour to facilitate this transition in the 19th and 20th centuries; see Neill, *A History of Christian Missions*, pp 510-539.

the sending church; and financial and prayer supporters. Idealism that pushes denominational oversight, sending church accountability, receiving church membership, or mission team belonging to the exclusion of the others is naïve and unrealistic.

Missionaries are not only potentially transient, but also come in as outside experts. Since missionaries have peculiar training, experience and gifts, they must acknowledge that this brings with it a certain kind of authority. The economic wealth, cultural influence or political power of their country of origin might add yet more layers of implicit authority. To ignore all this is to risk exerting more influence than intended, which could impinge on the genuine exercise of local leadership.

Expertise and seniority can be a good thing. The opposite of paternalism is not total abdication. The New Testament itself warns us against being "hasty in the laying on of hands" (1 Tim 5:22). The noble desire to appoint local people to leadership could obscure the fact that these locals are not practically prepared or spiritually mature. Paul's three missionary journeys (recorded in Acts 13-20) took place across the span of ten years, with repeated visits to the young churches and intense involvement and intervention—think about his letters to the Corinthians! How much more care might be needed in situations that are very different to the context of Paul's mission work: not every missionary context enjoys the common culture, shared language, and relative economic, political and technological parity that existed between regions in the Roman Empire. It is also a challenge to know how to equip young national churches to meaningfully interact in the wider international fellowship—theological and organizational complexity requires a different set of skills and experience from that which might be required for the local work.

This is not just about meeting some pedantic Western standard; it is about protecting the young church against bullying, corruption and heresy.[39] As Stephen Neill says, unless a church attains growth and maturity, "'independence' is only a synonym

39 LCWE Commission on Co-operation, Cooperating in World Evangelization.

for disintegration and decay".[40] It takes time to figure out what indigenous Christianity ought to look like in a new context. New converts may not always want to, or be able to, carry on exactly as they were before they came to faith.[41] So the goal of properly contextualized Christian maturity needs to be worked towards with determination, and with vigilance against cultural pride, racism, convenience and mere efficiency. The establishment of local leadership needs to be seen as a long-term goal, not a quick and easy feat.

Throughout this process, cross-cultural missionaries should work in partnership with local churches to keep advancing the evangelistic mission.[42] At its best, this type of long-term partnership ends up being another expression of the benefits of local churches and parachurches partnering together to bear fruit for the gospel.

---

40 Neill, *A History of Christian Missions*, p 206. Neill goes on to give the 'Native Pastorate' experiment in Sierra-Leone as an example of such failure. However, it can be argued in the long term it was successful in the formulation of African Christian identity, and that its failure was just as much due to lack of support from European church leaders and the death of Henry Venn. See JJ Hanciles, 'Missionaries and revolutionaries: Elements of transformation in the emergence of modern African Christianity', *International Bulletin of Missionary Research*, 2004, 28(4):146-152.

41 The new converts themselves may initially associate much of their own culture with their non-Christian past and desire to adopt and appropriate many of the cultural trappings that came with the gospel that was preached to them (cf. Neill, *A History of Christian Missions*, pp 534-539). Dana Robert talks about this kind of shift by referring to African historians Lamin Sanneh and Ogbu Kalu: "[Sanneh says] over-emphasis on the 'colonialism paradigm' in mission history effectively silences indigenous agents and ignores how they 'translated' the gospel into their own social and spiritual realities for the fulfilment of their own goals" (DL Robert [ed], *Converting Colonialism: Visions and realities in mission history, 1706-1914*, Studies in the History of Christian Missions, Eerdmans, 2008, p 4). Neill adds: "Missionaries have often been accused of unnecessarily separating Christians from the ordinary life of their people; but when converts have been cast out by their tribe, what is to be done? There seemed to be no remedy except that the missionaries should gather the little groups of the faithful into Christian villages" (Neill, *A History of Christian Missions*, p 349).

42 Goheen, *"As the Father Has Sent Me"*, p 320.

Conclusion

This topic is so complicated that entire books are dedicated to exploring it; this chapter can only scratch the surface. Simply appreciating the complexities is a good start. But what I hope I have shown is that cross-cultural missionaries are sent from local churches and remain accountable to those churches, while also having a need to be granted significant flexibility and autonomy. I have also shown that missionaries are equal partners with Christian converts while usually remaining distinct from those converts as somewhat transient and specialized outsiders. In thinking and working carefully in the light of these complications, we are seeking to honour two realities: the great importance of global evangelistic mission, and the enormous value of the local church. Our personal lives and organizational decisions must be shaped by these things, to God's glory.

Chapter 9: University student ministry and other local mission societies and discipleship groups

Ask Christians which organization has made the most profound impact on their lives, and many will mention the name of a parachurch ministry—a university Christian Union, a non-denominational conference, or some kind of discipleship network. Ask them to identify their true spiritual 'home', and many, if answering honestly, will answer the same way.

The local mission society or discipleship group[1] is the 'textbook parachurch' in many ways—the kind of group most readers would think about first. Such denominational or non-denominational groups were established to provide more focused discipleship and to facilitate more targeted evangelism than local churches might provide. Just as cross-cultural missionary societies exist to undertake evangelism and edification in other

---

1   I am using 'discipleship group' here to refer to parachurch ministries whose purposes (or at least part of whose purpose) is to provide in-depth spiritual, moral and theological maturity to its participants. They are usually both 'disciple*ship*' groups in seeking to help Christians follow Jesus, and 'discip*ling*' groups in promoting a culture of Christians being proactive in ministering to one another. As will be discussed in this chapter, local mission societies almost always have a significant discipleship component.

nations, local mission societies and discipleship groups undertake these things on home turf. Such groups include university student ministries, Christian workers' fellowships, Scripture teaching in schools, Bible study fellowships, men's and women's fellowships, and a range of youth camps and adult conferences and conventions. In this chapter, I will focus the discussion primarily on university student ministry, while drawing on examples from and applications for other groups along the way.

First, I will consider the benefits of university student ministry, before considering some of the issues relevant to these groups (and to other local mission societies and discipleship groups).

The benefits of university student ministry

University student ministries bring most of the benefits of parachurches mentioned in chapter 2. For one thing, *they facilitate broader forms of Christian unity and fellowship than local churches can or than a denomination should*, breaking down the barriers of denominational distinctives and tribalism. Young men and women enjoy the stimulating experience of interacting with Christians from Anglican, Baptist, Presbyterian, Pentecostal and independent churches of various stripes, and are challenged to reflect upon their own background and learn from the unique insights of others. This can also help students reach a healthy generosity in working together with others even where there is disagreement on secondary or tertiary matters.

At the same time, university student ministries also *facilitate narrower forms of Christian unity and fellowship than local churches can or than a denomination should*. A university group is largely restricted in focus to those studying at tertiary institutions, and also assumes a significant level of education. Such ministries are generally most popular among school-leavers and other young adults, rather than mature-age students, and so they are also narrow in their age demographic.

Some student groups are very explicit about their evangelistic purpose, their in-depth discipleship hothousing, or their specific strategies and programs. Not every Christian student might be enthused about the program or prepared to devote themselves to the strategies adopted—such as a heavy commitment to walk-up evangelism or an intensive 'missional' strategy. But even though it may turn away some potential participants, this type of special focus is still appropriate: their status as a parachurch enables a degree of specialization that may not be appropriate in a local church.

University student ministries certainly *are enormously effective at investing in Christians through discipleship and at training and releasing Christians for evangelism—and, in some cases, for good deeds as well.* Their narrow focus allows them to invest significant time in this work and to set up flexible programs and groups to meet the various needs of their own context. This benefit is often felt most markedly by Christians from small churches, which don't have the resources to provide these kinds of opportunities, or by those from larger churches that are not currently investing heavily in these ministries.

The relationship between university student ministry and local churches

Only one of the benefits listed in chapter 2 does not as obviously apply to student ministries: *parachurches can protect churches from mission drift and worldly entanglement.* This is because student ministries (and other local mission societies and discipleship groups) share the same basic purpose—gospel proclamation and discipleship—as local churches. For this very reason, and because they are not separated from local churches geographically, they can very easily begin to compete with and undermine the ministry of local churches. Therefore, these types of local mission societies need to conduct themselves with great care. Every point of advice listed in part 2 applies directly to these kinds of organizations. In their relationship to local churches, student groups and other similar societies need to uphold:

- the importance and responsibility of local churches
- the need for consultation and transparency
- the stance of being willing to serve but not judge
- a thoughtful approach to recruitment, support and discipline
- the principle that Christian activity should pay attention to God's pattern for church life
- the ideal balance of co-existing, comparing, contrasting and complementing without competing, and
- the necessity of programming and support-raising restraint.

Likewise, in their dealings with student ministries or other similar groups, leaders of local churches need to uphold:

- the primacy of the universal church
- the value of plugging into the wider gospel ecosystem
- the importance of humble, honest and loving communication
- the benefits of a proactive approach to prayer, promotion and planning
- the need for diligence in matters of ordination, support and accountability
- godliness and wisdom in listening, learning and leveraging, and
- a thought-through approach to financial support.

In the rest of this chapter, I will focus on seven further areas of concern that require special attention from university student ministries, local mission societies and discipleship organizations.

The triumph of pragmatism over principle

Parachurches are founded by entrepreneurial Christians who see a need and get on and do something about it. They are driven by gospel convictions, but often their real strength is in practical know-how and leadership charisma.[2] But as in every other area of life, it is not enough to do what works; we must do what is right. All Christian organizations must honour the Lord Jesus not only with fruitful results, but also with their godly conduct and theological faithfulness. Local mission societies can be governed far too much by doing what works rather than by theological and ethical principle. When parachurches explore sponsorships, offer incentives, manage their teams, design their program and market themselves, they need to carefully assess all such things from the perspective of beliefs, culture, values and principle.[3] Lack of theological depth (see below) certainly exacerbates the danger of pragmatism.

In their openness to innovation, university ministries and other such groups need to beware of the techniques they bring into their actual ministry practices. All their tactics should be subject to constant theological scrutiny.

Let's consider two examples where the danger of pragmatism has particularly reared its head.

1. Evangelistic techniques

Consider the evolution of techniques used in public evangelistic meetings. The Great Awakening preachers of the 18th century were innovators in many ways, such as holding evangelistic meetings based around passionate, forthright open-air preaching. These gatherings became massively effective at reaching large numbers of people who might never have come to a church

---

2   In fact, C Stacey Woods—the Australian who served as General Secretary of Inter-Varsity Christian Fellowship (IVCF) in both Canada and the USA, and later as General Secretary of International Fellowship of Evangelical Students (IFES)—was deliberate in appointing to boards not only ordained pastors and theologians, but business leaders with practical knowledge in how to manage and grow the organization—'doers not thinkers'; see AD MacLeod, *C. Stacey Woods and the Evangelical Rediscovery of the University*, IVP Academic, 2007, pp 61-62, 243.

3   The 19th-century movement of 'muscular Christianity' had the noble aim of re-engaging men with the gospel and mobilizing them for Christian ministry, but its culturally and historically British imperialist values and ideals needed to be subverted by Scripture; see Taylor, *Like a Mighty Army?*, pp 56-62. The same is true of other manifestations of 'muscular Christianity'.

building. They also freed the evangelists from dependence on the permission of local ministers and bishops.[4]

The leaders of the Great Awakening were also innovators in using publicity to promote public events, publishing periodicals, and writing new hymns that articulated the theological vision and heartbeat of their movement.[5] Mark Noll also observes another form of publicity that was a little less direct: the waves of revival experienced in the first Great Awakening followed something of a pattern modelled on the account of Jonathan Edwards.[6] A certain kind of preparation, including the expectations established by Edwards' account, seemed to facilitate these revivals. The Great Awakening was often accompanied by extraordinary emotional responses to the preaching, which further led many to be suspicious of the movement. This in turn provoked an important and heated discussion about the legitimacy of these various 'new measures' in evangelism. Edwards made a valuable contribution to this discussion in his *The Distinguishing Marks of a Work of the Spirit of God* and *A Treatise Concerning the Religious Affections* by seeking to differentiate between merely human emotional excess and truly spiritual things.[7] So also William Sprague offered a cautious assessment about appropriate new measures in revival.[8]

4   Noll, *The Rise of Evangelicalism*, pp 95, 139.
5   "They were, however, unusually gifted men: one of the greatest public orators of the century (Whitefield), one of the most effective organizers for one of the longest period of effectiveness (John Wesley), one of the pioneers in the management of publicity (William Seward), one of the most compelling popular troubadours (Charles Wesley), one of the most powerful thinkers (Edwards), several of the critical forerunners of printed mass communication (John Lewis, Thomas Prince, William McCulloch), and then scores of others who in their local spheres were sometimes even more memorable as preachers, networkers, hymnwriters, theologians and communicators" (Noll, *The Rise of Evangelicalism*, p 132).
6   Noll, *The Rise of Evangelicalism*, pp 83-84.
7   J Edwards, *The Distinguishing Marks of a Work of the Spirit of God, Applied to That Uncommon Operation That Has Lately Appeared on the Minds of Many of the People in This Land: With a Particular Consideration of the Extraordinary Circumstances with Which This Work Is Attended*, S Kneeland and T Green, 1741, accessed 23 September 2022 (name.umdl. umich.edu/N03831.0001.001); and J Edwards, *A Treatise Concerning Religious Affections, in Three Parts*, S Kneeland and T Green, 1746, accessed 23 September 2022 (name.umdl. umich.edu/N04635.0001.001).
8   WB Sprague, 'Lecture V: General means of producing and promoting revivals' in *Lectures on Revivals of Religion*, Banner of Truth, 1958 [1832], pp 115-152.

Other public evangelists brought new innovations with much more questionable theological tendencies. While some ministers were resistant to any innovation, engineering or emotionalism whatsoever, others went to the opposite extreme. The Presbyterian revivalist Charles Finney formalized a series of steps intended to prepare the way for revival.[9] He also introduced the 'anxious seat', to which those being especially affected by the meeting could come for personal prayer and ministry.[10] Finney was extremely confident in the science of revivals:

> *Religion is the work of man ...*
> I. A REVIVAL OF RELIGION IS NOT A MIRACLE ...
> It is not a miracle, or dependent on a miracle, in any sense. It is a purely philosophical result of the right use of the constituted means—as much so as any other effect produced by the application of means ...
>
> But means will not produce a revival, we all know, without the blessing of God. No more will grain, when it is sowed, produce a crop without the blessing of God ... [A] revival is as naturally a result of the use of the appropriate means as a crop is of the use of its appropriate means.[11]

Evangelists can easily begin to trust in a sequence of extra-biblical events intended to trigger revival. Leaders can also become too complacent about counting external responses to their ministry as marks of success, rather than looking for authentic and lasting spiritual fruit. So also their converts can begin to trust in the brute fact of having performed certain actions (such

---

9   CG Finney, *Lectures on Revivals of Religion*, Fleming H Revell Company, 1868 [1835], accessed 23 September 2022 (ccel.org/ccel/finney/revivals/revivals.i.html). Published only a few years after Sprague's lectures, not only the title but much of the content seems to have been taken from Sprague, but the theological emphasis dramatically changed.

10 Finney, 'Lecture XIV: Measures to promote revivals' in *Lectures on Revivals of Religion*, pp 238-262. This is the precursor of the modern evangelistic process of coming forward in response to a call to faith.

11 Finney, 'Lecture I: What a revival of religion is' in *Lectures on Revivals of Religion*, pp 9-21. Finney goes on to state that he believes that the outcome of a revival is more predictable than the outcome of farming.

as sitting on the anxious seat, coming forward for prayer or raising a hand), rather than the gospel of Christ.

In the 19th century, Dwight Moody and Ira Sankey brought other kinds of innovations by popularizing the use of music in public evangelistic rallies. Their events, featuring Moody's simple, anecdotal preaching and Sankey's emotional performances of popular Christian music, were massively popular as well as very influential on the shape of evangelistic meetings.[12] The use of music, the conjuring of an emotional atmosphere, and the provision of concrete opportunities to respond to a gospel appeal can all be used effectively and unobjectionably. But they can be imbued (even unintentionally) with great significance, even treated as spiritual methods and means with a power of their own, which come to distract from the fundamental importance of the plain preaching of God's word accompanied by Christian love and prayer (2 Cor 4:1-2; 1 Thess 2:1-6). The mechanics can become more and more sophisticated and elaborate, yet remain theologically unquestioned. At their worst, they can become techniques by which a congregation is manipulated more than persuaded.[13]

What is true of techniques for public evangelistic meetings is also true in the area of 'personal work', which might happen after larger gatherings or might be entirely separate from them. In the 20th century, more attention was placed on the best methods of personal evangelism, especially within university ministry.[14] Ironically, while personal work was considered to be a reaction against the manipulative techniques of public rallies,

---

12 Bebbington, *Evangelicalism in Modern Britain*, pp 163-164, 174. After the birth of modern rock music, the Jesus Movement pioneered its use for Christian evangelism with "a new form of evangelical itinerancy by a genre of intensely counterculture singer-preachers" (Smith, *The Origins, Nature, and Significance of the Jesus Movement*, p 78). These pioneers paved the way for the modern Christian music industry; see Smith, pp 133-139.

13 An evangelistic method becomes manipulative where non-rational influence or coercion is more powerful than a person's conscious, rational choice. Billy Graham's crusades were considered remarkable for their careful lack of manipulative techniques. See Piggin, *Spirit, Word and World*, pp 154-155.

14 D Belden, *The Origins and Development of the Oxford Group (Moral Re-Armament)* [PhD thesis], Oxford University, 1976, pp 41-55.

its quasi-psychological methods were open to the same charge of being manipulative and technique-driven.[15] Not only small groups but also weekend 'house parties' came to be an important part of this kind of evangelistic work.[16] In the end, the same type of risk can accompany large-scale preaching events or personal evangelism: too much confidence placed in particular techniques, and too little discernment applied to them.

2. Concern for reputation and influence

The size and scale of parachurch organizations can also bring the temptation to make decisions primarily to preserve the reputation and influence of the organization, even at the expense of honesty, morality or theological courage. This was one shameful aspect of the 18th-century Great Awakening in the American colonies. As Mark Noll describes it, the revivals were so successful that as they reached large numbers of slave owners, it became difficult for the evangelists to confront the problem of slavery.[17] Worse, George Whitefield began to advocate for the benefits of slavery, as Jared Wilson writes:

> As his popularity grew, so did his prestige and power ...
> There is something about bigness—and everything
> that comes with it—that can seduce anyone ... With
> power also comes the temptation to more pragmatic

15 Belden, *The Origins and Development of the Oxford Group*, p 237. These tendencies took an especially intense and eccentric turn in the therapeutic 'life-changing' of the Oxford Group; see Belden, pp 169-189, 227-231. They called it the "science" of "soul surgery".

16 The Oxford Group (see previous footnote) pioneered the 'house party': "Retreats and summer conferences had played important roles in Y.M.C.A. college evangelism. But [the Oxford Group's] use of the small conference as a primary means of converting enquirers and swiftly building them into a 'fellowship' was novel. The house-party was a psychologically effective means of combining the power of personal interviews and confessions with the need to create group consciousness and teamwork. In its psychological effect it bore resemblances to the more recent practice of the weekend or week long 'encounter group', as described, for instance, by the American psychologist Carl Rogers" (Belden, *The Origins and Development of the Oxford Group*, p 241). The name was chosen to appeal to the middle-class and upper-class target audience of the group: "you see, if we called it a "conference" some of the people would never come. The half-social aspect of it is what draws them in, because it hitches on to their own kind of experience" (quoted in Belden, p 239).

17 Noll, *The Rise of Evangelicalism*, pp 240-242.

thinking, where we will justify our own decisions in service of "the greater good." How did Whitefield justify his sin? Perhaps the same way many try to justify it today—his good outweighed his bad. His sin is put in the context of his success, effectively reducing it to an incidental blip on the massive radar screen of his exemplary evangelism.[18]

Likewise, the 20th-century evangelist Billy Graham was compromised by being too close to President Richard Nixon, which led to him being complicit in Nixon's personal character flaws and too closely associated with his administration.[19] The opportunities for gospel influence that might come from gaining access to powerful people are risky, because power can be intimidating and intoxicating. The Christian leader must be careful that they are not influenced by others more than they are themselves influential. Even if we are not meeting with presidents or founding orphanages, we can easily be tempted to please members, donors or wealthy stakeholders, members of government, respected academics, or local media and sports celebrities in a way that compromises our integrity.

Moral integrity

The informality, fluidity and intensity of parachurch ministries create opportunities for secretive immoral conduct to take a foothold. Ministries that involve a lot of travel are vulnerable to this

---

18 JC Wilson, 'Was George Whitfield a Christian? Dealing with the tainted legacy of American history's greatest preacher', *For the Church*, 23 May 2019, accessed 23 September 2022 (ftc.co/resource-library/blog-entries/was-george-whitefield-a-christian). Wilson reports that Whitefield saw the economic benefits of slavery for the orphanage he had established in Georgia, advocated for slavery in Georgia, and brought slaves there two years before slavery was legalized. See also Noll's larger assessment on George Whitefield in *The Rise of Evangelicalism*, pp 100-101.

19 A lapse of judgement he later regretted, and he was more careful in his dealings with subsequent presidents; see G Wacker, M Lee and M Galli, 'A Billy Graham biographer tells all!' [audio file], 22 February 2018, accessed 23 September 2022 (christianitytoday.com/ct/2018/february-web-only/billy-graham-podcast.html).

same temptation while on the road, too. As with megachurches (discussed in chapter 12), larger national and international parachurch organizations can bring with them additional temptations to abuse power, to give in to sexual immorality, to mishandle money, and to distort the truth—whether the truth about the credentials of their leaders or the success of their efforts.

Having criticized Billy Graham above, let me commend him for providing a positive example of diligence in this area. He and his team laid down some guidelines as a way of guarding against temptation:

> We determined to do all we could to avoid financial abuses and to downplay the offering and depend as much as possible on money raised by the local committee in advance ...
>
> We pledged among ourselves to avoid any situation that would have even the appearance of compromise or suspicion ... I did not travel, meet or eat alone with a woman other than my wife ...
>
> The tendency among some evangelists was to exaggerate their successes or to claim higher attendance numbers than they really had ... We committed ourselves to integrity in our publicity and our reporting.[20]

Sometimes, these kinds of approaches can have negative side effects or at the very least can be misinterpreted by outsiders.[21] And of course, no accountability framework or code of conduct will entirely prevent the deceitfulness of sin from gaining a foothold. As this book was being written, a string of scandalous

---

20 From Billy Graham's autobiography, cited in J Taylor, 'Where did the "Billy Graham Rule" come from?', *Evangelical History blog*, 30 March 2017, accessed 23 September 2022 (thegospelcoalition.org/blogs/evangelical-history/where-did-the-billy-graham-rule-come-from).

21 Graham's guideline around sexual purity has now become known as 'the Billy Graham rule' and has been criticized for overly sexualizing all male-female relationships, pushing women out of informal contexts for mentoring and influence, and being inadequate and unworkable for a range of reasons. Those who adopt this guideline need to find ways to correct against these legitimate concerns. At the same time, those who choose not to adopt it should be on guard against the inappropriate emotional intimacy and sexual temptation it is seeking to avoid; see K Cole, *Developing Female Leaders: Navigate the minefields and release the potential of women in your church*, Thomas Nelson, 2019, pp 201-245.

revelations about the recently deceased apologist Ravi Zacharias were made public. Zacharias ostensibly had a range of safeguards in place, but was wickedly ingenious in working around these safeguards.[22] But in most cases, thoughtful guidelines can provide a limited safeguard against immorality.

Financial integrity[23]

One area in which moral integrity is especially important, and where particular temptations are present, is that of money. Parachurches need to manage their finances beyond the basic standards of legal compliance and adopt policies that enshrine sound principles of wisdom and godliness. For example, while seeking to honour and care for those who work hard, we should question what level of remuneration and hospitality is inappropriately luxurious. As the Lausanne Commission on Cooperation wrote:

> While the Commission understands the need for stressing the interrelationship of money, time and energy, it regrettably notices that the life-style of some parachurch leaders leaves a lot to be desired if they wish to impress the Christian public with responsible stewardship. We need to be extra careful in differentiating between essentials and luxuries, perhaps especially in the area of travel.[24]

---

22 D Silliman and K Shellnutt, 'Ravi Zacharias hid hundreds of pictures of women, abuse during massages, and a rape allegation', *Christianity Today*, 11 February 2021, accessed 23 September 2022 (christianitytoday.com/news/2021/february/ravi-zacharias-rzim-investigation-sexual-abuse-sexting-rape.html). It is also worth asking where the accountability framework and code of conduct were inadequate, and where these frameworks were sound but were not diligently applied by others within his team.

23 This material was published in an earlier form on my blog: M Lynch, 'Church staff and external income', *Christian Reflections blog*, 24 July 2019, accessed 23 September 2022 (genevapush.com/blogs/xian_reflections/church-staff-and-external-income).

24 LCWE Commission on Co-operation, *Cooperating in World Evangelism*, p 70.

A basic starting point for a parachurch governing body to assess an appropriate level of remuneration and provision is for those who set such policies to research the average standard for relatively equivalent contexts.[25] Then the governing body can make its own judgement about whether the average might be too luxurious or too austere.

How should Christian leaders think about additional income that is earned through parachurch activity (such as wedding and funeral fees, book or music royalties, speaking or board member honorariums, consultancy fees, or part-time paid positions)? While there is no absolute biblical command on this matter, and there is a need for substantial freedom and diversity, a few aspects of the nature of gospel work are worth considering.

1. The nature of employment in Christian leadership

First, as with any employment, the Christian ministry worker "deserves his wages" (1 Tim 5:18) or her wages, and is fully justified in claiming this right for any work done (1 Cor 9:1-12).[26] Second, "the elders who direct the affairs of the church well are worthy of double honour, especially those whose work is preaching and teaching" (1 Tim 5:17), and so churches and parachurches should seek to generously provide for their paid leaders, rather than enforce "godliness with contentment" through low remuneration. Third, Christian leaders are paid to free them up to perform their gospel ministry—receiving a stipend rather than a wage (as illustrated in Acts 18:5).[27] Fourth, Christian ministries ought to have generous, spiritual interest in the wider kingdom of God beyond the bounds of their organization, and Christian

---

25 Researching beyond your immediate circle of ministries and denominations will provide a fuller picture.

26 A Christian leader is entitled to the same compensation whether or not they are married, whether or not their spouse works, and regardless of what prior income and assets they have or how many children they have. While personal circumstances might be a reason to consider paying someone more, it ought not to be a reason for paying them less.

27 Where a wage or salary is primarily compensation for the work being done, a stipend is primarily a provision for living expenses that frees a person to do the work.

leaders have a wider responsibility to God's work in the world beyond their formal employer.[28]

2. Risks of paid external ministry work

Work beyond the area of primary employment brings particular risks that need to be managed. First, additional external ministry can add a mental load that detracts from a Christian leader's primary ministry—the ministry for which they have been employed (somewhat like the situation Paul describes in 1 Cor 7:32-35). Second, the benefits a Christian leader gets from external ministry (not only money, but also respect and future ministry opportunities) can create a conflict of interest, which might distort their priorities and judgements: will they choose what is best for the primary ministry, or what is best for their external ministry? Third, in whatever way additional income is received, the Christian leader must flee greed and pursue generosity, for they should not think, "godliness is a means to financial gain. But godliness with contentment is great gain ... For the love of money is a root of all kinds of evil. Some people, eager for money, have wandered from the faith and pierced themselves with many griefs" (1 Tim 6:5-6, 10). Fourth, a Christian leader should always be concerned about commending the gospel by living in such a way that is seen to be "above reproach" (1 Tim 3:2).[29]

3. Ways to manage the risks of paid external ministry work

The good news is that these dangers can be managed in several ways. If the parachurch ministry is conducted within the con-

---

28 I believe that whether or not the church technically owns the legal copyright to a Christian leader's sermons, they should be granted a broad, perpetual licence to their use. The less the teaching content (such as training courses for a ministry team or a Bible study series) is tied to the individual author, the less entitled they are to such license of ownership. A church might choose to sell a Bible study series and so seek to prevent the author from changing or distributing that content freely. See B Smietana, 'Who owns the pastor's sermon?', *Christianity Today*, 8 January 2014, accessed 23 September 2022 (christianitytoday.com/ct/2014/january-february/who-owns-sermon-church-pastor.html).

29 This doesn't make a Christian leader bound to the judgements and assessments of everyone, but to the general impression created in their particular cultural context.

text and regular hours of a Christian leaders' ministry job, it is fitting for the organization for which the leader works to receive the income—or for the income to be given to some other church, parachurch or charity. The work was done in the context of their primary role and funded by their salary, so it should be seen as them fulfilling a different aspect of their primary role. However, if a Christian leader has additional personal needs that a church is financially unable to meet, additional income might be used for this purpose. In such cases, it is usually best for this to be formally approved by their employer.[30]

If a Christian leader does external ministry outside of their regular ministry context and hours, this raises questions around the nature of employment in Christian ministry. Christian leaders are paid to be freed up for the work of ministry. Therefore, it is appropriate for them to ask whether any additional capacity they have ought to be devoted to the ministry to which they are primarily appointed. In most cases, they should seek formal permission from their primary employer before taking on substantial amounts of external ministry work.[31] While recognizing there are many factors to consider here, it seems to me far wiser for any income related to a Christian leader's ministry to be thought of in the same way, whether done inside 'work hours' or in the leader's 'free time'. It is all part of them fulfilling their role in serving God's people. Why does a full-time Christian leader need any more income to be freed up to conduct their ministry? If the salary is inadequate, the board should adjust it appropriately.

If a Christian leader works across a variety of parachurch ministries, they need to declare these various activities as potential conflicts of interest to each leadership team to whom they are accountable. They cannot simply presume to use the public platform and mailing lists of one ministry to promote another parachurch

---

30 But see the next footnote.

31 In some ministry contexts, the pay may be so low and the governing body so stingy that the Christian leader is justified in discreetly taking on some extra work without consultation. This could be done in good conscience unless there were a specific clause forbidding it in their employment agreement.

ministry, especially if they personally benefit. For example, they need to examine their motivations before requiring team members to purchase books they have written, or to subscribe to services, or to register for conferences hosted by external organizations they are involved with. If employed by a local church, they must be careful not to privilege this church in the parachurch they work with, such as a church leader who also helps to lead a Christian Union inviting all the students to their church.

To avoid even the appearance of greed, if a Christian leader chooses to keep substantial external income, additional steps need to be taken. This might mean publicly declaring how much of their income they give away.[32] Or it might mean the establishment of a trust, whose trustees decide how much income might go to the Christian leader and what to do with the rest.[33] If a Christian leader can be freed up from relying on income from their primary employer, this obviously allows the money that would otherwise pay their salary to go to other good causes. Lack of financial dependence might even make such a leader a more courageous truth-teller, since they do not fear for job security. However, such freedom could also lead to an unhelpful autonomy that should be restrained by accountability and a clear set of expectations.

The less the parachurch work is the work of Bible teaching and disciple-making, the less directly these concerns apply. Being employed as a preacher is different than being employed as a

---

32 For example, megachurch pastor and best-selling author Rick Warren no longer draws a salary from his church and 'reverse tithes', giving away 90% of his income; see R Laura, 'Pastor Rick Warren is well prepared for a purpose driven retirement', *Forbes*, 21 March 2013, accessed 23 September 2022 (forbes.com/sites/robertlaura/2013/03/21/pastor-rick-warren-is-practicing-what-he-preaches-and-getting-ready-for-retirement); and BB Hagerty (presenter), 'Rick Warren: The purpose-driven pastor' [radio segment transcript], *Weekend Edition Sunday*, NPR, 18 January 2009, accessed 23 September 2022 (npr.org/2009/01/18/99529977/rick-warren-the-purpose-driven-pastor). This is a somewhat awkward violation of Jesus' principle "Do not let your left hand know what your right hand is doing, so that your giving may be in secret" (Matt 6:3-4), which brings with it the temptation to pride—but it may be justified in these circumstances.

33 So for example J Piper, 'Millions sold, no money taken: What John Piper does with his royalties' [video], *Desiring God*, YouTube, 5 October 2016, accessed 23 September 2022 (desiringgod.org/interviews/millions-sold-no-money-taken).

parachurch financial officer or a teacher in a Christian school. But even in these other cases, many of these principles are worth considering and applying as appropriate.

The risk of undermining local churches

1. Preventing new converts from meaningful involvement in local churches

University student ministries and other local mission societies usually have a proper interest in the follow-up and discipleship of any converts the Lord may bless them with. They also have a duty of spiritual care to Christian staff and volunteers who join them in the work.[34] But proper concern can expand in such a way that the parachurch hinders its participants from deep involvement in their local church. Student ministries and other discipleship groups which foster ongoing fellowship among those who are already Christians obviously run the same risk of becoming the primary spiritual home of their members.[35]

The Salvation Army is a major example of a parachurch ministry functionally taking the place of the local church and ultimately becoming an entirely separate denomination. This organization started as a mission led by William and Catherine Booth to reach out to the poor of London, changing its name to the Salvation Army in 1878. According to their sixth General, Albert Orsborn, they were "a permanent mission to the unconverted, one of the world's greatest missionary societies; but not an establishment, not a sect, not a Church".[36] The strict, military structure and high commitment to the Army meant that 'soldiers' (regular members) and 'officers' (leaders) were not meaningfully involved with

---

34 Moreover, "healthy, effective, faithful Christian witness requires biblical fuel—indeed, the whole counsel of God—not just pragmatic tips. It would be a mistake to conclude from the fact that a CU is a mission team that it should be fed solely on a diet of exhortation to evangelism" (Reeves, 'What is a church? What is a CU?', p 10).

35 Hill, *Officership in the Salvation Army*, pp 63-64.

36 Cited in Taylor, *Like a Mighty Army?*, p 101.

and submissive to a local church. It also proved difficult to integrate new converts from among the poor of London into the life of established churches. William Booth said:

> My first idea was simply to get people saved, and send them to the churches. This proved at the outset impracticable. 1st. They would not go when sent. 2nd. They were not wanted. And 3rd. We wanted some of them at least ourselves, to help us in the business of saving others. We were thus driven to providing for the converts ourselves.[37]

For a time, the Booths entertained the idea of becoming a kind of missionary religious order within the Church of England. But this never came to fruition, in part because they were unwilling to give up complete control over the Army.[38] The Booths' theological instincts placed little emphasis upon the formal particulars of the local church. Their concern was for ultimate spiritual realities and vital evangelistic efforts. Their spiritual purism considered the Lord's Supper and baptism to be mere rituals, unnecessary for the healthy Christian life.[39] Their missionary pragmatism gave them great freedom in the structure of their organization.[40] Like a religious order, the Salvation Army operated as a legitimate

---

37 Cited in Hill, *Officership in the Salvation Army*, p 84. "Fearing opposition of their 'respectable' parishioners … [the local clergy] arranged that The Salvation Army visits should be in the night, and as one consequence large crowds generally attended" (B Booth cited in Taylor, *Like a Mighty Army?*, p 85). See also RD Rightmire, *The Sacramental Journey of the Salvation Army: A study of holiness foundations*, Crest Books, 2016, p 16. In this, the Salvation Army is also an example of those groups who ask the question in the section below: 'What about when local churches fail to effectively serve new converts and support gospel mission?'

38 Taylor, *Like a Mighty Army?*, pp 66-70, 92-98. For a while, the Booths agreed to send Salvation Army soldiers to take communion at Church of England churches, but this never became widespread practice; see Taylor, *Like a Mighty Army?*, pp 84-85.

39 Taylor, *Like a Mighty Army?*, pp 76-92, 123-129. Curiously, though, these historical and biblical rituals were replaced by new ones: "the mercy seat, the love feast, the flag and Salvation Army uniform" (p 121). "Salvationists should reflect on whether Booth's lack of an objective theological compass, aggressively eliminated ritual, form and tradition, only to replace them with methods that were substitutes, that have become as ritualistic and traditionalistic as he viewed the High Church party of his own day" (p 92; cf. pp 210-211). See also Rightmire, *The Sacramental Journey of the Salvation Army*, pp 86-88.

40 "[A] 'lightweight' ecclesiology … which gives permission for the movement to be unfettered by such ecclesiastical tradition as is perceived to be burdensome in its mission" (Taylor, *Like a Mighty Army?*, p 119).

substitute for ordinary church life—or rather devotion to Christ's mission eclipsed interest in the theological significance of church community.[41] Their authoritarian structure and intense form of missionary activity, the strong personalities of their leaders, their peculiar practices and theological emphases, and their ambivalence about the importance of formal church community all combined to mean that they were functionally a separate denomination long before they described themselves this way.[42] Having functioned as a de facto church for a century, the Salvation Army eventually began to formally speak of itself as a church in 1998.[43]

In contrast to this, as discussed at length in chapter 5, I want to insist that parachurches need to be willing to set aside maximum organizational effectiveness for the sake of the broader and longer-term goals of a healthy gospel ecosystem. This means, for example: being explicit on theological distinctives, so that it is obvious when a parachurch might differ from local churches; regular, genuine consultation with churches and denominations; restraint in programming and recruitment; and clarity on the specific purpose of the parachurch, along with the discipline and good faith to keep within the bounds of this narrow purpose. Deeper and more important than any list of 'Dos and Don'ts' are the underlying biblical convictions and holy commitment to honour local churches and seek the best for the wider work of the gospel.[44]

---

41 Taylor, *Like a Mighty Army?*, pp 130-134. "The enjoyment of the community for its own sake is undermined. In particular, an army does not instinctively focus upon the reality that its own community life is an integral part of its mission; that the church is part of the gospel" (p 133; cf. p 262).

42 An admirer of the Booths, Cardinal Manning expressed his scepticism of the Army's stated desire to not become a separate denomination: "We have a conviction that the Salvation Army will either become a sect, or it will melt away. This world is not the abode of disembodied spirits" (cited in Taylor, *Like a Mighty Army?*, p 34; cf. pp 94-95). See also Hill, *Officership in the Salvation Army*, pp 66-67.

43 Taylor, *Like a Mighty Army?*, p 100.

44 David Belden has a helpful discussion about the difference between a sect and religion, where he proposes the category of 'pietist' type of 'anti-separatist sect'. He argues separatism is not "virtually inevitable" for such movements and says that separation is "at least partly avoidable", especially where the movement's emphases and practices affirm existing churches and churches where the denominational leaders are tolerant (Belden, *The Origins and Development of the Oxford Group*, pp 28-35).

2. Undue influence over participants

University student ministries and other similar groups can also undermine the local church through informal influence over their participants. The staff of student ministries often have more power over their members than the local church leadership does, because of the relational authority that comes with being instrumental in someone's conversion and spiritual maturity. Such authority is further heightened when the ministry takes place in the context of live-in hospitality, such as halfway houses and Christian hostels. There's nothing wrong with this in the short-term—in fact in many cases it's both normal and wonderful—but over time disciples need to be gently but firmly exposed to a wider sphere of influence, especially within the context of the local church.

Despite the formal policies of the organization, parachurch leaders and committed members can draw participants into a small pool of local churches, sometimes even enticing participants away from churches of which they were already members. While this kind of informal influence can never be eradicated, parachurch leaders can correct against it by proactively celebrating participation in a range of churches, diffusing enthusiastic advocacy of any one church, and discouraging people from urging others to change churches (except in exceptional circumstances, such as significant doctrinal disagreement). In some cases, the leadership of a parachurch might also consider adopting policies where certain roles cannot be filled by someone who already has a significant leadership role in a local church. For example, it might be hard for a church planter to resist the inappropriate urge to invite lots of people to join his core group if he is also the leader of an inter-denominational workplace ministry; the heightened excitement and lack of resources that accompany the early days of a church plant would create a major conflict of interest.

Local mission societies and discipleship groups can also influence the theological convictions of their participants, beyond even their stated doctrinal tenets. Such influence is not necessarily sinister;[45] it can be just one of the unavoidable effects of ongoing ministry relationships and the ebb and flow of the larger theological tide. Moreover, I don't think parachurch leaders must avoid ever teaching on secondary matters, nor do I believe that parachurches must ensure an equal representation of all possible views. Parachurch leaders should have the courage of their convictions, and should—with all humility and respect—teach their members what they understand the Bible to be saying.

Local church leaders and other concerned Christians need to take responsibility to research the formal doctrinal position of parachurch groups their members participate in, so that they can address any explicit areas of concern. For example, before adopting the popular Alpha Course, leaders should note the charismatic theology that is explicitly taught throughout it.[46] Slightly more difficult, but still important in the process of researching a parachurch, is to try to discover what other theological emphases and currents might be present beyond a ministry's formal doctrinal position. Church leaders must be generous and tentative in any conclusions they draw about such things, taking second-hand reports with a grain of salt and being careful not to define a whole ministry by a few of its members. Parachurch leaders can help this process and can allay suspicions by being explicit about their doctrinal stance and open about other theological influences and emphases.

Having said all this, it is also possible for parachurches to have an undue influence in the area of doctrine. This happens when its leaders teach on 'unofficial' distinctives with regularity, depth and dogmatism. It could be legitimate to explain one's beliefs about believers-only baptism, the ordination of women, creationism, or speaking in tongues; it is another thing to run

---

45 As is implied by Muriel Porter's claims that AFES is a "Trojan horse for Sydney Anglican teaching around [Australia]" and "an outreach of Sydney Diocese in all but name" (M Porter, *Sydney Anglicans and the Threat to World Anglicanism: The Sydney experiment*, Ashgate, 2011, p 5).

46 J Chapman, 'First things first', *The Briefing*, 1996, 184:8-10; cf. alpha.org.

an extended conference or preaching series advocating for a particular view. Furthermore, when talking about matters on which the parachurch allows diversity, leaders should make a point of communicating that there is a diversity of views on the matter.

3. Sidesteps biblical church discipline and whole church reformation

Parachurches are often founded within denominations, or even informally within local churches, to make up for perceived inadequacies in established churches or denominations. A fellowship of genuinely converted and spiritually awakened believers gather together from among the members of the church or denomination so that they might be strengthened in their faith and equipped in their ministry. The hope is that these fellowships will bring about spiritual reformation to the wider church. Martin Luther coined the term *ecclesiola in ecclesia*, 'little church within the church', to describe this phenomenon, a term then picked up by others such as the 17th-century Pietist leader Philipp Spener.[47]

Those who start groups like this often think: "If only we can gather together those who are spiritually serious and evangelistically concerned, we might be able to slowly influence the wider church." If institutional change is slow, there are great benefits to being able to move forward with those who are receptive, rather than all ministry and fellowship being muddied by lethargic, apathetic, nominal Christians.

Martyn Lloyd-Jones raised some strong warnings against this strategy: it can lead those outside the fellowship to be resentful rather than inspired; it is by its very nature divisive and, unsurprisingly, often ends in starting new churches and denominations; it creates confusion about the role of the formal church leadership; and it can lead to various kinds of excesses and spiritual pride. Fundamentally, Lloyd-Jones rejected this strategy because it sidesteps more fundamental issues. For example, the unbiblical concept of a 'state church'—where every citizen is presumed to

---

47 M Lloyd-Jones, 'Ecclesiola in ecclesia', sec I-II.

be a member of the church—obviously creates the problem of nominal Christianity and should be critiqued rather than worked around. Likewise, basic matters of genuine spirituality and godliness should be addressed through diligent gospel ministry and church discipline which bring about reformation in the whole church, not through launching breakaway groups to address these shortcomings.[48]

These warnings are very important to hear, but they remain warnings rather than requirements. Lloyd-Jones does not successfully establish any absolute theological reasons why sub-church renewal fellowships cannot play a part in church renewal. As discussed in the first two sections of this book, God's work through his people extends beyond the bounds of local churches. There is no reason why, even as church-wide reform is also being pursued, sub-church fellowship cannot also be fostered in a way that conscientiously guards against the problems that Lloyd-Jones highlights.

4. What about when local churches fail to effectively serve new converts and support gospel mission?

There are some cases where it seems that local churches and denominations fail to effectively care for new converts and support new evangelistic initiatives, and so local mission societies and discipleship groups feel a responsibility to fill this gap. This is usually complicated, as it might involve a cocktail of lethargy, legalism or heresy in established churches, driven and undiplomatic leaders in the parachurch, new converts from radically different social or cultural backgrounds, peculiar parachurch distinctives and expectations, and political manoeuvring and personality clashes. Perhaps some of these breakaway denominations might be avoided, but in other cases some kind of parting of the ways seems almost inevitable. Maybe some of this mess needs to be accepted as the imperfect reality of what happens when the Lord brings significant spiritual revival through

---

48 Lloyd-Jones, 'Ecclesiola in Ecclesia', sec IV-VI. See also Hammett, 'How church and parachurch should relate', pp 203-204.

gifted but flawed movements and leaders.

Methodism, for example, grew out of the evangelistic ministry of John Wesley during the time known as the first Great Awakening. In fact, the term 'methodism' first described all those involved in the Great Awakening.[49] Wesley was an Anglican minister and encouraged his followers to remain involved in the Anglican denomination.[50] But alongside their regular churchgoing, Wesley and other leaders organized informal 'society meetings' where members could gather to pray, read Scripture and talk about their spiritual struggles and aspirations.[51] No doubt many saw these society meetings and the movement they were a part of as their primary religious community long before any formal, structural changes took place.[52]

Existing within and alongside the Church of England became increasingly difficult, as many of the leaders in the established Church were critical of what they saw as extremism and a disregard for tradition and structure.[53] Wesley's ministry began to be marked by certain doctrinal distinctives around free will and Christian perfection, which gave the movement even more of a distinct identity.[54]

The massive growth of the Methodist movement also made it difficult for the established Church hierarchy to effectively integrate it. This was accentuated in America, where mission

---

49 A similar story on a smaller scale could be told of the Calvinistic Methodists who, under the leadership of George Whitefield and Lady Selena, Countess of Huntingdon, also organized into a 'Connexion'. After Whitefield's death, some churches from this tradition established an independent network. While few endured in England, they became the largest denomination in Wales; see Noll, *The Rise of Evangelicalism*, p 193; and Bebbington, *Evangelicalism in Modern Britain*, pp 29-30.

50 John Wesley discouraged his unordained preachers from celebrating the Lord's Supper as one particular demonstration of the fact that they were not to replace the established church; see Noll, *The Rise of Evangelicalism*, pp 116, 146.

51 Noll, *The Rise of Evangelicalism*, p 108.

52 "Methodism was an elaborate religious organisation that has no dependence, except for the sacraments, on existing ecclesiastical structures" (Bebbington, *Evangelicalism in Modern Britain*, p 28). Therefore, they are also an example of 'Preventing new converts from meaningful involvement in local churches', discussed above.

53 Noll, *The Rise of Evangelicalism*, p 147.

54 Noll, *The Rise of Evangelicalism*, pp 255-260.

was increasingly conducted in more geographically isolated areas in the context of a much weaker church infrastructure.[55] Wesley eventually felt compelled by the practical needs of American Methodists, allowing them to administer baptism and the Lord's Supper in 1784. This gave further impetus to similar practical pressures in Britain, and within a few years of Wesley's death (in 1791) the same took place there.[56]

After the American Civil War, American Methodists constituted as a separate church. Their itinerant preachers, known as 'circuit riders', would travel enormous distances, ministering to people on the fringes of Western habitation and facilitating the movement's astonishing sevenfold growth in the 1780s.[57]

It might seem that the intensity in this movement and its leaders, together with its level of organization, meant that the founding of a new denomination was inevitable. But this is not necessarily the case. Much of the difficulty could have been avoided if the bishops of the Church of England were more proactive in welcoming the movement and so had ordained Methodist leaders to keep pace with the wonderful growth that was taking place.[58] Even if the separation of Methodism in England and America was almost inevitable, its leaders demonstrated impressive restraint to hold off from formal separation for 40 years. At some point the greater concern to see the work of gospel preaching advance in a vigorous and holistic way rightly overcomes deference to established church institutions.

The 'Jesus Movement' of the 1970s provides diverse examples

---

55 Noll, *The Rise of Evangelicalism*, p 139.

56 Noll, *The Rise of Evangelicalism*, pp 192-193.

57 Noll, *The Rise of Evangelicalism*, pp 202-206.

58 A counter example is the legacy of the Great Awakening in Scotland. Here, the evangelistic work of Whitefield was welcomed and supported by Presbyterian leaders and hosted very much within Presbyterian structures. Noll writes: "The differences with America (where Whitefield functioned like a Dissenting preacher and with almost no attention to the sacraments) and England (where he helped construct a network of Calvinist cells partially in and partially out of the Anglican church) suggests why Scottish evangelicalism developed along lines different from evangelicalism in these two other regions where Whitefield also exerted such memorable influence" (Noll, *The Rise of Evangelicalism*, p 107). See also the discussion about inevitability with regard to both Methodism and the Salvation Army in Taylor, *Like a Mighty Army?*, pp 95-98.

of conflict and independence, as well as positive case studies of church leaders caring for new converts well and experiencing extraordinary revitalization as a result. The beginnings of the Jesus Movement involved spontaneous evangelistic activity in a very counter-cultural way. For many the questions of church or parachurch were moot, as the leaders were simply seeking to follow the Spirit and preach; they were not self-consciously being either church or parachurch.[59] As a result, plenty of small communities and independent churches and denominations were started from nothing.[60] In many cases, existing churches failed to welcome or adequately care for new converts.[61] On the other hand, some existing churches invested in these young leaders and movements, creating a fruitful partnership. It was out of this that many of the megachurches of the 1980s grew—such as Calvary Chapel, Vineyard, Sovereign Grace, and Harvest Fellowship. John Smith observes that "it is difficult to find the enduring success of Jesus Movement units where a cultural liaison was not developed between hippies and straights".[62]

The lessons to be learned from these patterns are that wherever possible both parachurch leaders and church leaders should make every effort to work together. Patience that is willing to allow the mission and the movement to slow down for the sake of respectful cooperation with existing churches is an honourable thing. Generosity that is willing to relinquish control and stability for the sake of investing in new works is also an honourable thing.[63] However, we need to allow that some-

---

59 The mode of ministry was often that of the 'wandering charismatic'; see Smith, *The Origins, Nature, and Significance of the Jesus Movement*, pp 59-104.

60 Smith, *The Origins, Nature, and Significance of the Jesus Movement*, pp 151-195.

61 Smith, *The Origins, Nature, and Significance of the Jesus Movement*, p 172.

62 Smith, *The Origins, Nature, and Significance of the Jesus Movement*, p 121 (cf. pp 266-299).

63 It is very important to try to resist the inevitable tendency for new movements to become domesticated. Smith writes: "Where conservative leaders opened their church doors to hippies, there was usually a domestication of the world view of previous radicals rather than political radicalization of the existing congregation" (Smith, *The Origins, Nature, and Significance of the Jesus Movement*, p 123). "Ironically, that which began as an aggressive outreach to an alienated generation gave rise to institutions in which successive generations of young evangelicals could be acculturated into mainstream society in terms of world view, institutionalized into their own comfort zone" (pp 138-139; cf. pp 140-142).

times close, long-term cooperation is not possible without hindering the advance of the gospel or causing people to violate their personal convictions and their conscience. The establishment of new churches and new denominations, although a sad necessity, might at times be the best course. Under those circumstances, dismissing such innovations as divisive and schismatic is itself a conservative kind of divisiveness. Far better to admit that, in the complexity of the real world, seeking to build the church and reach the world often leads to impasses. Acknowledging this reality can be the first step towards preserving generous and prayerful goodwill.

The homogeneous unit principle

One particular strength of many local mission societies is also one of its weaknesses: it ministers to a specific demographic. A local mission society can fine-tune its structures, events and style to best connect with a certain group of people: athletes, high schoolers, business professionals, those who are homeless, recent migrants, middle-aged men, and so on. They are leveraging what is known as the 'Homogeneous Unit Principle': that people are most likely to come to faith among those who are similar to them. Donald McGavran writes: "Peoples become Christian fastest when least change of race or clan is involved."[64] Or again: "people like to become Christians without crossing racial, linguistic or class barriers."[65] In many cases this is a matter not of optimal effectiveness but of necessity, such as when language barriers require an entirely different ministry to reach and serve a group of people. In other cases, targeting particular groups ensures that attention is given to their unique questions, difficulties and opportunities. In still other cases, it is important

64 DA McGavran, *Bridges of God: A study in the strategy of missions*, Wipf and Stock Pub, 2005, p 23.
65 DA McGavran, *Understanding Church Growth* (CP Wagner ed), 3rd edn, Eerdmans, 1990, p 163.

to equip and empower those who might be less privileged in the wider culture because they could otherwise be neglected.

But there is a theological problem with the Homogeneous Unit Principle: it doesn't reflect the reality that all people can be "one in Christ Jesus" (Gal 3:28). Since this is the goal of Christ's saving work, should this not be reflected in our Christian lives and communities? This leads to a range of potential practical problems. *First, those in homogeneous units are often not helped to live out their faith in overcoming social, cultural and ethnic prejudice.* As Paul urges in Colossians 3:

> Here there is no Gentile or Jew, circumcised or uncircumcised, barbarian, Scythian, slave or free, but Christ is all, and is in all.
>
> Therefore, as God's chosen people, holy and dearly loved, clothe yourselves with compassion, kindness, humility, gentleness and patience. Bear with each other and forgive one another if any of you has a grievance against someone. Forgive as the Lord forgave you. And over all these virtues put on love, which binds them all together in perfect unity. (Col 3:11-14).

In the worst cases, this could make it easier for church communities to get swept up in wider social conflicts, rather than protesting against them.

Second, potential converts and young believers also need to repent of the sins of racism, sexism, and other kinds of prejudice. As Paul argues in Galatians 2, seeing how the gospel breaks down human barriers helps us to appreciate "the truth of the gospel" (Gal 2:5, 14).

Third, we miss opportunities to commend the gospel to outsiders by manifesting its reconciling power. Even "pagans" and "tax collectors" love those who love them, but when we love our enemies, when we care for and relate to those with whom we have little in common, we are showing the love of God much more plainly (Matt 5:43-48).

Fourth, we miss out on the insights and experiences that those from different backgrounds can share with us. A divided humanity is ultimately a poorer humanity. This is true in the church as in the wider world. Demographically narrow ministries prevent different groups from benefitting one another and serving one another. Writing in *USA Today*, Michael D Lindsay observed how many prominent evangelicals are becoming less involved in church and more committed to various targeted (and sometimes invitation-only) parachurch ministries:

> I spent the past five years interviewing some of the country's top leaders—two U.S. presidents ... 100 CEOs and senior business executives, Hollywood icons, celebrated artists and world-class athletes ... I was shocked to find that more than half—60%—had low levels of commitment to their denominations and congregations ...
>
> [This] is deeply troubling. It signals the loss of one of the few social settings where average "Joes" used to rub elbows with the powerful, and where the powerful kept in touch with the concerns of average folks ... Otherwise, affluent believers will continue to leave their congregations—and their fellow believers—behind in their ascent, creating a gated community of the soul.[66]

Finally, different demographic groups will have different levels of openness to diversity. Those in fairly stable rural communities may be less open to cultural diversity than those in the urban centres. But then again, rural communities may be more open to mixing with those of different ages. Furthermore, inner cities can either flatten cultural difference among those of various ethnic backgrounds or produce quite isolated ethnic communities. Different cultures have different preferences around age and sex segregation, and these preferences vary depending on things like social status and geographical location. How much more will individuals differ on such things! All of this means that in some cases a greater degree of heterogeneity may prove more effective in reaching certain demographics.

---

66 DM Lindsay, 'A gated community in the evangelical world', *Home Is Where the Heart Dwells blog*, 1 April 2008, accessed 23 September 2022 (blogs.harvard.edu/guorui/2008/04/01/michael-lindsay%EF%BC%9Aa-gated-community-in-the-evangelical-world).

Despite these important concerns, it must be said that no single church or parachurch can be absolutely heterogeneous and representative of all of humanity. Geographical location alone will limit the ethnicities and education levels that are represented. Even those churches and parachurches that reflect the demographics of their area are therefore also reflecting the social divisions of the area. Moreover, those who criticize homogeneous ministries have often focused on some measures of homogeneity while ignoring others. A university ministry, for example, may be homogeneous in terms of age and education, but more diverse with regard to ethnicity; a neighbourhood church may be diverse with regard to age and ethnicity, but homogeneous in terms of wealth. If you look closely at most healthy Christian ministries, you will soon notice more diversity than a lazy glance might have concluded: homeless people attached to wealthy churches; new migrants welcomed in white suburban churches; mature-age students and faculty participating in campus ministries.

There are both benefits and risks to targeted ministries, and there is no way to avoid some limitation in any church or parachurch. What is needed is a set of values and practices that guard against the greatest risks.

Firstly, whatever the target audience of a ministry, strictly enforced homogeneity should be kept to a minimum. While some ministries are narrower by necessity—such as youth and children's groups, men's ministries or women's ministries, or language-specific groups—often there is no need to actively exclude those who do not conform to the primary target group. Which ministries to professional workers absolutely must restrict membership to those in executive positions of large companies? Which university ministries really need to exclude anyone not studying at a specific campus? What ethnic-focused ministries must be entirely closed?[67]

---

67 More complex and controversial: Christians need to think through and be clear about what faithful Christian discipleship looks like for those with gender dysphoria, even as we rightly create contexts for those of the same biological sex. And yet such theological and ethical clarity doesn't mean every single ministry and program must become a boundary mark for these issues. It is worth at least pondering: what men's and women's events really ought to be restricted to only those of the same biological sex?

Secondly, even where the ministry itself is homogeneous it can balance this by seeking partnership with other groups. For example, in the network of campus ministries I oversee, we have several separate ministries—for Australian-born students (and others with high English competency), for East-Asian international students, and for subcontinental Asian students. Each of these groups operates with a great degree of independence. But the ethnically diverse staff meet together weekly for prayer and encouragement, and the groups pray for one another, send staff and student leaders to serve one another, and send a number of visitors from each group to the others.

Thirdly, churches and parachurches can complement one another in the area of diversity. If someone is involved in an ethnically homogeneous migrant church, they could try to regularly attend conferences with a more diverse attendance. Students who are heavily involved in a university Christian Union might choose to be involved in a more diverse local church. The Promise Keepers men's ministry provides a good example: the movement has fostered spiritual friendships with men of different races in a way that is powerful in weakening racism.[68]

Lack of theological depth

A strength of parachurch ministry, as discussed in chapter 2, is that it can allow for a broader Christian unity than the local church can or should allow. An evangelistic organization is free from needing to make sharp distinctions around matters of church governance or around the nature of God's sovereignty and human responsibility. George Whitefield articulated the spirit of unity in fundamentals that became a mark of the evangelical movement: "It was best to preach the new birth, and the power of godliness, and not to insist so much on the form: for

68 LD Allen, 'Promise keepers and racism: Frame resonance as an indicator of organizational vitality', *Sociology of Religion*, 2000, 61(1):55-72; and P Glynn, 'Racial reconciliation: Can religion work where politics has failed?', *American Behavioral Scientist*, 1998, 41(6):834-841.

people would never be brought to one mind as to that; nor did Jesus Christ ever intend it."[69]

There is nothing wrong with this in and of itself. However, in a context where a parachurch has become very influential and local churches are not as vibrant, this narrow focus can lead to an overall thinning out of Christian theological conviction.[70] A generation of Christians predominantly influenced by university ministry rather than the local church might never form basic convictions around broader theological concerns. This may eventually weaken the local church if these people come into positions of leadership and influence in the church without having adequately supplemented the diet of teaching they received through parachurch involvement.

Parachurch leaders should also be careful in the way they explain and celebrate their 'gospel unity'. It is one thing to be undistracted by 'secondary matters'; but it is sloppy and reckless for leaders to imply that only 'gospel issues' are important in any sense whatsoever, or that any concern about 'secondary matters' is pedantic and divisive.

Theological eccentricity and heresy are also risks. Church and denominational ministries are not immune to these, of course, but parachurch ministry certainly provides a loose context where maverick leaders can entertain and propagate unusual theological ideas. 'Sinless perfectionism' is one such error that has thrived in various parachurches at various times. Stuart Piggin denounces this teaching:

> It is an aberration of the holiness movement of the nineteenth century, a caricature of evangelicalism, and a bastard growth of revivalism. It is an exotic growth

69 Cited in Noll, *The Rise of Evangelicalism*, p 12. The tenth General of the Salvation Army said that they never "developed a theology of the Church [because] ... we have been too busy doing the Lord's work to take time to think seriously about our precise position in His 'Body' ... Some day someone will tackle the task" (cited in Taylor, *Like a Mighty Army?*, p 102).

70 Stuart Piggin identifies this tendency in the legacy of Dwight Moody: "The gospel according to Moody was less exacting ... and preaching was made more palatable: more entertaining and simpler. Strongly reasoned, doctrinal sermons and catechising all but disappeared. This was bound ... to eat into the foundations of the strong Reformed formations ... to produce sickly offspring: theological illiteracy and indifference" (Piggin, *Spirit, Word and World*, p 58).

which can luxuriate in the hothouse of doctrines of the Spirit when uncorrected by the clear evidence of the Word and untested by the need to evangelise effectively in the real world. It is one of the weeds which can grow in the evangelical garden ...[71]

The freedom of the interdenominational student world ... provided a situation in which such spiritual dilettantism, linked to Christian responsibility beyond the theological competence of the individuals involved, was clearly dangerous. Such evangelical parachurch organisations generally contain an element of protest against denominational bureaucracy. They are usually therefore not very democratic, tending to selection by and for the elite. Ironically the 'freedom they generated was the very environment that bred spiritual dictators.[72]

The solution in both cases is usually not simply for the parachurch to become more comprehensive in its theological instruction, but to ensure that its participants are involved in a larger context of theological formation. Participation in the local church, formal theological education, and reading and learning widely are some of the basic ways that parachurch participants can receive a well-rounded education in the Christian faith.

Just as parachurches can become narrow in terms of theology, so also they can become narrow in matters of ethics and social vision.

Sidelines broader Christian responsibilities

A local mission society exists for the express purpose of engaging in evangelistic activity; a discipleship group usually has a narrow

---

71 Piggin, *Spirit, Word and World*, p 106. Piggin goes on to describe how a movement of sinless perfectionism was bound up with (and eventually expelled from) several Australian parachurches in the earlier 20th century, including the Sydney University Evangelical Union, the Inter-Varsity Fellowship, the Crusader Union, the South Seas Evangelical Mission and the Katoomba Christian Convention (pp 105-124).
72 Piggin, *Spirit, Word and World*, p 119.

focus on Bible knowledge, personal godliness and spiritual disciplines. While these priorities are fundamental for the local church as well, there is a danger: a sharp mission statement from a parachurch could give its participants the impression that there is nothing more to Christian life and responsibility than churchgoing, evangelism, Bible reading and prayer.[73] It is one thing to champion the great—even primary—importance of gospel preaching, but it is another to suggest that other duties of family life, productive work, cultural contribution, research and education, charitable action and political involvement are utterly insignificant.

At its worst, a failure to properly consider wider ethical and social responsibilities can lead wonderfully devout and zealous Christians to be blind to and complicit in the social evils of their day, as discussed above with George Whitefield's attitudes to slavery. Here is Mark Noll's assessment of Whitefield's ministry:

> Much of what Whitefield did was admirable by any standard, and his commitment to Christ-centred preaching was a shining beacon. But while his character and purpose possessed great integrity, there was no consistency to his broader actions, no depth to his thinking about culture. Ready-fire-aim was his style. In a word, much that would be best and much that would be worst in the later history of evangelicals in America was anticipated by Whitefield.[74]

In his book *Spirit, Word and World*, Stuart Piggin argues that the evangelical movement in Australia was at its healthiest when it found a synthesis of concern between vibrant personal spirituality, serious biblical commitment and energetic social action.[75] This kind of synthesis requires a broader theological and ethical vision than local mission societies often cast.

---

73 Such groups have a tendency towards quite a functionalist pattern of discipleship; see Smith, *The Origins, Nature, and Significance of the Jesus Movement*, p 175.

74 Noll, *The Rise of Evangelicalism*, p 101.

75 Piggin, *Spirit, Word and World* (although note Phillip Jensen's critique of how Piggin identifies these things in his history: P Jensen, 'A new vision of evangelical history', *The Briefing*, 1996, 178:3-10.

Conclusion

Local mission societies and discipleship groups are a valuable part of a healthy 'gospel ecosystem', and they can have a powerful turbo-charging effect on a Christian community or region. But they are not without their weaknesses. Nevertheless, I believe the dangers that such organizations bring are worth the risk. This means they should be managed carefully, rather than made a target for abolition or strict regulation. Three crucial values must be cultivated in and expected of local mission societies and discipleship groups: earnest striving for godly integrity; theological rigour; and healthy relationships with local churches and denominations.

Chapter 10: Theological formation: publishing, broadcasting and theological education

Alongside face-to-face ministry, publishing has played a hugely important part in the spread and renewal of the Christian movement. Since the writing, copying and distribution of the New Testament Gospels and letters, Christianity has always had an important place for written material, whether books, letters, creeds and confessions, handbooks, hymns, sermon transcripts, histories, journals, tracts, or extended theological works.

Publishing and distribution allow stories, ideas and practices to spread far and wide, uniting people and organizations across vast distances. In the providence of God, the newly invented printing press was a powerful force at the time of the Reformation.[1] A few centuries later, the circulation of printed stories of revival was very important to the spread of the Great Awaken-

---

1 N Campbell, 'Plundering gold from Egypt to contextually communicate the gospel of Jesus: A methodological survey from Solomon, Amenenope, Cicero, Paul, Augustine, Luther, and Grunig's "Four models of public relations", *St Eutychus*, 24 July 2013, pp 52-56, accessed 24 September 2022 (st-eutychus.com/wp-content/uploads/2013/07/Plundering-the-Gold-of-the-Egyptians.pdf).

ing.[2] In the 20th and 21st centuries, radio, sound recording, television and the internet have made it possible for the latest Christian ideas and activities to spread across the globe in an instant.[3] And then there is music. As with all music, Christian song-writing plays a special part in popularizing ideas, as the best hymns and songs transmit new ideas in memorable, emotionally resonant and culturally appropriate forms. All these types of publishing and broadcasting ensure not only the spread of ideas but also their preservation for future generations.[4] The power of media can obviously be used to have either a positive or negative impact—they can be harnessed to spread the life-changing good news of Jesus, but also to propagate unhealthy and heretical ideas and practices.

As we consider the power and influence of media, this chapter also examines the place of theological colleges alongside publishing and broadcasting ministries. For while they could be considered as a kind of focused discipleship ministry for emerging Christian leaders, theological colleges are also centres for the exploration and propagation of theological ideas, whether in essays by students, the gathering of influential theological works into large libraries, the development of curricula, or the publishing of journal articles and books by faculty.

I am very aware that I write as an outsider to the daily pressures and responsibilities of leading one of these organizations,

---

2 Noll, *The Rise of Evangelicalism*, pp 82-83.

3 M Driscoll and G Breshears, *Vintage Church: Timeless truths and timely methods*, Crossway Books, 2009, pp 269-270.

4 Tim Keller made this prediction about the 'emerging church' movement of the early 21st century: "Evangelicalism developed in the United Kingdom and the United States because of certain institutions: a couple of key seminaries laid the groundwork for the movement, and Crusade, InterVarsity, and Navigators raised up the foot soldiers. Because of this, evangelicalism created something different. But I don't see that in the emerging church—it's so anti-institutional, so afraid of authority, that I doubt very much that it can create those institutions and become a cohesive movement. There might be some sort of post-liberal/post-conservative theological party that comes together, and I think it could produce writers and lots of books, but I doubt that they're going to create churches or any strong communities and institutions" (J Piper, M Driscoll, T Keller and J Taylor, 'A conversation with the pastors', *Desiring God*, 29 September 2006, accessed 24 September 2022 [desiringgod.org/interviews/a-conversation-with-the-pastors]).

PART 3: CASE STUDIES

with all the freedom to criticize and offer suggestions from the sidelines. Writing as an onlooker and a stakeholder, I hope that I can pull together a range of common themes, issues and reflections that might at least provoke helpful reflection and reaction. I don't have a single model to champion for each of these types of ministry—I don't believe the issues are that simple. But hopefully, by surveying a few major issues, both existing models and new approaches can be helped.

Opportunity to serve the local church and the gospel mission

Publishing, broadcasting and theological education all bless local churches, denominations and the wider Christian community by gathering together a large volume of theological and practical resources and then making those resources available to the widest possible group. In this way, the whole gospel ecosystem is made richer and deeper and wiser than it would otherwise be if we were all restricted to our local church or denomination.

But, like all parachurches, *the healthiest publishing, broadcasting and theological education all have a strong commitment to serving local churches.* At the most basic level, this requires professors, authors, bloggers, musicians and podcasters to uphold the value of the local church, pointing their audiences back to genuine involvement in the church and encouraging godly submission to it. A simple example of this is the introduction that well-known preacher Matt Chandler includes at the start of his online sermons:

> This [online sermon] is never meant to substitute God's good plan for you to be in a community of faith where the word of God is preached and proclaimed. I want to encourage you to use this as a vitamin, not like a meal, so that you belong to a community of faith where you're being shaped by being known, by using your gifts, by receiving the word, by partaking in the

sacraments and by walking faithfully in accordance with the Scriptures ... So [I] just want to make sure we frame what this is and what it should not be.[5]

It would be wonderful if something like this became standard practice for all 'celebrity pastors' (and if something equivalent was employed by other Christian leaders and 'influencers').

The value of campus-based theological colleges needs to be balanced with a recognition that they usually pull students out of the local church. All parachurches do this to some extent, but theological colleges can be one of the most immersive. At the most extreme end, a four-year residential training program with a heavy study load and additional college responsibilities dramatically extracts students from ordinary church life—especially when this also involves a student moving to a new church where they have no pre-existing relationships.

In the worst cases, this can create a class of private, mercenary Christians who remain aloof from local church fellowship for the remainder of their lives, seeing themselves as hired hands who expect to move from one church to the next, rather than as fully immersed and involved members of the body of Christ in their current locale. When students have to move city or region, campus-based training also removes up-and-coming leaders from their local church and mission setting for several years, only to send them back significantly changed—perhaps even no longer 'one of us'.[6] And that's if they return at all!

Of course, these legitimate concerns are balanced by the enormous value of campus-based learning: it facilitates a more holistic learning environment than almost any local church can offer; it disciplines both theologians and students to function in spiritual community rather than merely pursuing educational qualifications; it forces future Christian leaders to develop a

---

5   M Chandler, 'Practicing prayer' [sermon video], *The Village Church*, 17 September 2019, accessed 24 September 2022 (thevillagechurch.net/resources/sermons/practicing-prayer).

6   This is not true of all campus-based tuition students. Those who live near their theological college don't experience the same kind of upheaval.

healthy independence of spirit separate from their home community and their mentors; it broadens the horizons of students by bringing them into contact with other Christians from all over the world; and it provides a wider ministry network for future Christian leaders.

Because of this mix of significant benefits and legitimate concerns, it's difficult to argue against developing a range of different training models and options, while giving preference to full-time, campus-based training, especially for those who are preparing for senior theological leadership in church or parachurch ministry.[7]

Moreover, *theological colleges can serve the Christian community in their cities and countries in many ways beyond the training of pastors.* Australian Bible colleges like Sydney Missionary and Bible College and the Melbourne School of Theology were expressly founded to provide rigorous, high-quality theological training to a wider group than those training for ordained ministry, including those planning to engage in cross-cultural mission work.[8] Over time, denominational theological colleges have also become open to a wider student body, so the distinction is much less clear than it once was. Beyond their major courses, theological colleges also serve the Christian community in many other ways: offering correspondence courses, evening classes and public lectures; attracting theologically astute staff and students who contribute to local denominations, churches and parachurches; providing auditoriums, classroom spaces and a theological library for wider use; and hosting guest lecturers who might serve the wider Christian community in teaching, training and evangelism.

At the same time, however, *theological colleges should be cau-*

---

7   I also wonder if campus-based study is most valuable for those students with less life experience, as the context of the college community provides extra depth to their personal formation. Mature-age students often bring greater life experience that they can integrate with their learning, even if conducted primarily by distance.

8   Piggin, *Spirit, Word and World*, pp 91-92. Piggin observes that although these colleges were established with a proactive vision, they also provided an alternative to the denominational colleges, many of which were dominated by liberal theology in the late-19th and early-20th centuries.

tious about multiplying events, courses and programs in a way that competes with other churches and parachurches or undermines the thorough training of church leaders. Out of a noble desire to bless the Christian community and maximize resources, colleges can run more and more events, courses and programs. When taken too far, this can crowd the local Christian event calendar and make unnecessary extra demands on the time and energy of local Christians. As Carl Trueman says:

> When seminaries were just teaching men for the ministry it was very straightforward—the line of demarcation between church and seminary. Seminary trained men for the ministry, and the men for the ministry trained everybody else. That was how it [went]. But the multiplication of degree programs renders that more complicated. The church, if you like, starts to get squeezed somewhat. One has to start asking whereabouts exactly does [theological education] fit in the pedagogical project ... Partly it connects to the rhetorical question ... "Don't we want people to know the Bible more thoroughly?" ... Yeah, but we want the churches to do that.[9]

While offering a range of courses to the wider Christian community can be an effective way to gain maximum benefit from a college's resources, in some cases it may be more than adequate to provide much of this training in the local church.[10] It is also important to preserve a clear expectation of a solid and general theological education as the standard preparation for ministry leaders, with a program covering Old Testament, New Testament, systematic theology, Christian history and biblical languages. Such training should not be replaced by a program dominated by electives and specialist courses.

9   CR Trueman, 'Follow the money' [audio], 2019 Den Dulk Lectures on Pastoral Ministry, *Westminster Seminary California*, 6 March 2019, accessed 24 September 2022 (wscal.edu/ resource-center/follow-the-money).
10 Trueman also argues that, because of the debt burden that formal theological study lays on people, "the multiplication of degree programs has moral implications"; see Trueman, 'Follow the money'.

Educators, authors and broadcasters should be careful about speaking too authoritatively from the sidelines. Yes, I realize the irony in me daring to speak from the sidelines about what others should and should not do—and I hope I have been sufficiently careful about not coming across as too authoritative! There are certainly many professors, bloggers and podcasters who have significant ministry experience and yet are still attentive to the insights and experiences of others who are busy 'on the ground'. Some remain engaged in a great deal of ministry activity alongside their writing, broadcasting, teaching or research duties.[11] Yet there are others who have had minimal first-hand ministry experience, or whose experience is now a distant memory, but who will still make all sorts of bold judgements about what Christian ministry ought to be like, or what evangelistic strategies ought to be pursued, in a context where their position of influence is out of proportion to their credibility to speak on these matters.

To best serve the wider Christian community, *colleges, broadcasters and publishers should resist the pressure to become too narrow.* Ministries inevitably develop characteristics and tendencies that are caused by all sorts of historical and social factors. These tendencies don't always betray a deceitful or negative agenda, nor must they all be actively resisted. But, as Carl Trueman points out, the pressure to differentiate oneself in the 'marketplace' can lead colleges to deliberately position themselves as representing one stance or party within a wider denomination.[12] Likewise, influential leaders can wrongly exert pressure for a college or broadcasting platform to champion their theological and strategic agenda. But a denomination is best served by a college that teaches within the broad bounds of its confessional standards. A Christian community is best served

---

11 See J Piper and DA Carson, *The Pastor as Scholar and the Scholar as Pastor: Reflections on life and ministry*, Crossway, 2011. It must be said it is very difficult to do both of these things equally well.

12 Trueman quotes Freud, who speaks of the "narcissism of the minor difference"; see Trueman, 'Follow the Money'.

by at least some media who publish items of interest from a wide range of perspectives and emphases. While there is certainly space for much more narrowly constituted publishing houses, media platforms and training institutes, the Christian community can easily become unnecessarily atomized.

Informal media serve the Christian community with rich diversity. Tracts, street papers, social media, podcasts, blogs and community radio all provide opportunities for ordinary, everyday Christians to share in a broader teaching ministry. Such Christians can have different theological insights and ministry experiences than the 'ordained' and the 'experts'. Christian publishing and broadcasting are industries like any other: certain people, ideas and styles come in and out of fashion. Informal media provide a context for less marketable people, ideas and styles. They also offer a way for 'ordinary' Christians to speak out against errors or abuses that more formal media may be unwilling or unable to address. Informal media can also draw everyday Christians into networks of shared needs, interests and experiences for immense mutual encouragement and instruction.

Such diversity and freedom are not without their dangers, of course, which I will come to below.

Academic freedom and confessional colleges

Academic freedom can serve the Christian community by helping theologians, Christian leaders and Bible college students to seek the truth, especially when the truth is contrary to received wisdom.[13] What is true for science or history is also true in the academic study of theology. Without allowing a significant amount of freedom, theological reflection can become stale, never moving beyond traditional formulas that may not have fully grasped God's

---

13 American Federation of Teachers, *Academic Freedom in the 21st-Century College and University: Academic freedom for all faculty and instructional staff*, AFT Higher Education, 2007, accessed 23 September 2022 (aft.org/sites/default/files/academicfreedomstatement0907. pdf).

truth and never finding ways to communicate God's truth effectively to new cultural contexts.[14] A free learning environment also encourages students to form sincere convictions rather than simply complying with a standard set of beliefs.

It's true that not all teaching and learning demands an environment of pure academic freedom, for there is also a proper place for teaching within the bounds of established knowledge.[15] However, the freedom to research and explore ideas at the boundaries of established knowledge and to question orthodoxies is usually needed to make major new advances in human knowledge. In addition, ambitious explorations often lead to less remarkable but nevertheless valuable discoveries. This process of free enquiry certainly can open the door for scepticism, heresy and unbelief. But rather than seeing academic freedom as nothing more than a threat to Christian faith and the Christian church, we should see it as the means by which the church may arrive at a fuller grasp of the truth.

The nature of the university in the Western world has shifted over the past millennium from being largely religious to largely secular. For much of Christian history, intellectual endeavour and instruction often took place in monasteries or cathedrals.[16] Early universities were often founded or sponsored by churches and were at least nominally under the authority of the local bishop or monastery. In practice, both state- and church-sponsored universities had significant independence from their sponsor.[17]

14 RW Southern, *Western Society and the Church in the Middle Ages*, Penguin history of the Church (O Chadwick gen ed), vol 2, Penguin, 1990, p 296.
15 Charles Curran says academic freedom "distinguishes a university from a propaganda institution or a center of indoctrination" (C Curran, 'Academic freedom: The Catholic university and Catholic theology', *Academe*, 1980, 66:(3):127). However, these are not the only possible options, or at least more neutral words than 'propaganda' and 'indoctrination' ought to be used. John Dewey distinguished legitimate "teaching bodies called by whatever name" from "the university proper" (cited in GM Marsden, *The Soul of the American University*, Oxford University Press, 1996, p 298). Much of the teaching that takes place even at the undergraduate university level is also largely within the bounds of established knowledge.
16 Southern, *Western Society and the Church in the Middle Ages*, p 277. But there were always exceptions to this. For example, the University of Bologna (arguably the oldest Western university) was originally a cooperative of students and professors (cf. pp 202–203).
17 H de Ridder-Symoens (ed), *Universities in the Middle Ages*, A History of the University in Europe (W Rüegg gen ed), vol 1, Cambridge University Press, 1992.

In the past few hundred years, many major European and American universities have become more secular, public institutions. For example, the University of Paris was shut down after the French Revolution and re-established by Napoleon; Acts of Parliament removed religious entry tests from the universities of Oxford, Cambridge and Durham in the mid-19th century;[18] and the universities of Harvard and Yale in the late-19th and early-20th centuries gradually secularized through changes in administrative policy, intellectual ideals and social needs.[19] This shift has not been absolute. Some divinity schools, such as Berkeley Divinity School (Yale University) and New College (Edinburgh University), remain denominationally associated. Some universities, like Princeton, preserve ties to neighbouring seminaries. And some universities have Christian colleges attached, for example Wycliffe Hall at Oxford University.

In addition to the secularizing of religious universities, more and more public universities have been established with no religious affiliation at all. Yet even secular universities serve the church as they do the wider community by providing an environment for expansive academic freedom in every area of human knowledge, including theology, philosophy and ethics. Theological faculty attached to more secular universities often do not have any formal obligation to uphold a fixed doctrinal position. This makes them most able to capitalize on the full freedom of academic exploration, but also leaves them vulnerable to drift from traditional theological moorings. Christians can genuinely recognize the merit of this kind of freedom, even if it might at times radically undermine Christian beliefs and values. Our theological convictions should give us a concern for individual freedom of conscience and for encouraging the open pursuit of the truth.[20]

---

18 Universities Tests Acts 1871 (UK)

19 See Marsden, *The Soul of the American University*.

20 Abraham Kuyper's concept of 'sphere sovereignty', which argues for different spheres of power in human society that ought not to interfere with one another, is a helpful one. A totalitarian or theocratic society might be neater and tidier, but at the cost of massive invasion church life, family life or education. Independent, mediating institutions safeguard freedom and truth. See JE McGoldrick, *God's Renaissance Man: The life and work of Abraham Kuyper*, Evangelical Press, 2000, pp 163-166.

By contrast, theological colleges established to uphold a particular doctrinal stance provide a narrower scope for academic freedom. The secularization of major universities, together with the rise of theological liberalism (especially in the 19th and 20th centuries), created a perceived need for theological colleges that would promote academic research and provide theological training from within a confessional framework. This led to the founding of new theological halls and Bible colleges.[21] Most such colleges aim to be not merely training centres but also legitimate tertiary research and educational institutions. Protection of academic freedom is therefore necessary to ensure intellectual integrity as well as to preserve government recognition. This freedom is more difficult to maintain for confessional colleges.

Perhaps it is easiest to consider each component of academic freedom in turn: freedom to learn; freedom to teach and research; freedom of speech; and institutional autonomy.

In order to safeguard the academic freedom to learn, a separation can be made between academic assessment and qualification for ordained ministry. Because of this, it should be possible for a student to be at the top of the class academically and yet fail to be accepted as a candidate for ministry.[22] Theological colleges therefore serve the dual functions of educating and assessing their students' academic performance while also contributing to their preparation as ministers of the gospel. Godly and faithful ministers are far more important for the cause of Christ than straight-A students. And yet students thoroughly educated in a solid, biblical curriculum will also be well equipped for their teaching ministry.

Confessional theological colleges and their sponsoring denominations can *uphold significant scope for the academic freedom of their faculty by clarifying the confessional boundaries around*

---

21 See also Marsden, *The Soul of the American University*, pp 74, 99, 197; and Piggin, *Spirit, Word and World*, pp 91-92.

22 N Ormerod, *Academic Freedom in a Theological Context*, Occasional Paper 4, *The Australian College of Theology*, Sydney, July 2008, accessed 16 October 2022 (issuu.com/ alphacruciscollege/docs/neilormerod).

academic freedom. Within these pre-defined boundaries, freedom should be preserved.[23] Defining theological boundaries and affirming a commitment to academic freedom protects faculty from ongoing arbitrary external interference from denominational leaders. There is no way to entirely remove this point of tension; indeed, some degree of ambiguity is not necessarily a bad thing.[24] Theological reflection should lead us to concede that, at some point, a historic confession or traditional practice may need adjustment. This isn't always a process of theological compromise; after all, creeds and confessions are fallible, subordinate standards to the infallible Scriptures, and can be critiqued in light of the Bible. Managing some degree of tension serves the church by enabling her to be always reforming in the light of the word of God.[25] Academic freedom is not the same as academic anarchy. It has its own restraints: the formal standards of academic discipline and the public critique of academic colleagues provide checks and balances that are separate from (church or secular) government control. Furthermore, academic ideas can be critiqued and opposed by individuals, local church leaders and denominational bodies in a range of ways that stop short of formal censure. In extreme cases, new academic ideas might prompt church authorities to formally rule on their orthodoxy. Such rulings are not in principle

---

23 This is argued for in Ormerod, *Academic Freedom in a Theological Context*. The analogy drawn between confessional theology and constitutional law is not a perfect one, since a constitutional law academic can still vigorously express their disagreement with a nation's constitution. See also Marsden, *The Soul of the American University*, pp 292-312, 434-435.

24 The American Association of University Professors' *1915 Declaration of Principles on Academic Freedom and Academic Tenure* denied the legitimacy of such restrictions on academic freedom, whereas their 1940 statement allowed for it; see AAUP, 'General report of the committee on academic freedom and academic tenure', *Bulletin of the American Association of University Professors (1951-1955)*, 1915, 1(1):15-43, accessed 24 September 2022 (doi.org/10.2307/40216731); and AAUP, *1940 Statement of Principles on Academic Freedom and Tenure with 1970 Interpretive Comments*, AAUP website, n.d., accessed 24 September 2022 (aaup.org/report/1940-statement-principles-academic-freedom-and-tenure). The 1970 comments on the 1940 statement do not endorse this exception (see *1940 Statement of Principles*, fn 5). Marsden rightly challenges these assertions as making no room for religious pluralism at the level of university institutions and scholarship; see Marsden, *The Soul of the American University*, pp 436-440.

25 William Hodgson, the first principal of Moore Theological College in Sydney, said he was aware of the weakness of "Colleges exclusively" to have a "tendency to foster a hard narrow repulsive ecclesiasticism"(quoted in Piggin, *Spirit, Word and World*, p 37).

oppressive, since new theological ideas and formulations can sit between the cracks of existing confessional statements—they need to be addressed as they arise.

It should be noted that academic freedom is related to but separate from broader claims about freedom of speech. For example, where an academic is outspoken on matters beyond their area of theological expertise—such as expressing their (church or secular) political opinions—this is not clearly a matter of academic freedom.[26] General freedom of speech issues should be considered on their own merits, and it is fitting for universities and theological colleges to grant substantial freedom of speech to academics beyond their area of expertise.[27] The American Association of University Professors' 1940 *Statement of Principles on Academic Freedom and Tenure* makes a balanced case along these lines:

> College and university teachers are citizens, members of a learned profession, and officers of an educational institution. When they speak or write as citizens, they should be free from institutional censorship or discipline, but their special position in the community imposes special obligations. As scholars and educational officers, they should remember that the public may judge their profession and their institution by their utterances. Hence they should at all times be accurate, should exercise appropriate restraint, should show respect for the opinions of others, and should make every effort to indicate that they are not speaking for the institution.[28]

There are many good reasons for theological colleges, like other universities, to be places where staff and students can openly explore and express all sorts of ideas.

26 Stanley Fish makes a strong case along these lines; see S Fish, *Versions of Academic Freedom: From professionalism to revolution*, Rice University Campbell Lectures, University of Chicago Press, 2014.

27 Australian National University, *The Australian National University Statement on Academic Freedom 2018*, ANU website, 2018, accessed 24 September 2022 (anu.edu.au/files/committee/ANU%20Statement%20on%20Academic%20Freedom.pdf).

28 AAUP, *1940 Statement of Principles on Academic Freedom*.

Institutional freedom is another important element of academic freedom. Institutional freedom is about giving universities discretion in matters such as staff appointments, student admissions, course offerings, teaching methodology and assessment. Too much pressure around such matters ends up distorting the freedoms already mentioned and potentially compromising the quality and culture of the institution. Denominational colleges are ordinarily established with a significant degree of autonomy, and it is good for this to be maintained.[29] Independent theological colleges enjoy autonomy from the church authorities, but need good governance to protect them from interference by outspoken donors, who can also threaten institutional freedom.

There is also a threat that the civil government will interfere with institutional autonomy. This can be done indirectly through apportioning funding, but also directly through over-regulation. It is possible that one day confessional limitations on academic freedom will no longer be accepted by government legislation in countries that currently enjoy this freedom. In such cases, colleges will face difficult decisions about whether it is better to forego recognition as a higher education institution in order to preserve a distinct confessional identity.[30]

One final note related to academic freedom and theological colleges: there are many pressures that undermine the work of academic research. Like all tertiary institutions, *theological colleges need to strike a balance between the work of tuition and the work of research.* Training pastors and missionaries clearly has much more immediate and obvious benefit for the cause of Christ than publishing journal articles and debating esoteric

---

29 It is good for the denomination to have healthy institutional freedom from its theological colleges. The denomination's formal theological reflections and formulations should not be entirely outsourced to theological faculty. Ordination standards should not be controlled by the staff of theological colleges, who have a vested interest in the college institution, which may cloud their judgement.

30 After all, a formal government recognition is not necessary for an excellent education. While countercultural education is likely to have significant blind spots and weaknesses, it also has unique strengths. See for example L'Abri and Christian World Liberation Front; and Smith, *The Origins, Nature, and Significance of the Jesus Movement*, pp 163-165.

ideas with theologians and historians who may not even share the same theological convictions. Christians rightly have a biblically motivated suspicion of intellectual elitism and the aimless vanity that can accompany it. The more we are concerned with winning the respect and acceptance of the intellectual elite, the greater the temptation to theological compromise.

On the other hand, there is also a danger of thin populism that is more concerned with tribal boundaries than the pursuit of the truth. If we're not careful, we can become vulnerable to superstition, mindless dogmatism or tribal conservatism. The opposite risk to theological liberalism and worldly elitism is theological fundamentalism and ignorant Philistinism. Although it is pathetic to seek to jump through hoops to earn the respect of the world, this is very different from conducting ourselves with godly intelligence and competence that gains a genuine hearing for the gospel. For this reason, it is important that we safeguard a very important place for theological research. There is a financial dimension to this as well, since tuition fees incentivize teaching over research. College administrations need to budget for theological research, and gospel patrons need to invest in it.

Freedom of the press

Freedom of the press serves churches and parachurches by holding us to account. The media is often spoken of as 'The Fourth Estate': a separate branch of public life that holds the other three branches to account.[31] Something similar operates within the narrow context of the Christian community. The demands of truth, justice and mercy might interfere with the strategic priorities of a church or denomination, but we must not ignore these demands. A free Christian press can force

---

31 Traditionally, the other three branches are defined as the clergy, the nobility and the commoners; see K Gill, 'What is the fourth estate?', *Thought Co.*, 16 January 2020, accessed 24 September 2022 (thoughtco.com/what-is-the-fourth-estate-3368058).

Christian leaders to deal with such things as they ought. In this way the interests and reputation of institutional churches might be interfered with, but the ultimate wellbeing of God's people is preserved. Therefore, there is an important place for Christian publishing and broadcasting in both formal and informal ways, using traditional and new media, free from tight control by secular or church authorities.

Accountability of theological colleges, publishing and broadcasting

Theological education, publishing and broadcasting institutions need to be held to account, just like any other parachurch, for how effectively they are serving the local church and the gospel mission. Theological college professors who undermine the confessional stance of their denomination should be called to account; Christian authors or songwriters who undermine sound biblical doctrine should be publicly critiqued.

Theologians, authors and journalists are not simply motivated by a noble pursuit of the truth. Just like church leaders, they can become compromised for various reasons. Like all of us, they too have vested interests they can bring to their work: the economic pressure to attract students, sell books, draw an audience or build a reputation; the political pressure to support a particular agenda in the church or the world; or the social pressure to be considered sophisticated or courageous among their peers. Speaking the truth, even if it has a catastrophic short-term effect on a church's reputation, is often the right and noble thing to do. At other times, speaking the truth can be more about mischievously generating controversy. In the first instance, accountability is best pursued through the formal structures and policies of these various organizations—assuming they have good policies and structures in place. Churches, denominations, parachurches and even individuals should urge these institutions to be diligent in their internal processes, especially if those processes appear to be inadequate. In some extreme cases, especially where these structures fail, the local church or denomination might eventually engage in direct discipline of one of their members for their actions as a publisher, broadcaster, theologian or educator.

These institutions also need to be held to account for professional breaches. Many countries have laws in place to regulate such institutions and to ensure their integrity in matters of honesty, accuracy, clarity, transparency, balance, attribution, privacy, defamation and diversity. Other independent regulatory bodies and professional associations add further accountability and pressure to uphold standards of integrity. Christians can usually be thankful for the existence of such regulations for the whole community, including Christian organizations. We should establish and maintain bodies that diligently comply with all relevant legal regulations (unless conscientious objection might prevail) and seriously consider subscribing to other widely recognized statements of principle and codes of conduct.

Informal media also need some degree of accountability. The downside of informal media is that they don't have the same checks on integrity, accuracy and expertise. As a result, high-quality content and healthy networks can co-exist with substandard or misleading content and toxic networks. It is not always obvious to individual Christians which is which. This creates additional urgency for Christians to be taught discernment and for church leaders to be alert to various ideas and movements among informal Christian media. Christian leaders can also model this by showing discernment in their own interactions with various sources of news and ideas.[32] Much of this accountability can and should take place as part of the ordinary Christian life and through the oversight of the local church, as Jesus outlined in Matthew 18:15-20. Fellow Christians can provide feedback, correction and rebuke to one another for their contribu-

---

32 This could mean finding contexts for things like: book/podcast/blog reviews; providing training on discernment, on how to evaluate the credibility of an information source, and on identifying bias in yourself and others; and correcting commonly repeated disinformation.

tions on social media, blogs, podcasts, radio and so on. Serious issues can be brought to the attention of their local church.

For this to be effective, Christians should identify themselves in their publishing and broadcasting (rather than using pseudonyms or remaining anonymous). They also need those in their immediate circles to be aware of their work. Of course, there will be exceptional and difficult situations in which an author wishes to remain anonymous because they are exposing misconduct—perhaps even a situation where they feel threatened or unsafe. Like all cases of conscientious disobedience, this presents its own ethical and practical difficulties.[33]

As in the modern secular landscape, some Christians become very influential through informal media. The equal access of informal media is somewhat illusory: not everyone actually has an equal voice. Informal media operates in its own economy where certain things become disproportionately popular and influential. Christian leaders must make an effort to understand and interact with these influential ideas and leaders. For those few who do become significantly popular and influential through informal media, there probably comes a point where it is wise to proactively seek out or establish some kind of accountability framework.[34]

33 Difficulties include knowing how to determine when such disclosure is justified, and how to evaluate and investigate anonymous accusations. Many countries have legislation that seeks to protect 'whistleblowers', as they are called, and many organizations have now adopted such policies. But these types of laws and policies don't remove all the difficulties.

34 Andy Crouch offers his own practice as an example of what external accountability for influential Christians might look like: "I have joined an organization I did not found, led by a CEO to whom I report, who in turn reports to a serious, empowered, independent board of directors, and I spent 12 years before that working for another organization. I have submitted all my travel and speaking decisions to my CEO as well as to [my wife] Catherine, and was finally able, gladly, to shift from a freelance speaking career, with income flowing to my sole proprietorship, to one where all fees flow to the organization. I publish my speaking fees and terms online. I minimize my use of agents who would have a financial incentive to increase my celebrity and would interpose themselves between me and the churches and ministries that wish to engage me as a speaker. (I do have a literary agent, but she is eminently and unshakably sane.) At conferences that offer speakers a 'green room,' I use it only for prayer and preparation immediately before I speak. The rest of the time, I sit in the audience like everyone else. At events that use name tags, I wear one" (A Crouch, 'It's time to reckon with celebrity power', *The Gospel Coalition US Edition*, 24 March 2018, accessed 24 September 2022. thegospelcoalition.org/article/time-reckon-celebrity-power).

Conclusion

Freedom and accountability are the two themes that dominate this chapter. Both are needed for Christian publishing, broadcasting and theological education to be a substantial blessing to local churches and denominations. If these organizations are overly constrained, they won't stretch, challenge and deepen the Christian community and its institutions as needed. But if there is no responsibility or accountability, they can undermine the local church and denominations and lead God's people astray.

Chapter 11: Chaplaincy

We come now to one of the oldest forms of distinct parachurch ministry: chaplaincy. The idea of chaplains may be so obvious, so easily taken for granted, that perhaps we don't even conceive of them as parachurch. Yet chaplaincy has many of the same features as other kinds of parachurch organizations. Chaplains and chapels exist to provide Christian ministry where there are no local churches but where Christian work and witness is especially needed. For example, one of the earliest forms of chaplaincy was in the military, where the need for spiritual blessing, support and counsel was strongly felt, for obvious reasons.[1] Chaplains initially provided religious duties, counsel and support to kings and other military leaders. As more modern forms of chaplaincy began to be established in the 19th century, their duties evolved to also include care for the sick and support of regular troops.[2]

---

1   The actual name 'chaplain' comes from the story of Martin of Tours, the fourth-century solider turned monk (and later bishop) whose torn cloak (Latin: *cappella*) became a relic that was brought on military campaigns, escorted by *cappellani* and housed in temporary religious structures called *cappelle*; see M Gladwin, *Captains of the Soul: A history of Australian Army chaplains*, Big Sky Publishing, 2013, pp 2-3.
2   Gladwin, *Captains of the Soul*, pp 6-10. From the 17th century, every British royal ship was supposed to have a preacher on board, which brought chaplains into much closer proximity to regular sailors; see R Strong, *Chaplains in the Royal Australian Navy: 1912 to the Vietnam war*, UNSW Press, 2012, pp 1-9.

The same kinds of needs are experienced in hospitals, where people are unable to engage in regular church life. Understandably, those suffering serious illness and those facing death feel a special need for targeted spiritual care. Hospitals in fact grew out of the monastic hospital care that thrived from the 11th century, where the sick were brought into the life of a religious community. It was only after the Protestant Reformation of the 16th century that this model was reconfigured for hospitals to become state-governed institutions with clergy appointed to work within them.[3]

Chaplains also provide intensive, targeted Christian ministry to areas of society where people who can regularly attend local churches still feel the need for additional, targeted ministry. For example, political leaders and religious leaders, and more recently sportspeople, might engage personal chaplains, while educational institutions often appoint chaplains to their communities. In such establishments, dedicated meeting rooms and buildings might be set aside. These are not church buildings for the gathering of local churches, but 'chapels' for the special supplementary services held by chaplains.[4] In many ways, then, chaplains and chapels function as the formal denominational analogue to parachurch ministries.

The distinctive of chaplaincy, then, as opposed to church or other kinds of parachurch, is its focus on formal or ceremonial Christian activity and targeted spiritual support and counsel, but in an exceptional context. Not all these features might be equally dominant in a chaplain's role; in many settings, a chaplain has regular public and formal Christian duties. In such cases, they are usually clergy appointed to a different kind of role, but still

3   C Swift, *Hospital Chaplaincy in the Twenty-First Century: The crisis of spiritual care on the NHS*, Explorations in Practical, Pastoral, and Empirical Theology (LJ Francis, J Astley and M Percy eds), 2nd edn, Ashgate, 2014, pp 9-27.

4   The English word 'chapel' can also be used to simply mean 'small church building', and so is also used for some church buildings. In the late Middle Ages, 'chantries' also sprang up. These were foundations established to ensure that the Roman Catholic ceremony of the Mass was performed for the benefit of people already in purgatory. See Peters, *The Story of Monasticism*, pp 195-196.

ordained by and accountable to their denomination or church. In other contexts, a chaplain is primarily appointed to provide spiritual support and counsel, but with much less emphasis on formal Christian ministry—such as hospital chaplains or leaders within the modern Australian National School Chaplaincy Program (who explicitly "must not proselytize").[5] In some of these cases it is not expected that the chaplain be an ordained minister, and their accountability might primarily be to a parachurch committee or simply through endorsement by their local church.[6]

In still other settings the exceptional context is the primary thing. Richard Johnson, the first chaplain to Australia, was appointed as chaplain to the First Fleet and subsequently to the New South Wales colony because no local church had yet been established.[7] He was expected to be an evangelist and church founder, not merely to conduct services on board the ships or on public occasions in the colony.[8] As a gospel patroness, the Countess of Huntingdon appointed George Whitefield and other Calvinistic Methodists as 'chaplains', facilitating their innovative ministry outside normal church structures.[9]

Kate Bradford, a former CMS missionary in Tanzania who also has extensive experience in various chaplaincy roles, has developed a helpful matrix to describe the different types of

5   Federal Financial Relations, *Project Agreement for the National School Chaplaincy Program*, FFR website, 29 October 2018, p 4, accessed 27 September 2022 (federal financialrelations.gov.au/agreements/national-school-chaplaincy-program).

6   So in the Australian National School Chaplaincy Program, a chaplain is defined as "an individual who ... is recognised through formal ordination, commissioning, recognised religious qualifications or endorsement by a recognised or accepted religious institution". The minimum qualification requirements for program chaplains is a Certificate IV in Youth Work, Pastoral Care, Chaplaincy and Pastoral Care or equivalent. See FFR, *Project Agreement for the National School Chaplaincy Program*, p 8.

7   The 'First Fleet' is the name given to the fleet of 11 ships that left England in May 1787 and arrived in present-day Sydney in January 1788, bringing over 1000 convicts (as well as many free people) and establishing the British colony in Australia.

8   Like many other chaplains of the colonial era, this was very specifically the vision and intention of Richard Johnson's appointment. It was financed by members of the evangelical 'Clapham Sect', a group that included leaders such as John Newton and William Wilberforce, with the express purpose of "planting and propagating the gospel in Botany Bay" (Quoted in Piggin, *Spirit, Word and World*, p 6).

9   Bebbington, *Evangelicalism in Modern Britain*, p 29.

Christian ministry that can take place within a Christian or secular space, whether directed by Christian leaders or in response to a need:[10]

	Ministry directed by ordained clergy and authorized laypeople	Client- or patient-directed ministry in response to a need
Christian space	Pastoral ministry to a congregation	Pastoral care/hospitality
Secular space	Chaplaincy/mission	Christian care/public Christianity

Table 4: Different types of ministry

Even in this simplified version of Bradford's analysis, we can see that the matrix is helpful in locating chaplaincy: it sits within the secular space where ministry is primarily directed by clergy and authorized laypeople. This distinctive sphere of ministry means that chaplains often face unique challenges and require very particular skills. They do not have the luxury of being able to focus purely on preaching, prayer, discipleship and evangelism. They may have to be heavily involved in the machinery of a secular institution while at the same time being proficient in not only theology, but also in professional counselling and even philosophy as they engage with very diverse worldviews. Sitting in these very different contexts, the various types of chaplains have both unique opportunities and unique vulnerabilities.

The unique opportunities of chaplaincy

Firstly, the chaplain has access to those whose 'life package' separates them from regular churchgoing or who might not otherwise go to church at all. While chaplains may not always enjoy a great deal

10 K Bradford, '2x2 grid', 2019, personal communication. Presented here in a simplified form.

of freedom to preach the gospel in the most unfettered manner, in one way or another they all have opportunities to say something where otherwise there would be no gospel witness at all —sometimes speaking to the most privileged or the most underprivileged in society. Along with the charitable parachurches I will discuss in chapter 14, chaplains can speak to isolated people in our community who are simply not accessed through local church efforts such as friendship evangelism, Christmas Carol nights, letterbox drops and Facebook promotions.[11] Chaplains also provide encouragement and counsel to brothers and sisters in very challenging circumstances and careers—people to whom the local church often cannot minister in a very deep way.

Secondly, chaplains can provide targeted spiritual input for those whose 'life package' brings unique challenges. It is a wonderful honour to apply the comfort of the gospel and demonstrate the love of God to distressed and lonely elderly people, to be an unfazed and agenda-free pastor to a public figure, or to bring joy, hope and humanity to frightened and disheartened soldiers. Michael Gladwin includes many stories from Australian army chaplains, including this account from Anglican Great War padre Kenneth Henderson:

> I ... do all I can to help [promote] inner tranquillity and fortitude, so I proceed as quietly as possible about my Father's business ... A man shaken by shock and pain of his wounds needs strength of will and peace of mind above all. He knows not how severe his injuries are. Wide-eyed he faces eternity and gropes in the loneliness of pain and shock for sympathy and confidence. He is not to be questioned or worried, but to be reassured in his great loneliness and darkness that the eternal arms of God's love and mercy are about him, and helped to feel the grip of Christ's pierced hands— the Christ who has been through it all Himself.[12]

---

11 Australian Defence Force chaplaincy "is probably the largest Christian youth outreach in the country" (Gladwin, *Captains of the Soul*, p 263).

12 Gladwin, *Captains of the Soul*, p 60.

In these contexts, chaplains not only serve people through formal religious ceremonies and professional counselling appointments; there is also an important place for the 'ministry of presence' as an 'intimate stranger'.[13]

Thirdly, chaplains might have the overwhelming but unique opportunity to 'speak truth to power'. Chaplains don't only provide comfort and support. Sometimes they might also have to boldly speak up for what is good and right and true. Sometimes, like Queen Esther they might feel they are the only person who can speak in this way, and "who knows but that you have come to your ... position for such a time as this?" (Esth 4:14). Among the various metaphors for describing pastoral care in *Images of Pastoral Care* are 'the circus clown' and 'the wise fool', both of which point to ways that, like the idealized Tudor court jester, the chaplain might bring unique insights as an outsider.[14] The chaplain plays an important humanizing and spiritualizing role in large institutions that can easily become technocracies—ruled by systems and experts to the neglect of individual humans and their needs.[15] In correction against the professionalization of healthcare chaplains, where the industry can define them primarily as professionals who provide 'spiritual care',[16] Christopher Swift attractively argues that ambiguity is part of the value of the chap-

---

13 RC Dykstra, 'The intimate stranger', in RC Dykstra (ed), *Images of Pastoral Care: Classic readings*, Chalice Press, 2005, pp 123-136. Another expression quoted by Michael Gladwin is "loitering with intent", which I am told is increasingly falling out of favour, sadly because of potentially predatory connotations; see Gladwin, *Captains of the Soul*, p 291.

14 H Faber, 'The circus clown', and AV Campbell, 'The wise fool', in Dykstra (ed), *Images of Pastoral Care*, pp 85-93 and 94-107. However, David Carlyon observes that often the ideal of the court jester is more wish fulfilment than reality. It is just as likely for a jester to become tamed by their position of power and lapse "into the conservative nature of comedy to reinforce power"; see D Carlyon, 'The trickster as academic comfort food: Jesters, Dan Rice, and the alleged hero-fool', in R Sugarman (ed), *The Many Worlds of Circus*, Cambridge Scholars, 2008, p 199. There's clearly something in the type that resonates with us, even if the formal role rarely functions this way.

15 "The most important people in the Army are the Nursing Sisters and the Padres—the Sisters because they tell the men they matter to us—and the Padres because they tell the men they matter to God" (Bernard Montgomery, quoted in Gladwin, *Captains of the Soul*, p 119).

16 See for example SB Roberts, *Professional Spiritual & Pastoral Care: A practical clergy and chaplain's handbook*, Skylight Paths, 2012.

lain: he or she can function as an outsider, a "heretical fragment", often with unusual dress and speaking with the "formality and spaciousness" of biblical language. Their marginality can give them an ability to cut across the organization, give significance to difficult events, and provide an important ethical perspective.[17] "Put simply, the chaplain's epistemic fragment has potential to confer gravitas and significance onto events which could be described in quite different terms."[18] Where chaplains can become influential, not only are people better cared for but the institutions themselves often function in a much more holistically healthy fashion.

Fourthly, chaplains are entrusted with a role as 'public Christians', thinking through how the truths of God's word apply to politics, health care, education, sport, the entertainment industry and much more. They find themselves brought into informal conversations and formal committees where other Christian ministers may rarely find themselves. And they are there explicitly in their capacity as Christians. Although there have been times of war when Christian leaders, including chaplains, have largely adopted the attitudes of the wider culture, military chaplains have increasingly provided ethical reflection and challenge on the just causes for war and on conduct within war.[19] Another opportunity for public Christianity has been seized by army chaplains who offer tours or lectures when service brought soldiers close to sites connected with biblical history.[20] In some recent occupation and peacekeeping contexts, army chaplains have also provided additional help in promoting sensitivity to local religious concerns.[21]

---

17 Swift, *Hospital Chaplaincy in the Twenty-First Century*, pp 123-130 and 166-173. See a similar discussion in Gladwin, *Captains of the Soul*, pp 272-275.

18 Swift, *Hospital Chaplaincy in the Twenty-First Century*, p 126. Or again: "The appearance of the chaplain denotes the emergence of an unorthodox space in the fabric of care" (p 130).

19 Gladwin, *Captains of the Soul*, pp 237-242, 314-317.

20 Gladwin, *Captains of the Soul*, pp 53-54 (at times even making archaeological discoveries!), 105, 302.

21 Gladwin, *Captains of the Soul*, pp 318-320.

Sarah Coakley offers an example of the complicated ethical and theological issues facing a prison chaplain:

> I was struck that in my time in the Boston jail I was up against a nexus of issues which no one seemed adequately to have probed in relation to one another—or at least no one seemed to have probed theologically. There was the harsh legal response to minor drugs offences; the racialized policy of policing in the 'black' area of Boston; the deliberate brutalizing and further criminalizing of young men in impossibly cramped cell conditions in the jail; and the scarcely-veiled threat by the jail authorities towards chaplains and other well-wishers that any dimensions to their ministry that might be construed as politically subversive would be harshly riposted and repressed.[22]

While these are highly complex issues, and while it takes great wisdom to judge how and when to speak, chaplains may find themselves in the rare and privileged position of offering a gospel-shaped response to complex social problems. To take one other example, health-care chaplains can be part of a larger discussion about the role of spirituality in the holistic care of patients, ensuring that spiritual and religious affiliations are treated as very significant parts of a person's identity and needs.

Fifthly, because of their experiences, chaplains can bring unique insights and expertise to the wider Christian community regarding matters such as secularization, modern spirituality, ethics and pastoral care. Swift writes:

> Chaplaincy is fascinating, and in its minute detail it is possible to trace connections to questions about the nature of life; personhood; pastoral power; resistance to medical culture; religious fragmentation and spiritual hope ... Chaplains stand in a place of significant

22 S Coakley, 'Can pastoral theology be saved? Reflections on the practice of theology inside the university and out', *ABC Religion & Ethics*, 21 June 2021, accessed 27 September 2022 (abc.net.au/religion/can-systematic-theology-become-pastoral-again-and-pastoral-theol/10095582).

intersection between the historic present of the Church in public spaces; secularization; contemporary spiritual expression and close engagement with life-changing effects of illness ... [There is potential here for] real learning and growth that would arise from a more honest and integrated engagement with a ministry that is in the forefront of some of the major questions of the twenty-first century.[23]

Sixthly, chaplains can provide personal, moral and spiritual support to people within an institution, but in a way that transcends the regular hierarchy and formal human-resource structures. This is especially true in those cases where chaplains do not have any other institutional status. A chaplain can contribute to the vibrancy and wellbeing of the community and foster trust and understanding within the community as a 'permanent guest', with few strict disciplinary or reporting duties and no administrative agenda.[24]

For this reason, the uniform, duties and rank of chaplains in the armed forces has historically been an important point of discussion.[25] School chaplains who are also part of the teaching staff likewise must strive to preserve a space to perform the chaplain's unique role. It is sometimes claimed that chaplains offer nothing that cannot be provided (with more professional expertise) by trained social workers and counsellors. But not only do chaplains provide support for the people's spiritual needs (which cannot and must not be reduced to 'psychological needs'); they also often provide their support within an entirely different kind of relationship. Gladwin writes:

23 Swift, *Hospital Chaplaincy in the Twenty-First Century*, pp 7-8.

24 Their unique role also means that chaplains can provide 'workaround' solutions to practical and relational problems, sometimes going outside more inefficient or rigid formal channels.

25 Until World War II, the Australia Navy had no official uniform for its chaplains, and has continued to give them no assigned rank. By contrast, the Australian Army has provided a uniform for its chaplains and assigned classes of chaplains that correspond to relative ranks in the army hierarchy. On the one hand, it is important to stress the unique role of the chaplain; on the other hand, in a highly formalized context, uniform and rank provide clarity and help get things done. See Strong, *Chaplains in the Royal Australian Navy*, pp 79-83, 142-145, 155-156; and Gladwin, *Captains of the Soul*, pp 28, 91-93, 259-266.

The incarnational nature of the chaplain's ministry—of living and sweating with soldiers in their units at home or in patrol bases while on operations—means that the chaplain performs a radically different role from the psychologist and the social worker. Because chaplains are posted to units, ships and formations they experience the impact of incidents and deployments ... The relational and spiritually grounded nature of chaplaincy also stands in potential contrast to the clinical distance and humanist assumptions of many psychologists and social workers.[26]

Finally, chaplaincy can open an official door for more modern forms of parachurch activity. For example, in some settings a modern parachurch might have limited access to certain institutions. However, when in partnership with an officially recognized denominational chaplain, the parachurch could enjoy privileges such as making room bookings, operating with more freedom and promoting events to a wider audience.

But while there are many wonderful opportunities, there are also some unique risks and challenges that chaplains face.

The unique vulnerabilities of chaplaincy

Firstly, chaplains can become tamed by the institution that they serve. Since they are ordinarily appointed by, or at least authorized by, a secular authority, chaplains can feel great pressure to conform to the standards of that authority. It could be said that in times of apostasy and corruption this is exactly what happened to the prophets and priests in Israel: they became 'pet prophets' of the monarchy, prophesying peace when there was no peace, giving spiritual legitimacy to the ungodly leaders, endorsing their

---

26 Gladwin notes the experience of army chaplains that "soldiers and veterans are more likely to seek spiritual or moral counselling from chaplains than clinicians" (Gladwin, *Captains of the Soul*, p 274).

policies and superstitiously granting divine blessing.[27] While there is nothing wrong with tact, it can easily become a cover-up for cowardice. Chaplains need to practice a degree of spiritual detachment from the secular institutions in which they serve, even if the leaders of the institutions are professing Christians. Chaplains are especially responsible for bringing a spiritual, Christ-centred perspective into their situation. They must be careful not to find themselves remaining silent when they ought to speak, or worse, entirely conforming to the priorities of a human institution.

Christopher Swift gives several examples of how chaplains have been used to serve a disciplinary purpose for the larger institution—a purpose which may not be in the best interests of the individual nor the most glorifying to God. This might manifest itself in seeking to help provide moral instruction and supervision as part of a program to manage vagrancy and criminality, endorsing political parties in parish churches, "[reconciling] the sick to the power of the workplace within Victorian society", or encouraging compliance with the treatment priorities of medical staff.[28] In the case of military work, chaplains run the risk of being reduced to agents for boosting morale and promoting organizational compliance.[29]

It is not wrong for chaplains to be involved in caring for the welfare and moral conduct of those whom they serve. This is often a natural outworking of Christian concern, and can provide meaningful points of contact. But it is sad when a chaplain is reduced to merely a kind of social worker.

Likewise, there are perfectly legitimate reasons to profession-

---

27 Lesslie Newbigin similarly commented that in the centuries of European Christendom, Christianity became the folk religion of Europe: "the church has become the religious department of European society rather than the task force selected and appointed for world mission" (cited in Goheen, *As the Father Has Sent Me*, p 193).

28 Swift, *Hospital Chaplaincy in the Twenty-First Century*, pp 17-25, 32-33, 39, 44-45, 79.

29 Gladwin describes various ways in which Australian Army chaplains have fulfilled roles such as organizing entertainment for the troops, leading courses in leadership and character, and even education around venereal disease. In these kinds of ways, he says they have served as "force multipliers". See Gladwin, *Captains of the Soul*, p 29.

alize chaplaincy—pursuing more thorough research, consistent procedure, training, goal setting, accountability and inclusion in the institutional hierarchy. This can enable chaplains to be disciplined and effective in their ministry, and can also ensure they are understood, valued and empowered members of their respective institutions.[30] But the professionalization of chaplaincy runs the risk of distorting both the very nature of religion and the role of the chaplain: they are reduced to experts in delivering the service of meeting the spiritual needs of the individual in pursuit of their overall wellbeing. Swift warns against this approach to chaplaincy:

> [In this approach] chaplaincy is to be managed and applied within the same concept of personhood and society used by the state wherever it has authority over institutions. Those who seek the service are consumers of faith-based products, and chaplaincy must therefore be branded and graded according to a centrally determined set of standards.[31]

> Increasingly, the chaplain no longer comes to colonize the experience of the patient, or build the patient's story into a tool for professional power. This may become a temptation for chaplains as their sense of professionalism grows, but I suggest that it should be resisted. Chaplains need the kind of structure and identity required to remain within health care—but they do not need to recruit patients into a campaign for professional aggrandizement. If that were to be done, they would find that they have lost the marginality that makes them uniquely useful to patients who are exploring what it means to live in a post-Christendom world.[32]

---

30 So argue: SB Roberts, DW Donovan and G Handzo, 'Creating and implementing a spiritual/pastoral care plan'; B Peery, 'Outcome oriented chaplaincy: Intentional caring'; and J Overvold, 'Quality improvement: A chaplaincy priority'; in Roberts (ed), *Professional Spiritual & Pastoral Care*, pp 61-80, 342-361 and 372-386.

31 Swift, *Hospital Chaplaincy in the Twenty-First Century*, pp 63-64; see also pp 68-69, 143-150.

32 Swift, *Hospital Chaplaincy in the Twenty-First Century*, p 178.

This can also become an issue when a chaplain takes on additional formal duties in the life of the organization they serve.

At the other end of the spectrum, chaplains can be tamed by focusing too much on rank-and-file members in a way that morally compromises the chaplain or undermines the institution they are supposed to be serving.[33]

Secondly, chaplains can experience great pressure to endorse a nominal, inclusive and ritualistic function, rather than one faithful to devout religious convictions. All human beings, no matter what their religious beliefs, have a desire to mark important occasions in some kind of ceremonial manner.[34] Religion can be appropriated to serve this psychological and sociological need, but without any real interest in its truth claims or personal demands. Secularists object to what they see as the pseudo-scientific spiritualizing of psychology: "[our] main aim is to reconfigure the spirituality-in-nursing debate and to position it where it belongs: in the literature on health psychology and social psychology, and not in a disciplinary cul-de-sac labelled 'unfathomable mystery'."[35] Religious people and those more sympathetic to religion object to the "dumbing down of the spirit"[36] and the promoting of a universalistic spirituality that doesn't match the religious experience or needs of many religious people.[37] Nominally religious schools value the gravitas of a chapel service but consider a clear proclamation of the gospel to be in poor taste. Faced with these challenges, chaplains need great wisdom to judge how much

33 Gladwin, *Captains of the Soul*, pp 232, 311. However, Gladwin notes throughout that these cases have always been in the minority.

34 See the important article RN Bellah, 'Civil religion in America', *Daedalus*, 1967, 96(1):21. Civil religion might be a meaningful and useful thing, but Christianity must not be reduced to a civil religion. In this regard, it is interesting to note that one of the defining days in Australian and New Zealand civic religion, ANZAC Day (a memorial day for all Australians and New Zealanders who died in combat) was established in a form drafted by David Garland, an Anglo-Catholic minister from Brisbane: "it had to be a holy day, not just a public holiday" (Piggin, *Spirit, Word and World*, p 87).

35 John Paley quoted in Swift, *Hospital Chaplaincy in the Twenty-First Century*, p 147.

36 Stephen Pattison quoted in Swift, *Hospital Chaplaincy in the Twenty-First Century*, p 78.

37 Swift also observes that there are significant differences between those who hold to some non-institutionalized spirituality and adherents of religion; see Swift, *Hospital Chaplaincy in the Twenty-First Century*, pp 69-70.

they can soften their preaching to suit the expectations of the institution before they are no longer acting in good conscience. Local churches face similar questions when they serve a kind of chaplaincy function in the community at Easter and Christmas, or when conducting weddings, baptisms and funerals.

Another manifestation of this danger is the ecumenical or inter-religious service.[38] Often nominally religious people aren't aware of important differences between Christian denominations and other religions, let alone between the various Christian denominations. Chaplains need to gently but firmly explain the need to respect the conscience and honour the goodwill of those who cannot in good faith participate in certain inter-religious or ecumenical services. They need to explain that these points of difference are not an expression of hostile intolerance, but simply one aspect of respecting the many religions of the world. In fact, to insist that chaplains must participate in inter-religious services is to (perhaps accidentally and ironically) trample on sincerely held religious convictions.[39]

At the same time, chaplains should generously explore ways of fostering genuine collegiality with people of different denominations and different religions—without compromising their convictions, of course.[40] Offering prayers on behalf of your own religious community in an inter-religious ceremony is at a different point on the spectrum than officiating or fully participating

---

38 Often called 'inter-faith' services. 'Faith' is an unfortunate term used to describe different religious traditions, since it is very much a Christian-centred term. Many religious traditions don't place 'faith' as central to their religious framework in the way that Christianity does. As a result, the term both obscures the uniqueness of Christianity and misrepresents other religious traditions. I have chosen to use the term 'inter-religious' here instead.

39 Gladwin, *Captains of the Soul*, p 263.

40 Gladwin records the legacy of ecumenical relations between chaplains in the Australian Army, which nevertheless upheld certain important points of difference: "We were ecumenical before we even knew how to spell the word", said one chaplain from the mid-20th century; quoted in Gladwin, *Captains of the Soul*, p 253. By contrast, Strong focuses on the ways in which denominationalism often betrayed territorialism in the Royal Australian Navy; see Strong, *Chaplains in the Royal Australian Navy*. Perhaps this is partly a matter of authorial emphasis, although it does seem that different factors were at work in the navy. Ship size, for example, means that there is less space to carry chaplains from multiple denominations.

in a deliberately inclusive ecumenical or inter-religious service.

Beyond shared public ceremonies, there is a great deal of scope for building harmonious and respectful relationships with fellow chaplains without the need to claim fundamental religious agreement. In some cases, chaplaincy roles are structured to provide general 'spiritual care' to all, regardless of religious affiliation. In such cases, it is important for the sake of clarity and conscience to acknowledge that 'spiritual care' means something very different to the evangelical Christian than it does to the secular administrator, the Muslim, or even to the liberal Christian.[41] In these contexts, Christian chaplains can participate in what others may see as 'spiritual care', but they will be looking and praying for opportunities to engage in what they understand to be gospel-shaped 'pastoral care' or 'soul care'.[42]

Thirdly, chaplains often have a limited scope for ministry. This is often just the reality of their position, attached as auxiliaries within larger institutions—especially secular or nominally religious bodies. Where their role is primarily general 'spiritual care' with restrictions on 'proselytizing', the chaplain will need to be content to do good within the framework of the role. As Martha Jacobs warns: "If I cannot support a patient (or family member or staff person) in his or her theology, then I cannot serve as a multi-faith chaplain."[43] So also David Plummer writes:

41 The Association of Professional Chaplains' definition of 'spiritual care' is: "Interventions, individual or communal, that facilitate the ability to express the integration of body, mind, and spirit to achieve wholeness, health, and a sense of connection to self, others, and[/ or] a higher power" (cited in G Handzo, 'The process of spiritual / pastoral care: A general theory for providing spiritual / pastoral care using palliative care as a paradigm', in Roberts (ed), *Professional Spiritual & Pastoral Care*, p 24.

42 "An intentional Christian ministry that is concerned with the whole person, and that knows that the deepest personal wholeness is ultimately found through a restored relationship with God the Father, fellowship with others and forgiveness through Jesus Christ" (K Bradford, 'Recovering a vision for soul care through a Reformed evangelical lens', *Lucas: An evangelical history review*, 2019, 2.13:94-95. Bradford's definition fits into the category of what is now called 'pastoral care', as distinct from 'spiritual care'. See also Handzo, 'The process of spiritual / pastoral care', p 24.

43 MR Jacobs, 'Creating a personal theology to do spiritual / pastoral care', in Roberts (ed), *Professional Spiritual & Pastoral Care*, p 5.

Integrity is also violated when the pastoral caregiver affirms a commitment to religious pluralism to gain employment and be placed in a position of trust, only to betray that trust by attempting to proselytize to the caregiver's belief system and/or cultural values.[44]

In many contexts, there is a great deal of ambiguity around the role, which creates the potential for chaplains to become lazy, undisciplined, frustrated, over-worked, or a combination of all these.[45] To be personally content and practically useful in their work, chaplains need to draw on a range of skills. They need to be creative and flexible to find the best ways to serve, to connect with people and to be available to people.[46] They need patience and contentment, trusting that God will use them in his timing. They also need shrewdness and 'hustle' to carve out roles and resources for themselves, sometimes presuming to step forward in grey areas where they may not have been explicitly invited.

The reality of role ambiguity also means that both religious and secular assessment of chaplaincy needs to tread carefully. Positions may not offer an obviously valuable return on investment for institutional effectiveness or gospel mission. While chaplains should not overstate what they are able to deliver, onlookers must realize that the long-term, qualitative impact of chaplaincy roles

---

44 DB Plummer, 'Creating a personal theology to do spiritual / pastoral care', in Roberts (ed), *Professional Spiritual & Pastoral Care*, p 14 (note that this article and the article previously cited are separate pieces with the same title).

45 Swift gives the example of the Rev Frederick Pocock, a 19th-century full-time hospital chaplain, who neglected basic chaplaincy duties while running a private school from his home; see Swift, *Hospital Chaplaincy in the Twenty-First Century*, pp 36-37. Swift also summarizes the findings of a 2000 report by Helen Orchard, which found that work of English hospital chaplains was capricious, inconsistent and vague (p 61). See also Peery, 'Outcome oriented chaplaincy'.

46 Dykstra, *Images of Pastoral Care* is valuable for the sake of its evocative chapter titles alone, as it provides a richly diverse list of ways to think about the ambiguous role of chaplain: for example, 'The Solicitous Shepherd', 'The Self-Differentiated Samaritan', 'The Wounded Healer', 'The Circus Clown', 'The Wise Fool', 'The Intimate Stranger', 'The Ascetic Witness', 'The Diagnostician', 'The Moral Coach and Counselor', 'The Indigenous Storyteller', 'The Agent of Hope', 'The Gardener', 'The Midwife, Storyteller, and Reticent Outlaw'.

cannot be easily observed and must not be quickly dismissed.[47]

On the other hand, where chaplains have a great deal of freedom and influence, they face the opposite danger: *fourthly, chaplains risk facilitating the neglect of ordinary churchgoing among those they serve.* Chaplains are not appointed to be a substitute for local church membership, but a supplement to it. They need to reinforce this to those they serve, and when appropriate should urge people to find a spiritual home in a local church.

Fifthly, chaplaincy can lose its distinctively Christian theological and ethical depth. The less a chaplain functions as a minister of religion, the less immediately obvious it is that the role requires rigorous theological education. Training in counselling and other forms of personal care can seem much more necessary for the kind of work many chaplains perform. Added to this, some move into chaplaincy because they don't fit comfortably in local church ministry due to various eccentricities; such misfits can shape the overall professional culture of chaplaincy.[48] Sadly, professional development for chaplains can be a mixed bag of secular counselling training and ethical papers on hot-button issues along with devotional content drawn from different Christian and religious traditions. Sarah Coakley writes of her experience:

> The theology that was on offer to accompany the profundity of the "living documents" I encountered was thin gruel indeed: if this was "pastoral theology" then I felt I could well do without it. Most of it was warmed-over tid-bits from an earlier generation of systematics, one which had in any case signally failed to re-ignite

47 In *Professional Spiritual & Pastoral Care*, Roberts demonstrates a strong commitment to professionalism, which has many helpful structures and recommendations: as simple as advocating careful note-taking and having some basic plans and pathways in place. However, I cannot wholeheartedly agree with the strong insistence that this is the only legitimate way for chaplains to justify their presence in the modern hospital, for example; see Handzo, 'The process of spiritual / pastoral care', p 22.

48 Swift, *Hospital Chaplaincy in the Twenty-First Century*, pp 157-158. Swift also cites 2008 research showing that 80% of English healthcare chaplains were theologically liberal and 20% or more are in same-sex partnerships (p 7). He ponders what the causal relationship might be: is this primarily because their experiences and theology incline them to such roles, or because such people feel like "refugees" within the mainstream church?

excitement about pastoral ministry in itself. The rest of it was light-weight spirituality, so-called, which acted as a sort of palliative but did not probe the big theological and philosophical questions about unjust suffering and untimely death that any CPE [Clinical Pastoral Education] candidate will inevitably encounter in the wards.[49]

What is missed is that digging deeply into a book of the Bible or a systematic theological topic can also have all sorts of relevance to the day-to-day work of chaplaincy. While there are some advantages to having a lower bar for entry to chaplaincy, there is ultimately a significant loss if chaplains are not trained, equipped, and deepened in their theological and ethical thinking over time. Drawing on the Bible, and on other deep and ancient theological resources, will greatly enrich the chaplain's ability to offer personal care, spiritual encouragement and evangelistic engagement. Neglecting these resources will subtly distort the chaplain's practice and counsel over time. More still, depth in these disciplines will enable chaplains to contribute to a robust development, critique and reformation of institutions where needed.

Conclusion

Chaplaincy is a strange and diverse phenomenon, ranging from roles that closely resemble that of a cross-cultural missionary, right through to roles that are much more like that of a social worker. The unique issue facing many forms of chaplaincy is the chaplain's 'dual citizenship': seeking to offer an authentic Christ-centred witness, while being funded by—or at least formally answerable to—a secular organization whose primary purpose is something other than the ministry of the gospel. Where the funding organization shares the chaplain's Christian theology and purpose, the work is much easier—though chaplains still need to ensure they are being faithful, even if that

---

49 Coakley, 'Can pastoral theology be saved?'

means pulling in a different direction than their host organization would have them go.

Where chaplains are embedded in secular institutions, they often find themselves in difficult positions: 'how do I best conduct myself in a way that is faithful to Christ and his gospel, while also respectful of those in authority over me and appropriate to the context in which I am ministering?' Understandably, some will conclude that they are unable to accept certain roles in good conscience, while others will understandably question the appropriateness of gospel ministers being employed by the government and other secular bodies. The Scriptures do not speak specifically about such matters, but they do establish a distinction between the church, the work of the gospel, and the business of this world and its governing authorities—perhaps most famously in Jesus' extraordinary insight in Matthew 22: "give back to Caesar what is Caesar's, and to God what is God's" (Matt 22:21).[50] Where chaplains serve in these contexts, they need to be wise and courageous.

But even though much chaplaincy work is problematic, it also continues to have enormous potential, even in a pluralistic and secular society. It is a wonderful thing to bring a primarily God-centred perspective and agenda into both Christian and secular organizations. As we have seen in this chapter, chaplains can be a blessing to their community in special ways, even producing eternal fruit through the ministry of the gospel.

---

50 See also, for example, Acts 5:29; 1 Cor 5:9-13; 1 Thess 2:5-6; 2 Tim 2:4.

Chapter 12: Megachurches, multi-site churches, evangelical networks and the ecumenical movement[1]

There's the universal church, the local church, and the denominational association of local churches. But in the gaps between each, there exist many other kinds of organization. It is to these types of groups that we turn our attention in this chapter as we consider the place of megachurches, multi-site churches, evangelical networks and what is usually known as the 'ecumenical movement'.

Some of the ministries I have in mind look very similar to denominations. Others look a lot like local churches. Sometimes it's unclear what comparison we could make or what we should call them. Are they churches? Denominations? Parachurches?

For example, a large city-wide event in my home town is called 'Church Together', positioning itself as a single manifestation of the church of Christ in southern Tasmania.[2] Even

---

1 Earlier versions of this material were delivered in sermon form in 2019 at Crossroads Presbyterian Church, Hobart, Summerleas Christian Church, and the Camp Clayton Easter Festival, Ulverstone.
2 See churchtogethertasmania.com.

bigger still is the World Council of Churches, which describes itself as "a community of churches on the way to visible unity in one faith and one eucharistic fellowship, expressed in worship and in common life in Christ".[3]

What do we make of these kinds of church networks that are not-quite-denominations, or more-than-denominations? What are the benefits of such networks? The theological principles that should guide them and our participation in them? The problems and risks they bring with them?

Megachurches and multi-site churches

Ever since the first Christian church started in Jerusalem, there have been very large churches.[4] But the late-20th and early-21st centuries have been characterized by an enormous increase in the number of very large churches, not to mention the sheer size of some of these churches (at time of writing, the largest 'church' in the United States is around 85,000 people, and the largest in the world around 480,000).[5] In part, this can be explained by the growing number of people who now live in cities, as well as by advances in all sorts of transport and communications technology.[6] While some churches regularly meet as one congregation in enormous auditoriums, most are made up of multiple services, increasingly across multiple venues—and sometimes spread across multiple cities, states or even countries. This growing

3   World Council of Churches, *What is the World Council of Churches?*, WCC website, 2022, accessed 27 September 2022 (oikoumene.org/about-the-wcc).
4   A megachurch is normally categorized as a church which has a weekly attendance of at least 2,000 adults and children; see W Bird, 'World's first megachurch?', *Leadership Network*, 4 May 2012, accessed 27 September 2022 (leadnet.org/worlds_first_megachurch).
5   S Thumma, *Exploring the Megachurch Phenomena: Their Characteristics and Cultural Context*, Hartford Institute for Religion Research website, n.d., accessed 17 October 2022 (hirr.hartsem.edu/bookshelf/thumma_article2.html). See also Hartford Institute, *Database of Megachurches in the U.S.*, Hartford Institute website, n.d., accessed 17 October 2022 (hartfordinstitute.org/megachurch/database.html); and W Bird, *2022 Global Megachurches—World's Largest Churches*, Leadership Network website, accessed 17 October 2022 (archive.leadnet.org/world).
6   Driscoll and Breshears, *Vintage Church*, pp 269-270.

phenomenon offers some great strengths as well as presenting some significant challenges.

In the section that follows, I will examine the ways in which megachurches and multi-site churches push the boundaries of the definition of the 'local church' and the ways in which they often initiate a range of ministries that are very similar to para-churches. But I will also take the time to reflect on some of the potential benefits and risks of megachurches and multi-site churches. These broader comments will, I hope, highlight the effects that these ministries can have on local churches, denominations and parachurches, as well as drawing out lessons that are relevant to denominations, parachurches and even churches of a much smaller size.

The benefits of megachurches and multi-site churches

A clear strength of megachurches is their efficiency, which comes from economies of scale. Complex systems like finances and payroll, and costly resources like staff and facilities, can be shared among a larger number of people at a lower cost per person—whereas small churches usually have their own finance committee, their own pastor, and their own church building. The multi-site approach, where a church starts satellite 'campuses' in different locations while still operating under a unified leadership, maximizes the same efficiency for the purpose of church planting: a campus is less costly in money, thought and effort than a regular pioneering church plant. While denominational associations offer some of these efficiencies, they tend to move more slowly due to traditionalism and a more democratic structure.[7]

Megachurches use the gifts of extraordinary leaders. Unusually capable administrators, compelling preachers, visionary strategists

---

7   Some versions of Presbyterianism also see no problem with a network of churches that have no individuated elderships.

and persuasive evangelists are able to use their gifts for the benefit of a larger number of people on a regular basis. While this can also happen within denominational associations and parachurch fellowships, the opportunities these ministries provide are rarely quite as intensive and regular as those provided by the megachurch. If a megachurch starts multiple campuses with a multi-site strategy, then the exceptional strengths of their ministry model and church culture can be transmitted even further afield.

Megachurches are typically able to provide deeper levels of care, community and ministry than a smaller church. The caricature of the megachurch is that of a 'celebrity pastor' together with a professionalized ministry team serving a passive crowd of consumers. While this is sometimes the case, many megachurches are deep and rich, full of carefully planned small-group ministries, inclusive care structures, and a variety of opportunities for members to use their gifts to build the church and reach the world. In the best megachurches, staff are not the ones who do all the work, but the ones who train and oversee the members to share in the work together. In fact it is possible for a small church, with staff and church members stretched across multiple ministries and rosters, to have less effective small groups and less thorough and accessible pastoral care structures.[8]

The size of megachurches requires and enables the development of best practices, not only in ministry activities, but also in governance and safety. Part of the charm of smaller churches is their more casual and informal character. There can be a greater tolerance for dips in quality and more flexibility with bureaucracy because personal relationships provide a glue for the community and the organization. But there is a serious limit to the level of quality that a small staff and volunteer leadership team can achieve, which in turn leads to a greater reliance on external resources to

---

8   See W Bird, 'Do megachurches provide a better religious experience than smaller churches?', *Leadership Network*, 3 October 2018, accessed 27 September 2022 (leadnet. org/do-megachurches-provide-a-better-religious-experience-than-smaller-churches).

plug the gaps. By contrast, a larger church can become more specialized in all sorts of areas of church life, ministry and evangelism. In the best cases, this also means that megachurches can develop some of the most robust and thorough policies on issues of finance, governance, privacy and safety, which not only help them function as healthy institutions but might also be shared for the benefit of other churches and organizations. Of course, some of these same benefits can also be achieved through denominations, with less temptation to bend policies to the convenience and self-protection of a single church.

Megachurches also pioneer and support new ministries of various kinds. Large churches are more likely to establish counselling ministries, outdoor ministries, outreach in schools, training colleges, journals, and much more. In preparation for writing this book, one of the resources I found most helpful was *The Church and the ParaChurch: An Uneasy Marriage* by Jerry White. I had the chance to meet Jerry in person when he visited Australia. When I asked him what he thinks has changed since he wrote his book in the 1980s, he spoke of the rise of the megachurch, and how it really is a kind of "conglomerate of parachurches". Willmer, Schmidt and Smith similarly write:

> What is different about these [very large] churches is that they have managed to combine the strength of the parachurch with the strength of the small traditional church and have avoided the weaknesses of both. The firmly drawn dividing lines between church and parachurch are partially blurred by the megachurch.
>
> The megachurch resembles a constellation of generalized church ministries and specialized church ministries ... The megachurch has expanded the definition of local church ministry to include what was, for decades, the parachurch's work. In addition, it has created an entrepreneurial environment whose 'parachurch founders' are often given the freedom to express their vision—within the boundaries of the local church. In essence, the megachurch undoubtedly has and will continue to keep some parachurch ministries from

independent operation by incubating and sustaining them within the church's boundaries.[9]

This kind of activity can lead to fruitful evangelism to whole new groups of unreached people and new ways to bless the community, which gives God's people more diverse ways to use their gifts for the good of others. All this raises the question of whether these ministries would be more effective or more impartial as independent organizations, which I will consider below.

Megachurches provide an upward pressure for the denomination to be restrained in its reach. Smaller churches are more likely to be organizationally and even financially dependent on their denominations, whereas megachurches are more self-sufficient; they don't need the denomination. As a result, they can challenge a denomination which becomes overly controlling and bureaucratic, and they might be better able to resist doctrinal decline into liberalism. Phillip Jensen expressed this, with provocative humour, at the Evangelical Ministry Assembly in 1988:

> If the pastor is in passive subservience to episcopal bureaucrats [bishops], then the congregation will be passive and subservient to episcopal bureaucrats … Their [the bishops'] job is to keep peace. They always oppose change and always avoid conflict … They spend their time spreading the resources evenly across the land so every church has the same resources. That way, they minimise the number of churches that complain to them about them. That way, they make sure there is no rival power structure to oust their position. We mustn't let them chart the course … Don't wait for the bishop to send you a curate. The bishop will only send you a nong. He won't send you a good man. He doesn't want to build your work up. He wants to spread the manure far and broad, not gather it in any place that will cause a smell in the diocese.[10]

9   Willmer et al., *The Prospering Parachurch*, pp 194-195.
10 P Jensen, 'Why bishops are deacons' [audio file], *Proclamation Trust*, 1988, accessed 27 September 2022 (proctrust.org.uk/resources/talk/396).

Perhaps the same might be true to some extent in relation to the civil government. Megachurches might be big enough to, at times, express resistance to state interference or government overreach in religious matters, just as denominational leaders are sometimes able to do.[11]

Danger areas

The megachurch and multi-site phenomenon has, of course, attracted its critics. Some of the criticisms are rightly directed at peculiar kinds of megachurch, such as those multi-site churches which almost exclusively broadcast sermons to their various campuses, or megachurches that have very glamorous yet aloof 'celebrity pastors'. But these criticisms do not rightly apply to all expressions of the diverse megachurch or multi-site phenomenon.

Other criticisms focus on high-profile scandals. While there are doubtless many unique temptations that megachurch leadership brings (which I will explore below), and corruption in a well-known megachurch can have a much more catastrophic impact, sinfulness lurks in the hearts of elders in the smallest church or most traditional denomination. These criticisms are not criticisms of the megachurch in principle, but only of particular megachurches.

Still other criticisms are of a more principled and theological nature: where might these ministries fail to be structured or conducted in a healthy and biblically faithful way? It is on these types of criticisms and concerns that I will primarily concentrate.

First, attention must be given to the temptations faced by leaders of megachurches in areas such as power, money and sex that are amplified by the sheer size of megachurches. Just as megachurches

---

11 Certainly churches and other religious organizations serve as 'mediating institutions' between individuals and families and the government, and so provide protection and advocacy for their interests; see MR Gornik, *To Live in Peace: Biblical faith and the changing inner city*, Eerdmans, 2002, pp 18-19. Gornik warns, however, that the church must not let itself be reduced to *merely* a 'mediating institution' serving a social function.

can magnify a healthy spiritual culture and an effective evangelistic impact, they can also magnify the pursuit of applause and
power, feeding our sinful desires and affording new opportunities to hide our sinful actions and satisfy our sinful cravings.
Further, when serious sin is committed in a larger institution,
the destructive impact can be magnified for a range of reasons,
including the number of members directly affected and the
higher likelihood of widespread bad publicity, which results not
only in a loss of reputation for the megachurch, but also in the
gospel itself being brought into disrepute. Furthermore, the
instinct to preserve the institution and its uniquely gifted leaders rather than deal properly with sin can also be felt more
intensely because of the size and influence of the church. Some
of these dangers can also be found in positions of influence
within denominations and larger parachurch networks.

*Second, we should honour and learn from megachurches without
attributing disproportionate authority to them.* The authority that
capable and successful leaders accrue is perfectly normal and
healthy: the skill and wisdom required to lead a megachurch,
even if the church is in what appears to be an 'easy patch', can
rightly be respected. In addition, megachurches will have the
capacity to contribute to a range of concerns beyond mere survival.[12] But their fellow elders in sister churches must not give
megachurches and their leaders undue authority. They are still
forgiven sinners with flaws and blind spots. They enjoy fruitfulness because of skill and wisdom, but also because of unusual
giftedness, peculiar context, and the extraordinary blessing of
God. Their doctrine and ministry practices must be tested with
discernment against the word of God, not merely received as
good and right because they seem to 'work'. For all these reasons, megachurch leaders need to check their rhetoric and

---

12 Sometimes, smaller churches facilitate this same wider investment: if there is little progress in the growth of the local congregation, the elders might have more ability to serve
the other churches and parachurches, although in this case the elders must beware that
their interest in broader and more stimulating contributions is actually making them
neglect the work that would help grow their local congregation.

guard their public actions to ensure that they are heard and received in an appropriate way.

Third, megachurches must continue to uphold gospel faithfulness, moral purity and spiritual humility as being of the greatest worth. The pressures of a public profile and a big budget can become alluring, so that decisions are made more for the sake of 'optics', for economic return, or in order to meet key performance indicators, rather than because they deeply reflect Christian values.[13] A celebrity culture, fuelled by social media, can further distort the nature of true Christian leadership and ministry.[14] To be sure, smaller churches have their own versions of this temptation—for example, a wealthy or vocal member who comes from one of the church's founding families can hold a church to ransom and effectively tame the preacher of the gospel; or perhaps the pressure to play along with a local inter-church network can pressure churches to compromise on matters of principle for the sake of small-town courtesy. Whether in small rural church or urban megachurch, we must all persevere in godliness, faithfulness and humble devotion above all.

Fourth, efficiency and effectiveness need to be considered alongside other theologically driven values about the nature of church and ministry. A vivid example is the multi-site church that shows a video of the 'big-name' preacher across its multiple campuses.

13 See DA Carson, *From Triumphalism to Maturity: A new exposition of 2 Corinthians 10-13*, Baker Book House, 1988; and DA Carson, *The Cross and Christian Ministry: An Exposition of Passages from 1 Corinthians*, Baker, 2004. These two books are wonderful expositions of 2 Corinthians 10-13 and 1 Corinthians 1-4 respectively, applied powerfully to these concerns. Ben Tertin's article about the demise of Mars Hill Church, Seattle, is a sobering warning of how this can slowly start to happen in the ministry culture of a church; see B Tertin, 'The painful lessons of Mars Hill', *Christianity Today*, 8 December 2014, accessed 27 September 2022 (christianitytoday.com/pastors/2014/december-online-only/painful-lessons-of-mars-hill.html). For more on Mars Hill, see the excellent podcast from Mike Cosper (host), *The Rise and Fall of Mars Hill*, Christianity Today, 2021, accessed 28 September 2022 (christianitytoday.com/ct/podcasts/rise-and-fall-of-mars-hill).

14 See Andy Crouch's very helpful article about celebrity culture, 'It's time to reckon with celebrity power'. But note the qualifications to this by Mark Dever in a podcast episode on celebrity pastors: J Leeman, *J Leeman interviews Mark Dever: On T4G and Celebrity Pastors* [interview audio file], Pastors' Talk episode 47, 9Marks, 10 April 2018, accessed 27 September 2022 (9marks.org/conversations/episode-47-on-t4g-and-celebrity-pastors).

In some cases, other parts of the church meeting might also be broadcast to other locations. This is not necessarily a problem; it could simply be an upgraded version of books of homilies, singing along to a karaoke-style video of recorded church music, or a small-house fellowship without a pastor of their own listening to recordings of another preacher.[15] In a large multi-site church, this technology also offers the ability to foster a united experience for all the campuses, and takes all sorts of pressures off the new campuses: pastors don't need to spend hours and hours preparing and delivering sermons at every location, but instead can focus on the local needs of the congregation and the community.

But technology is never entirely neutral; it shapes us in a range of ways.[16] Critics of this approach question how it changes the nature of preaching and leadership: is it healthy for our main preaching pastor to have no local presence with the community of believers? Is it fitting for the on-the-ground leaders of the local community to have minimal roles in leading that community through the preaching of the word?[17] Does the very nature of a television screen subtly (or perhaps not so subtly) enhance the presentation of an unhelpful celebrity persona for the preacher? I suspect these considerations are part of the reason why only a minority of multi-site churches predominantly use video preaching. This is one example of the kind of careful thinking that needs to take place to ensure that a model's practi-

---

15 Note, however, that it is questionable to draw an analogy between what a small, under-resourced church does out of necessity and what a large, well-resourced church deliberately builds into their ministry model for the sake of efficiency.

16 For more on our relationship to technology, see N Campbell, 'Plundering gold from Egypt'; A Crouch, *Culture Making: Recovering our creative calling*, IVP, 2013; Crouch, 'It's time to reckon with celebrity power'; and J Ellul, *The Technological Society: A penetrating analysis of our technical civilization and of the effect of an increasingly standardized culture on the future of man* (J Wilkinson, trans), Vintage Books, 2011 [1954].

17 Critics also point out how the video-venue strategy is short-sighted, because it reduces the number of preachers being equipped and raised up. It must be recognized, however, that a megachurch will have more 'pulpits' than just the Sunday morning: other ministries within the larger church (youth, men, women, training) might have 'congregations' as big as the Sunday gathering of a small or medium-sized church. On the other hand, these other opportunities are still qualitatively different than preaching to a gathered church on a Sunday morning.

cal efficiencies don't have unintended ripple effects in the kind of culture that is created.

Fifth, megachurches need to honestly assess whether they should more properly think and act like a denominational unit rather than a single church. As soon as a church begins a second service on a Sunday—which is not intended to be a 'double dip' for the one community, but rather a separate congregation—important questions are raised: in what sense is this still one church if it no longer gathers as one church? Do we rather have two churches that share one building, budget and leadership structure? Multi-site churches make these questions even more obvious, for geographical distance and lack of shared space means that the overlap between campuses becomes more and more restricted to the budget, branding and the highest levels of leadership.[18]

At this point, honest reflection on the theological principles around the nature of church and denomination (see part I) must come into play. This reflection has led some to choose not to adopt a multi-site model, nor even a multi-service model.[19] And yet it has led others to adopt a multi-site model with a long-term goal of releasing the campuses as independent churches— a kind of glacial-pace church planting strategy.[20] Still others have changed the terminology they use to speak about their multi-site ministry: for example, they are leading a family of churches (plural), not a single church.

Two issues are worth considering here. *First,* given the

---

18 Can a single church be constituted simply by shared leadership, mission and resources? Instead of the ancient saying *ubi episcopas, ibi ecclesia* ("where the bishop is, there is the church"), perhaps we could say *ubi* lead pastor and corporate branding, *ibi ecclesia*? The Westminster Assembly argued that it is legitimate for a number of congregations to be led by a single presbytery, with no localized elders at all. I am unpersuaded by the wisdom of this.

19 The *9Marks Journal* focused on this topic in 2009. See, for example, J Leeman, 'Theological critique of multi-site'.

20 For example, K Shellnutt, 'Matt Chandler's Village Church ends multisite era', *Christianity Today*, 28 September 2017, accessed 27 September 2022 (christianitytoday.com/news/2017/september/matt-chandler-village-church-end-multisite-campuses-dfw.html); and R Pope, '3 reasons we stopped doing multisite church', *Christianity Today*, 6 July 2015, accessed 27 September 2022 (christianitytoday.com/pastors/2015/summer-2015/3-reasons-we-stopped-doing-multisite-church.html).

importance of gathering as a part of what it means to be church, planning for occasional combined gatherings of multiple services should not be considered a gimmicky, momentum-building exercise, but a sincere manifestation of a theological principle.[21] And *second*, if it is more accurate to describe a megachurch or multi-site ministry as a family of churches, then governance should be evaluated to reflect this reality. A mature and respectful leadership might foster genuine interdependence and equality in its manner of relating—but should that leadership be protected in the actual constitution and organizational hierarchy? In the end, who has coercive power in the network of campuses or congregations? Just as denominations ask careful questions about governance, autonomy and control, it would be consistent for megachurches and multi-site ministries to do the same, even if the necessary changes might slow down some of their efficiencies.

Sixth, some kinds of mission and ministry will be much more difficult for megachurches to do effectively. While large ministries can do many things with more efficiency and polish, the pressures and necessities of being large can also make them blind, or even stupid in some ways. Moreover, as a megachurch grows, it generalizes; even its specialized ministries may have a certain generalized quality to them. For example, will it make economic sense for a megachurch to undertake a really good, faithful work among small ethnic groups or among other niche demographics? Perhaps, with a great deal of discipline and conviction, it will. But often certain demographics are left behind. This doesn't make the megachurch bad or the boutique church good; it means both are needed.

Lastly, megachurches need to be aware of the unhelpful ways they might compete with smaller churches and parachurches. The excel-

---

21 This act of gathering as a whole community reminds us that the whole community—not simply the leadership, the programs, or the branding—constitutes the church. Leeman, however, considers this as "anaemic, not to mention disobedient", undermining church discipline and separating discipline from the ministry of the word; see Leeman, 'Theological critique of multi-site'.

lence of staff, facilities and programs, the diversity of people, and the sheer excitement of a megachurch can understandably draw Christians away from smaller churches. This is not entirely a one-way process, of course, as some Christians leave megachurches because they are attracted to the intimacy, slower pace, or different style of gathering they might find in a smaller church. Nevertheless, this 'black hole effect' can be discouraging and damaging for the churches in the catchment area of a megachurch. Smaller churches may already be unhealthy or unviable, and the growth of a megachurch simply exposes these vulnerabilities.

Megachurch leaders and members should adopt a default setting of urging 'church shoppers' to go back to their current churches. Moreover, megachurches might also think about how they can generously invest in lifting up churches in their region, not only when it suits their own expansion through mergers, but simply to be a blessing to others.[22] When it comes to para-churches, the megachurches do well to stop and ask whether they should launch a new ministry or invest in an existing para-church ministry. Willmer, Schmidt and Smith appear to argue that it is better for parachurches to be housed and supported within the structure of a megachurch than to exist as independent organizations.[23] But this is not necessarily the case, especially if there are good ministries already in existence: why not use the resources and expertise of the megachurch to strengthen existing work without having that work subsumed into the megachurch?

---

22 This is not to say that church mergers are always a bad thing; they can be a wonderful way to give struggling and dying churches a new lease on life. What's more, smaller churches need to realize that healthy megachurches often struggle with a lack of resources as much as smaller churches do. It's not as if megachurches enjoy a leisurely life with all the volunteers, staff and finances in the world. They are often scrambling to plug gaps—just on a larger scale.

23 Willmer et al., *The Prospering Parachurch*, pp 194-195. But they do acknowledge that "Prudent parachurch organizations will see megachurches as worthy partners for more ministry impact. Despite their independence and the huge defences that most mega-churches erect, partnership is possible" (p 195). White is also largely positive about parachurch functions being taken on by churches large enough to resource them, provided these ministries are "a real need and not just a response to a current fad" (White, *The Church and the Parachurch*, p 135).

Even if a megachurch sees a need to launch a new ministry, they ought to ask if it should be housed under their brand and governance, or if they should spin-off an independent parachurch that other churches might also share in. While in-house parachurch ministries might create efficiencies and synergies and help to build the brand of the megachurch, the new venture might have more integrity and longevity if it is independent.

Evangelical networks

A much looser expression of Christian partnership is the 'network', 'alliance' or 'fellowship' that brings together pastors, churches or individuals across a region. When the gospel ecosystem is healthy in an area, Christians work together well, both within and beyond their denominations. This might be something as simple as a monthly pastor's brunch, a combined Christmas carols or Reformation Day service, or a quarterly prayer meeting. Or it could be a more formal association with a constitution and governing body—for example, The Vision 100 Network, a church planting network I helped establish in Tasmania, is an incorporated association.

Interdenominational work is not easily identified during much of church history, because denominations as we know them today did not really exist before the Reformation, and rarely featured in stable and sizeable numbers in a single city, social class or country before the 19th century.[24] Still, Kevin DeYoung shows that even before this time there were 'extra-ecclesial' fellowships, which served as a precursor to interdenominational networks.[25] The first Great Awakening in Brit-

---

24 Bebbington, *Evangelicalism in Modern Britain*, p 18; and Piggin, *Spirit, Word and World*, p 34. Piggin notes that the interaction of various denominations was from very early on a particular characteristic of both the United States of America and Australia.

25 'Extra-ecclesial' fellowship refers to networks that went beyond institutional church; see R Kelly and K DeYoung, 'Extra-ecclesial gospel partnerships: A mess worth making', *Foundations*, 2014, 66:4-24, accessed 27 September 2022 (affinity.org.uk/foundations/issue-66/issue-66-article-1-extra-ecclesial-gospel-partnerships-a-mess-worth-making).

ain and the American colonies in the middle of the 18th century led to the proliferation of interdenominational partnerships and extra-ecclesial fellowships, for while much of the revivals of this time took place in the context of local churches, the period was also marked by many inter-church prayer meetings, small-group networks, and enormous public preaching events. These awakenings are, in many ways, the origin of the modern identity and pattern of 'evangelicalism' as we still know it today, which, among other things, is marked by an openness to partnerships that transcend denominational institutions.[26] But more than being a mere social and historical novelty, I suggest that wherever there is vibrant biblical Christianity, there will be expressions of extra-ecclesial fellowship.

These broader networks provide a basic vehicle for genuine, ongoing relationships between Christians of shared convictions. They help to create a 'hothouse' effect that can allow genuine listening, learning and constructive conflict, and which leads to inter-church and interdenominational enterprises for Christian ministry and good deeds. They also facilitate the support of parachurch ministries, as the evangelical network endorses parachurch ministries to a larger group of churches, broadcasts their communications, or mediates their programs in a contextually appropriate way. Another way to describe all this is to say that evangelical networks help to promote a healthy 'gospel ecosystem', as already described in this book.

---

26 David Bebbington captures some of the distinctive flavour and dynamics of the evangelical movement in his famous fourfold description of what characterizes it: biblicism, conversionism, cruicentrism, and activism; see *Evangelicalism in Modern Britain*, pp 2-3. Both 'conversionism' and 'activism' critique nominal, institutional Christianity, and so can motivate an interest in seeking out other Christians who share the experience of genuine conversion and a commitment to zealous action for Christ, wherever they may be found. 'Crucicentrism' encourages an ordering principle to theological convictions, which supports the process of deciding which theological matters are of primary or secondary importance. The social context of weakening influence of historic institutions and relationships also made this emphasis more plausible and useful. See also Noll, *The Rise of Evangelicalism*, pp 136-143. To this historical and sociological description I also want to add conservative Protestant theological convictions. See MA Noll, 'What is "Evangelical"?', in GR McDermott (ed), *The Oxford Handbook of Evangelical Theology*, Oxford University Press, 2010.

'Movement Day' is one very explicit example of this kind of vision:

> A city's Christian vibrancy is in direct proportion to the depth of unity between its people. Defined as its "gospel eco-system," and comprised of churches, agencies and leaders, the goal of a MD expression is to see that eco-system mature in all its diversity.[27]

This movement seeks to 'accelerate gospel expansion' in cities by gathering urban networks of church, not-for-profit and business leaders in prayer, research, leadership development and bold vision setting.

Dangers for evangelical networks to avoid

Lacking clarity of purpose. Meeting just for the sake of fellowship, unity and prayer can be a lost opportunity. Having some special focus brings a tangible benefit to those in the network while also delivering the by-product of fellowship and unity. Such clarity of purpose also guards against the endless expansion of the activities of such networks, as discussed in chapter 7 (under 'Programming and support-raising restraint'). It guards against masses of money and effort being expended to gather Christians simply for the purpose of being together.

An example of a network with a very clear purpose is the Proclamation Trust: "to teach the Bible to preachers in order that they can in turn teach it to others", along with "a further aim … to provide a fellowship of like-minded evangelicals across the denominations for encouragement in an exacting work".[28] Another example is the Vision 100 Network in Tasmania, which exists "to gather and resource a network of church leaders" who

---

27 Movement Day, *What Is Movement Day?*, Movement Day website, 2020, accessed 27 September 2022 (movementday.com/what-is-movement-day).

28 Proclamation Trust, *About Proc Trust*, Proc Trust website, 2022, accessed 27 September 2022. proctrust.org.uk/about

will "raise up and train the next generation of church leaders in order to plant evangelistic, church-planting churches".[29]

Once an evangelical network grows sufficiently large—with a deliberately representative leadership and broad purpose—it can begin to share a lot of practical similarities with the ecumenical movement. Groups such as the National Association of Evangelicals or The Gospel Coalition start to function as a combination of network, peak body and publishing house.[30] Much of the discussion throughout this section, as well as in the next section ('The ecumenical movement'), will be relevant to such networks.

Casting the theological net too wide for the fellowship to be useful. The purpose of an evangelical network is to unite around common convictions and common causes, in the spirit of Paul's exhortation to the Philippian church:

> Whatever happens, conduct yourselves in a manner worthy of the gospel of Christ. Then, whether I come and see you or only hear about you in my absence, I will know that you stand firm in the one Spirit, striving together as one for the faith of the gospel without being frightened in any way by those who oppose you. (Phil 1:27-28a)

There comes a point, though, where differences in theology and practical priorities make regular interaction and cooperation less beneficial. The exact degree of diversity will differ depending on a range of factors, including the culture, personality and preferences of local leaders, and the purposes and activities of the evangelical network. But involvement in the same formal

---

29 Vision 100 Network home page, n.d., accessed 27 September 2022 (vision100.org).

30 "We are a fellowship of evangelical churches in the Reformed tradition deeply committed to renewing our faith in the gospel of Christ and to reforming our ministry practices to conform fully to the Scriptures … Our desire is to serve the church we love by inviting all our brothers and sisters to join us in an effort to renew the contemporary church in the ancient gospel of Christ so that we truly speak and live for him in a way that clearly communicates to our age" (The Gospel Coalition, 'Preamble', *Foundation Documents*, TGC US Edition website, 2016, accessed 27 September 2022 (thegospelcoalition.org/about/foundation-documents).

network is not the only way to fuel a connection between Christians. Other kinds of interaction can be proactively explored between those with whom we have significant points of disagreement on secondary and tertiary matters, those with radically different understandings of Christianity, and even those of other worldviews and religions. For example:

- evangelistic, polemic debating and dialogue, where we seek to respectfully correct and persuade one another
- co-belligerence and cooperation, working together in matters of common practical and social concern where we agree, or caring appropriately for members who might move between our groups
- learning: other Christians can teach us true and beneficial things on many levels, and we can reflectively bring these ideas back into our own networks
- inviting and visiting: we don't need to fully agree with one another to benefit from books, events and programs that others might offer.

In these cases, it is important to respect the consciences of all involved by not minimizing our differences for the sake of a sentimental niceness. For example, it is not necessary to say "all religions are basically the same" to have peaceful relationships with people of other religions, nor is it necessary to assume that conservative Protestants and Roman Catholics consider one another fellow Christians to be loving and respectful.[31]

Being defined by representation rather than purpose. The strength

---

31 This is the problem with the 'Evangelicals and Catholics together' statement from 1994. Its admirable ambition to work together on issues of common social concern is coupled with assertions like "All who accept Christ as Lord and Saviour are brothers and sisters in Christ. Evangelicals and Catholics are brothers and sisters in Christ ... However imperfect our communion with one another, however deep our disagreements with one another, we recognize that there is but one church of Christ" (Various authors, 'Evangelicals and Catholics together: The Christian mission in the third millennium', *First Things*, May 1994, accessed 27 September 2022 [firstthings.com/article/1994/05/evangelicals-catholics-together-the-christian-mission-in-the-third-millennium]). See also the well-intentioned attempts to say that Muslims and Christians worship the same God, such as: Royal Aal al-Bayt Institute for Islamic Thought, *A Common Word between Us and You*, A Common Word website, 2007, accessed 27 September 2022 (acommonword.com/the-acw-document).

of evangelical networks is that they can be organized in the best way to serve their purposes, rather than to satisfy the needs of equitable denominational and regional representation. In other words, they are *non*-denominational rather than *inter*denominational. While it can still be very wise to include a cross section of denominations and geography (along with age, sex, and culture), this is not always necessary. Phillip Jensen (over)states the case in favour of parachurches being non-denominational:

> Organizational unity instead of Gospel unity is death. The failure of Christian ministries, be they church or para-church, commences when they lose their direction and become organizations that demand organizational unity over theological unity in the service of the gospel ...
>
> The slide from 'non' to 'inter' usually happens un-noticed as politically sensible decisions are made. We are looking for a new committee member or a speaker for a conference, and it is pointed out that if we had somebody from denomination 'X' they would be able to bring greater support to our cause. The politics are right—broadening our base can bring greater strength to our organization, but the basis for the decision is poisonous to the whole ministry.
>
> For a non-denominational ministry to stay on course it must always seek contributions from the person most committed to their cause and most able to make the contribution needed. Genuine non-denominational ministries are totally unconcerned whether every speaker comes from the same background or different ones, for the only concern is whether the new person will be most effective in advancing their cause. When people of less ability are included because of their denomination, the ministry is weakened. When people of great ability who do not share the common theology or vision are included the ministry will inevitably be weakened.[32]

---

32 P Jensen, 'In what are we united?', *Phillip Jensen*, 26 July 2013, accessed 27 September 2022 (phillipjensen.com/in-what-are-we-united).

While he is wrong to insist that a representative interdenominational network *cannot* keep theological and strategic focus, he is right to say that this is a danger. He is also right to point out one great benefit of the non-denominational approach: the focus can sit squarely on building a leadership structure around spiritual giftedness and commitment to the mission.

Expecting participation from everyone. It is not appropriate for an evangelical network to establish itself as compulsory. Like all parachurches, these bodies must be optional enterprises for the benefit of Christians and churches if they choose to take advantage of them. But it can be so easy for those who really benefit from a parachurch network to put undue pressure, and even condemnation, on those who choose not to participate. Carl Trueman bemoans how ...

> ... those who do join parachurch groups as a way of seeking unity often regard those who refuse to be involved in a negative light. Such naysayers are often vulnerable to the accusation from members of that group that it is they who are subverting Christian unity and dividing the body. That is both unfair and wrongheaded.
>
> It is unfair because of the arbitrary nature of the claim. Somebody somewhere decides to form the next big organisation for carrying the gospel forward. They manage to obtain funding for setting up an infrastructure, and then spread their influence via the web, plush conferences and a regular cast of high-profile figures to be the public face of the organisation. This is the perfect context for making demands that everyone else hop on board or get out of the way. Such an approach fails to take into account that [for] those involved in confessional denominations ... it is inappropriate to have the personal vision of a handful of self-selected individuals trump or outflank historic—and biblical— ecclesiastical commitments.[33]

33 Trueman, 'Parachurch groups and the issues of influence and accountability'.

PART 3: CASE STUDIES

I have already mentioned the Tasmanian parachurch event 'Church Together', which describes itself as a gathering of 'the church in southern Tasmania'. The problem with such a vision is that, out of thoughtless enthusiasm, it implies that it is an interdenominational council of *all* the churches in southern Tasmania—therefore, any churches that are not involved or don't share the same enthusiasm for this event are functionally excluded from 'the church in southern Tasmania'. It's not intentional, but it is unfortunate, to my ears at least. A better, fairer (but less catchy) name would really be 'Church*es* Together'.

On a related point, the Lausanne occasional paper on church/para-church relations warns against parachurch leaders setting themselves up as "self-appointed rulers":

> Para-church leaders frequently try to bring together pastors and church leaders, or those in similar ministries in a certain geographical area. Although the response is often most gratifying from the vantage point of apparent Church unity, there are not lacking those who inwardly resent being herded by some self-appointed ruler.[34]

There is a balancing consideration here, however. The reality of Christian community, like any human community, is that patterns of relationship and participation come to be generally understood as matters of courtesy and collegiality. It is often foolish to insist on one's freedom not to attend a pastors' prayer breakfast if doing so just comes across as rude. Likewise, it is unavoidable that certain people will come to have a degree of influence that surpasses formal and obligatory church and denominational governance structures. To stubbornly refuse to acknowledge the role of such leaders at all is both naïve and a potential rejection of a gift Christ has given for the wider benefit of his people.

Meddling in church affairs. The larger the parachurch, and the more formal its membership, the more it can feel the pressure

34 LCWE Commission on Co-operation, *Cooperating in World Evangelization*, p 55.

or pull to be more involved in church affairs than is appropriate. Carl Trueman warns:

> We might say that [the parachurch] can fulfil hand-maiden functions that help the church but they should never seek to lead or control the church.
>
> Yet in all of this, the leadership of these groups needs to demonstrate a clear understanding that they are to serve the church. They must be careful to limit their own power to those boundaries which their account-ability to churches requires. On the whole, that means they should have very limited and modest ambitions. They must make it clear in deed, and not simply in the occasional act of verbal throat-clearing, that they are not the church, do not seek to be the church, and must not be regarded by anyone as the church.[35]

In reality, this prohibition is far from absolute. Leaders and other participants may have many good and justifiable reasons to seek to comment on or influence formal church life. For example, they may be members and office holders in local churches and denominations; they may have areas of expertise that would be useful; they may be invited to address church leaders on a net-work's platform, either through speaking or writing; they may share people, places and issues of overlapping concern; or the parachurch may have been founded in part to function as a kind of 'Fourth Estate', helping to hold local churches and denomina-tions accountable.[36] And yet upholding the unique place of the local church (and, secondarily, the denomination) ought to be a value of all parachurches and a recurring point of evaluation and restraint. There will be plenty of matters about which those

---

35 Trueman, 'Parachurch groups and the issues of influence and accountability'.

36 In the article just cited, Carl Trueman insists that the particular mechanisms of account-ability in churches and denominations are much more transparent and reliable than the structures of parachurch organizations; "Massive influence disconnected from ecclesiasti-cal accountability, whether we are talking individuals or organisations, is unknown in the New Testament". While I agree that church governance is good and right, I am not per-suaded this is the only noble approach. Besides, the level of congregational accountability that Trueman assumes only covers some denominational governance models.

involved in networks might hold strong opinions and even hold vested interests, but where it is still right to keep silent and allow those responsible to do their thing.

The ecumenical movement

In addition to the evangelical movement and the Pentecostal movement, one of the great missionary movements of the 20th century was the ecumenical movement, which sought to envision and facilitate greater organizational and spiritual unity between different denominations, with the hope of bringing about the merging of denominations wherever possible, to heal the fractured institutional state of global Christianity.[37] This movement not only had a missionary ambition but in many ways grew out of missionary activity, as its leaders sought a better way to approach the reality of global Christianity, which they saw as being cluttered with too many denominations and missionary societies. The growing impetus to empower indigenous leaders presented an opportunity to restructure the church scene in many places around the world for a more productive missionary effort.[38]

Reading about this movement from a distance, it seems now to be quaintly marked by the spirit of its age (as all Christian movements are, to some extent). It is hard not to draw parallels with other optimistic attempts to bring the world together in harmonious cooperation, such as the League of Nations and the United Nations.[39] The movement was also marked by a particu-

---

37 As an example, one of the best-known fruits of the ecumenical movement was the creation of the World Council of Churches in 1948.

38 Neill, *A History of Christian Missions*, pp 554-558. "If the Churches knew what they were doing at New Delhi, they have committed themselves to a revolution in their theology, in their understanding of the nature of the Church, in the organization of their manpower, in the distribution of their financial resources" (p 558).

39 Michael Goheen observes how the World Council of Churches and Vatican II share common interest in a united church as being a sign of global unity for the wider world: "the growing recognition that the world is one interlocked unit. The process of modernization, westernization and globalization was sweeping the world into one current of world history" (Goheen, *"As the Father Has Sent Me"*, p 210).

lar ethos and theology: a conviction that it was morally and spiritually necessary to work towards visible, institutional unity across all churches and denominations. This, it was claimed, would further assist world mission by commending the gospel, in keeping with Jesus' prayer:

> My prayer is not for them alone. I pray also for those who will believe in me through their message, that all of them may be one, Father, just as you are in me and I am in you. May they also be in us so that the world may believe that you have sent me. I have given them the glory that you gave me, that they may be one as we are one—I in them and you in me—so that they may be brought to complete unity. Then the world will know that you sent me and have loved them even as you have loved me. (John 17:20-23)

Some ecumenical exhortations are both gushingly idealistic in their hopes and damningly critical of those who are not willing to work towards them. For example, the World Council of Churches' 1962 New Delhi statement declares:

> We believe that the unity which is both God's will and his gift to his Church is being made visible as all in each place who are baptized into Jesus Christ and confess him as Lord and Saviour are brought by the Holy Spirit into one fully committed fellowship, holding the one apostolic faith, preaching the one Gospel, breaking the one bread, joining in common prayer, and having a corporate life reaching out in witness and service to all and who at the same time are united with the whole Christian fellowship in all places and all ages in such wise that ministry and members are accepted by all, and that all can act and speak together as occasion requires for the tasks to which God calls his people.[40]

---

40 Cited in Goheen, *"As the Father Has Sent Me"*, p 209.

More negatively, Lesslie Newbigin declared:

> The disunity of the church is a public denial of the sufficiency of the atonement. It is quite unthinkable that the church should be able effectively to preach that atonement and to become, in fact, the nucleus of the reconciled humanity, while that denial stands. So long as it stands, the world will see in the church not the one place where all men may at last come home, but a series of separatist bodies, each marked by a whole series of cultural peculiarities and idiosyncrasies of belief and practice.[41]

The ecumenical movement was a welcome corrective to the narrow tribal silos and shameful competitiveness on 'the mission field' as well as closer to home. It's such a pity and waste when almost identical denominations, missionary societies and theological colleges preserve distinctives not only on matters of secondary or tertiary importance, but often on things of quaternary and quinary importance! We have to ask: at what point are our 'distinctives' actually just matters of cultural and historical preference?[42]

Ecumenism is also a welcome prompt to continue reaching beyond the comfort of our Christian tribe. It provokes us to make an effort to connect with other Christians. It is right to hope and pray that sometimes, just sometimes, we might come to substantial and robust agreement with fellow Christians by sitting down together and discussing things in love. At the very least, we should be eager to unearth unfair misrepresentations

---

41 Cited in Goheen, *"As the Father Has Sent Me"*, p 213.

42 "Movement-oriented churches think more about reaching the city, while institutionalized churches put emphasis on growing their church's particular expression or denomination. In general, leaders of churches with movement dynamics have a high tolerance for ambiguity and organizational messiness. What matters is that people hear the gospel and are converted and discipled, which results in cooperation with people from outside their own membership and involves learning from them. As always, balance is crucial. A sectarian, highly institutionalized church or agency may refuse to cooperate with bodies that don't share all its beliefs, including secondary and tertiary ones. We rightly criticize this posture as being antithetical to movements. But so is the opposite posture. It is important to be doctrinally vigilant and willing, when necessary, to respectfully contend for important theological truths when we believe that ministry partners are losing their grasp on those things" (Keller, *Center Church*, pp 349-350).

of other people's beliefs and practices in the name of truth and righteousness.[43]

The ecumenical movement also points out to us that institutional allegiance and interaction cannot be entirely separated from personal relationships. Institutions are made up of individuals and represent the values and priorities of those individuals. Institutions function in symbolic and paradigmatic ways, showing what should and could be worked out in our personal and social lives. If nothing else, it is right to move away from an institutional church environment marked by suspicion, hostility and ignorance. In many cases, just as with narrower evangelical networks (see above), the simple act of spending time together, talking, worrying, praying and dreaming can be a catalyst for wonderful new ventures which we can meaningfully pursue together, despite our differences.

Problems with the ecumenical movement

The advocates of ecumenism do not make a strong case for large-scale institutional unity. It is no surprise that this movement resonates naturally with those Christians who believe in an institutional expression of the visible church beyond the local congregation.[44] Advocates of ecumenism take Bible passages that speak about unity in local church fellowships but apply those passages broadly to denominational mergers; Bible passages which describe the ultimate spiritual oneness of the universal church are applied to the work of creating one national or global institution. This is the context in which Broughton Knox and Donald Robinson's emphasis on the heavenly church and the local church (see part I) was formulated and propounded so vigorously.[45]

---

43 See a good discussion in Tuit, *A Study and Comparison*, pp 177-182.
44 For a discussion of these matters, see chapter 3.
45 Kuhn, *The Ecclesiology of Donald Robinson and D. Broughton Knox;* so also Kuiper, writing of John 17, says it is plain that "Jesus was thinking primarily of the *spiritual* unity of believers" (Kuiper, *The Glorious Body of Christ*, p 42).

I believe that diversity of denominations is unavoidable—not to mention important, so that the consciences and convictions of different groups can be honoured.[46] Open discussion across denominational divides might, in fact, facilitate more genuine loving unity than the unity created by institutional mergers.

The reality of ecumenical unity is often much less glorious for the average Christian and the watching world than is claimed. Forbearance and reconciliation among diverse Christians in a local fellowship is inspiring and intriguing to the watching world; likewise, inter-church efforts in charitable work. But hierarchical officials meeting in hotel conference rooms to co-sign formal statements and pose for cameras in their suits and robes is much less so.

Such 'peace talks' are absolutely necessary for political peace, because world leaders actually command armies and control borders. By contrast, representatives of various church organizations have much more modest influence. Even where the result is the amazing achievement of merging two denominations or an agreement on new rules of engagement in missionary work, such decisions remain primarily institutional and ceremonial in nature. I do not want to deny that occasional ecumenical negotiations really have resolved significant practical issues in local churches, mission fields and wider society. Nor do I want to diminish other wonderful trickle-down effects that can flow from these initiatives—the beautiful personal friendships they can facilitate, or the majestic gatherings of corporate proclamation, prayer and praise. But I do want to suggest that the more

---

46 For this reason, I am unpersuaded by the strong case by John Frame that all denominations are the result of sin and so should be repented of; see J Frame, *Evangelical Reunion: Denominations and the one body of Christ*, Baker Book House, 1991. (See the similarly strong case made by Spykman: "All attempts to justify disunity are therefore contraband. This includes appealing to ecclesiastical 'invisibility' as a way of escape into a docetic concept of the church" [Spykman, *Reformational Theology*, pp 443-444].) Of course, sin often causes division, or at least makes it worse. But the complexity of managing agreement and disagreement across large groups of human beings is unavoidably fraught for more practical reasons. For a recognition of the importance of respecting freedom of conscience, as well as the benefits that can come from diversity in denominations, see Bavinck, *Reformed Dogmatics*, pp 604-605.

institutional the ecumencial movement becomes, the less wonderful it tends to be.

Large ecumenical movements can lead to a distortion of the nature of Christian ministry. In order for ecumenical institutions to be established and maintained, pastors, bishops and missionaries need to give a significant amount of time to administrative processes, travel, and various kinds of committee meetings. It is hard to maintain all this while serving in a local church or parachurch ministry. Often, the result is that a new caste of Christian leaders is established: ecumenical diplomats and administrators. Sometimes, these leaders have retired from grassroots ministry and have lost touch with its challenges and priorities. But the laudable desire for representation from younger Christian movements can backfire by pulling their leaders out of local mission work and into the world of hotel function rooms and business lunches. Denominations and parachurches can create the same kind of phenomena.

The important thing is to emphasize that these wider structures and their leaders exist to serve the local church and mission. The ecumenical movement, with its emphasis on institutional unity, is especially likely to miss this. Phillip Jensen's theological subversion of Anglican ecclesiology captures this idea:

> In the New Testament the bishop is the elder ... the two words are used interchangeably ... Today, who fits the role of bishop? The Lambeth bishops don't ... What is the Lambeth bishop, then? He is a denominational administrator. He is an administrator of the association of churches. He is the one who is involved in the licensing of properties. He is a real-estate agent—a trustee of the trust deeds of properties around the land—set aside for committees that look after widows and orphans. He is a deacon.[47]

---

47 Jensen, 'Why bishops are deacons'. Jensen is using the title 'Lambeth bishops' to designate those who are traditionally called 'bishops' in the Anglican Communion (and who are usually therefore invited to the decennial Lambeth Conference). In context, he is using this term to differentiate them from the leaders of local churches, who he says are what the New Testament describes as 'bishops'.

Even those persuaded by a traditional version of Episcopalianism should, I think, grant that they best fulfil their work when they recognize that their role is to serve the needs of the local church as meekly and unobtrusively as possible.[48]

Beware an unsatisfactory drift towards lowest-common-denominator theology. Unity between organizations and denominations requires navigating theological differences. The ever-present risk is that important matters are sidelined for the sake of unity, whether by being removed entirely from confessional statements or through ambiguous wording. For example, 'Evangelicals and Catholics Together' removes the controversial word 'alone' from its statement on justification: "We affirm together that we are justified by grace through faith because of Christ." In an environment of relational warmth and social pressure, it takes leaders of strong principle to think clearly and to stand firm, even at the risk of seeming petty and divisive. In this way, ecumenical movements threaten to both violate the conscience of brothers and sisters who are more rigid in their theological views and to presume to condemn them for having a 'sinful party spirit' and for 'dividing the body of Christ'.

Ecumenical efforts eventually reach a point of diminishing returns. Since institutional unity is not the imperative that many in the ecumenical movement claim, a certain degree of godly realism ought to be employed in assessing any ecumenical enterprise. While there is some value to pursuing mutual understanding and cooperation, there surely must come a point where further ecumenical efforts should be declared a waste of

---

48 See 'The limits of the denomination in serving the wellbeing of local churches' in chapter 3. Bruce Ballantine-Jones outlines ways in which the Anglican Diocese of Sydney seeks to do this, while also highlighting other dynamics (such as investment income and organizational size and complexity) that have led to increased centralism; see Ballantine-Jones, *Inside Sydney*, pp 1-27. He writes: "In Sydney, the Archbishop has to share ... power with a democratic and often independently minded synod ... Limiting factors to that power are the security and tenure of clergy, the presence of strong-minded, theologically astute lay leaders and the effects of legislation which distributes functions away from the Archbishop." On the other hand, "the Archbishop ... is the single most powerful political element in the Diocese. He makes clerical appointments, has control over regulations relating to worship centres and variations to statutory services, and he can veto legislation of the Synod" (p 14).

time and effort and a distraction from the cause of the gospel. RB Kuiper writes:

> Neither extreme denominationalism nor extreme unionism has a remedy for division within the church of Christ. The former has no interest in a remedy and would let the disease run wild. The latter offers a remedy that is more fatal than the disease. Must we conclude that there is no remedy? The answer of *realistic idealism* to that question remains to be presented ... On the one hand, we must see to it that our idealism remains realistic; on the other hand, it is no less important that our realism remain idealistic.[49]

49 Kuiper, *The Glorious Body of Christ*, pp 49-51. He goes on to give several great practical suggestions: 1) Refuse fellowship with heretical denominations; 2) confront in-roads of heresy in orthodox denominations; 3) conservatives should accept their failures in overly rigid theology, traditionalism and sectarianism; 4) members of different denominations should seek to learn from one another and cooperate with one another; 5) those denominations which are extremely similar should work towards organizational unification; see pp 51-55.

Chapter 13: The Christian household and informal ministries[1]

t might seem strange to include a chapter on Christian house-holds in this book. After all, the household is hardly a parachurch, is it? Marriage and family are institutions of the created order, rather than new covenant institutions like the church. How can we speak about the family as 'parachurch' when we're simply born into it? How can we speak about the household as parachurch when this is the place where we eat, sleep, read, and sit around watching TV?

Despite these questions, a moment's reflection tells us that the Christian household is one of the first contexts in which much non-formal ministry and mission can happen. In fact, it seems that many of the very first Christian churches met in houses, and many continue to do so today.[2] Moreover, let's return for a moment to the definition of parachurch I offered in chapter 2: *organized Christian activity which is distinct from the visible, institutional church.* Family devotions, share-house Bible

---

1 An earlier version of this material was delivered in sermon form in 2019 at Mount Stuart Presbyterian Church, Hobart.

2 For examples of house churches recorded in the New Testament, see Romans 16:3-5, 1 Corinthians 16:19 and Colossians 4:15.

studies, and deliberate efforts to invite a mix of Christian and non-Christian friends into the home with the goal of talking about serious and spiritual things all fit within this broad definition. I deliberately proposed a very elastic definition, for it seems to me that without such a definition there is a risk of ignoring the interface between the local church and these kinds of informal contexts for ministry and mission.

Perhaps the biggest risk in pushing the boundaries of this broad definition to include households is the initial jarring confusion that says, "I thought 'parachurch' meant Christian unions and missions societies, not family devotions!" True, we may be pushing our definition to its limits to include the household. What's more, even the idea that 'churches sometimes meet in households' has its limits, for as soon as a household welcomes outsiders for church-related purposes, there is a sense in which the 'household' has become a 'house church'; the two things remain distinct. Therefore, we need to bear in mind the boundaries and the complex interplay between church relationships and household relationships.

But while there are limitations and potential pitfalls to including households in our analysis, there are also significant benefits. For one thing, it offers us a fresh way of looking at an issue and a great starting point for considering the whole range of organic, informal parachurch activity.[3] As we will see again and again in this chapter, many of the important principles for household ministry are also highly relevant to other informal parachurch structures, such as: small-groups and one-to-one discipling ministries in a local church;[4] discipleship ministries conducted by parachurch organizations; and historical examples like the 18th-century Methodism 'societies'.[5] Rather than treat-

---

3   There is a risk with many of the various types of parachurches discussed in this book that we fail to observe significant differences between each of them. This is one reason why part III of the book is necessary.

4   My definition of 'parachurch' is intentionally broad enough to include subunits of a local church, such as a Bible study group, women's ministry or leadership team.

5   Methodism was the name given to the movement that grew out of the 18th-century Great Awakening revivals in the British Isles and the American colonies.

ing these other structures separately, I will simply highlight points of particular relevance in the process of discussing the Christian household as the primary case study. They are, of course, not exactly the same as households, but the points of similarity are illuminating.

Perhaps more importantly, this topic forces us to consider how the relationships we are most likely to take for granted could prove to be fertile ground for rich, wonderful, intentional Christian ministry. And because the purpose of this book is to discuss ministry and mission beyond the local church, it would be a significant oversight to omit the ways in which ministry and mission take place in our families, our households, and even in friendship circles and a range of other fellowships that are much less formal than a typical parachurch organization.

First, however, a point about terminology.

'Family' is a slippery word

I have deliberately chosen to primarily use the word 'household' rather than 'family' in this chapter. This is because I want to recognize that there are kinds of households other than nuclear families and co-habiting extended families. Indeed, even nuclear families might involve others as members of their households. 'Family' has also become a slippery word in politics and ethics, where it can refer to:

- biological relation
- legal relation, such as adoption and 'in-law' relations
- a stable home/household, which might involve all sorts of configurations, including nuclear family, extended family, bachelor and/or spinster siblings, same-sex parents, a boarding school, an army unit, or a monastery
- a moral assessment of a legal or biological relation (for example, an illegitimate child might legally be considered 'not part of the family', but calling a household a 'family' can function as a kind of moral affirmation)

- a community of belonging, such as a sporting community
- a community of shared cause, such as a workplace or political group
- membership of the spiritual family of God.[6]

Moreover, the word 'family' also carries with it emotional overtones and associated expectations, drawn from our personal experience and cultural background. Each familial relationship has different rights, duties and dynamics, with significant diversity across cultures.

Because of this ambiguity in the meaning of the word, it is not immediately clear what it means to say, for example, "This same-sex-parent couple is a legitimate family, too". Does this statement mean that we should acknowledge that such households exist? That they are entitled to legal rights and protections? That such households can do a good job of loving and providing for their members? Or that such households are an equally desirable structure of social organization?

Similarly, when someone says "the church should be a family", they might be seeking a casual informality that marks the small nuclear family, or a level of commitment that they believe is currently lacking, or the intimacy of a close family, or perhaps they are reacting against formal employment practices.[7] Likewise, when the leader of a Christian organization asks their employees to go above and beyond because "we are family", the appeal blurs together the sense in which the employees are brothers and sisters in Christ, the sense in which they are members of a fellowship in a shared cause, and perhaps also some expectation of loyalty and sacrifice attached to associations with biological family and the household. But as Carl Trueman says

---

6   I first explored these ideas on my blog: M Lynch, '"Family" is a slippery word!', *Christian Reflections blog*, 7 August 2016, accessed 28 September 2022 (genevapush.com/blogs/xian_reflections/family-is-a-slippery-word). See also 'We need a Venn Diagram for family, home, marriage and legal significant other', *Christian Reflections blog*, 16 September 2017, accessed 28 September 2022 (genevapush.com/blogs/xian_reflections/we-need-a-venn-diagram-for-family-home-marriage-and-legal-significant-other-2).

7   For example, P Jensen 'Catching eggs', *Phillip Jensen*, 18 October 2013, accessed 28 September 2022 (phillipjensen.com/catching-eggs).

when speaking of his leadership in theological education:

> I stopped using the language of family ... First, because families don't fire people. Businesses fire people occasionally. So the analogy breaks down. Secondly ... families only have to remind themselves that they're families when they're dysfunctional ... We need to be aware of the way language often functions in Christian environments ... Pious language is co-opted in a way that makes it impossible to think clearly about the issue at hand.[8]

Perhaps a better way of thinking about institutional church relationships is that the church is like a family business—family members involved in a formal enterprise together.[9]

So the word 'household', as I am using it here, is broader, more concrete, and less ideologically ambiguous than 'family'. 'Household' includes *all those participating together in a stable living arrangement.* The household is not restricted to biological and legal family, nor to a sedentary (as opposed to a nomadic) lifestyle—a 'household' doesn't need a 'house' of bricks and mortar. To identify something as a household is not to make any preliminary value judgements about it. It is, in the first place, a descriptive label.

The importance of families and households in Scripture

In the Old Testament, God's word is often directed to the household. Take, for example, the directives to instruct children about

---

8   Trueman, 'Follow the money'. See also Cole, *Developing Female Leaders*: "There is often pressure for church staff members to have this kind of personal connection ... They feel they must 'do life together' or 'want to hang out together' to be productive teammates. I think this creates unnecessary pressure on teams and relationships, and it sets up our working dynamics to 'feel less,' even though we are being very effective for our churches" (pp 220-221).

9   Miroslav Volf proposes the category of 'sibling-friend' to describe the uniqueness of church relationships; see Volf, *After Our Likeness*, p 180.

the meaning of the Lord's saving work in Exodus 12:24-27 and Deuteronomy 6:20-25, or the instruction from a father to a son in the book of Proverbs.[10] The law of Moses also accepts and reinforces larger family and tribal units. These ideas are further reinforced when we remember that the Old Testament people of God were not only a religious community but also a geographical, political and ethnic nation. The promises of the Lord were in the first instance made to Abraham and his descendants (Gen 12:1-3). In the New Testament, this same reality is seen in the accounts of household conversions in Acts, the references to household churches in Paul's letters, and in the fact that Christian discipleship includes living out the gospel in the context of marriage, the biological family, and the household.[11]

Among the documents from the 17th-century Westminster Assembly, we find not only the Confession of Faith, the Catechisms, and *The Directory for Public Worship*, but also *The Directory for Family Worship*, which begins by recognizing the power of godly Christian households:

> By God's mercy, public worship has been established in this land in great purity. Besides this however, it is both expedient and necessary for each person to be involved in "secret worship", and for families to worship together privately as a family. By this, along with our national reformation, the profession and power of godliness, both personal and domestic, shall be advanced.[12]

---

10 It seems that, within the structure of Deuteronomy 12-26, the 5th commandment is taken as a heading for all kinds of human authority and life 'in the land' (16:18-18:22). See the discussion in JH Walton, 'The Decalogue structure of the Deuteronomic Law', in DG Firth and PS Johnston (eds), *Interpreting Deuteronomy: Issues and approaches*, IVP Academic, 2012, pp 93-117.

11 For example, see: 1 Cor 7:1-16; Col 3:16-4:1; Eph 5:18-6:9; 1 Tim 5:1-8; 1 Pet 3:1-7. These observations are taken to have even greater theological importance for those who hold a kind of covenant theology that says children of believers share (in some way) in the new covenant and so should be baptized as infants and considered members of the church.

12 Westminster Assembly, *The Directory for Family Worship (modernised)*, Evangelical Presbyterian Church in England and Wales website, 1647, accessed 28 September 2022 (epcew.org.uk/resources/the-directory-for-family-worship-1647-modernised).

Now that we have laid the groundwork, we can explore some of the many benefits that come from recognizing the importance of ministry in households.

1. The Christian household is a natural context for ministry

The Christian household provides many opportunities for "teaching, rebuking, correcting and training in righteousness" (2 Tim 3:16), as well as for evangelism and all sorts of practical and emotional care. Because households are made up of a relatively small number of people, usually in regular contact, there is significant potential for intimate and personalized ministry. The New Testament is full of exhortations to hospitality, which, in addition to being a noble activity in its own right, can also bring many other benefits.[13] In the chaos of life, parents of young families often feel like they are failing to do good deeds or real ministry because they are so busy just keeping the family afloat. It is important for them to remember that by providing well for their immediate family, they are offering a stable unit of care so that the wider church or society is not burdened (2 Thess 3:6-13; 1 Tim 5:16). By living out a godly example, teaching the word of God (whether conversationally or more formally) and praying, they are doing invaluable gospel work.

The same is true of informal parachurches. It seems that genuine conversion and spiritual growth depend more on having the gospel ministered to you in the household or other informal contexts than on mere attendance at a Sunday church

---

13 S Chan, *Evangelism in a Skeptical World: How to make the unbelievable news about Jesus more believable*, Zondervan, 2018, pp 39-51, 115-118. See also R Butterfield, *The Gospel Comes with a House Key: Practicing radically ordinary hospitality in our post-Christian world*, Crossway, 2018; and T Chester, *A Meal with Jesus: Discovering grace, community, and mission around the table*, Re:Lit series, Crossway, 2011.

gathering.[14] One of the best 'next steps' for someone investigating Christianity, struggling to grow as a Christian or seeking to develop as a leader is to bring them into some kind of informal ministry connection. The invitation to meet regularly with one or two others to talk about God's word or to join a small group can make all the difference in someone's spiritual life. Moreover, there are some special needs and stages of life at which a person will be best served in the household or some other informal ministry, rather than through the formal structures and meetings of the local church. Those with serious illness, special needs, language barriers, unusual career demands and other such circumstances often need to rely heavily on informal ministry. And that's okay, because—as we have seen throughout this book—there is much more to God's work in the world than the formal structures of the local church.

2. Building blocks of the local church

Just as the household functions as a building block for the wider society, the Christian household usually functions as the building block for the local church and other parachurch ministries. Church leaders can slip into thinking of their ministry in terms of its organizational structures such as small-group ministry, men's ministry, women's ministry, or youth and children's ministry. But it is important to remember how powerful, foundational and beneficial the Christian household is in the life of the local church.[15] Programs should strengthen and leverage

14 Ed Stetzer and Eric Geiger's research into small groups in the United States discovered that 67% of regular group attenders read their Bible regularly versus only 27% among non-group members; 64% of regular group attenders pray for their church and/or church leaders regularly, whereas only 30% of non-group attenders do; 82% of group attenders pray for fellow Christians versus 54% of non-group attenders; and 79% of group attenders confess sins to God and ask forgiveness, compared to 54% of non-group attenders. See E Stetzer and E Geiger, *Transformational Groups: Creating a new scorecard for groups*, B&H Publishing Group, 2014, p 43.

15 At many times in history, the household has operated in the same way that small group structures do today. *The Directory for Family Worship* certainly speaks of the family in very similar terms. Perhaps one reason for the increasing need for small-group ministry is the greater transience of modern urban life.

Christian households, not undermine or overlook them.[16] When the local church nurtures and upholds the household, these healthy households will boost the overall health and vibrancy of the church. Likewise, in cases where families are broken, unhealthy or in crisis, it shouldn't be surprising that the local church will experience the effects of this brokenness.

Although our identity in Christ supersedes our biological family or our social position as our primary identity (see, for example, Jesus' deliberately shocking words in Luke 14:26), it doesn't erase it. While there "is neither Jew nor Gentile, neither slave nor free, nor is there male and female" in Christ Jesus (Gal 3:28), we continue to live out our Christian faith in this age in the context of ethnic (Rom 15:26-27), social (Eph 6:5-9) and familial relationships (Eph 5:21-6:4), serving Christ's kingdom purposes in and among the kingdoms of this world.[17] Even the local church is both a sacred and a secular institution,[18] and to the extent that the local church is part of this present age (the original meaning of 'secular') its structures conform to the God-given created realities of this age (seen most clearly in biblical instructions about the participation of men and women in church leadership).[19] This is true, even as we reject human categories of ethnic, social and economic division.

---

16 *A Declaration of the Complementary Roles of Church and Family* says, "*We deny/reject* the current trend in churches that ignores the family unit, is blind to strengthening it, systematically segregates it, and does not properly equip her members to be faithful family members" (Church & Family Life, *A Declaration of the Complementary Roles of Church and Family*, Church and Family Life website, 2020, article XI, emphasis original, accessed 28 September 2022 [churchandfamilylife.com/about/276]). While I am uncomfortable with the shrill tone of the introductory remarks of this declaration, and don't believe the church must be as integrated as its authors think, much of its content is very balanced and helpful.

17 There is no biblical reason to think that we cease to be male or female, or Jew or Gentile, in the new creation. The marriage, family, social, economic and national structures attached to these characteristics pass away, but not the characteristics themselves.

18 The church functions as a "temporal-eschatological" entity; see Allison, *Sojourners and Strangers*, pp 148-157.

19 "If gender does shape the structure of authority relationships to the degree that a relationship is itself grounded in gender difference, and church is familial in nature, then gender is going to be a factor in how relationships in church work" (M Baddeley, *Authority and Gender* [unpublished lecture notes], Queensland Theological College, 2014, p 37).

As an example of the enduring power of the structures of this age, Jack Sparks, the founder of a ministry that experimented with Christian communalism in the 1970s and 80s, observed how the realities of human relationships influenced their efforts:

> Mostly they succeed where there is a centering around a family. You ordinarily do not succeed where you have families having to share all their facilities all the time. You have to plan for privacy for families and you have to have a sensitivity to others' needs.[20]

Just as church leaders do well to align the church to family and household relationships, so informal ministry leaders do well to align their activities with the local church: they work best when they come to operate as building blocks of the local church, rather than operating in independence from the wider church. Training small-group leaders, for example, to work at building alignment with the whole church will strengthen the whole church. This will be reflected in announcements, prayers, and possibly even a teaching program that is integrated with the Sunday preaching. There are great opportunities for the local church to go with the flow of the various informal dynamics at work in congregational life.

3. Protects us from unhelpful or even dangerous patterns of church life

Local churches can become unhealthy when they presume to dominate the lives of their members, or when their members expect too much of them. One unhelpful pattern is to place high expectations on what it means for the local church to function as a family. While family and household metaphors are used to describe the church, these metaphors do not dictate that the local church should function exactly like a biological family or household in every respect. The sheer number of 'brothers

---

20 Quoted in Smith, *The Origins, Nature, and Significance of the Jesus Movement*, pp 158-159.

and sisters in Christ' means we cannot share the same degree of intimacy and inter-dependence as biological siblings or a household. Being a spiritual family means we should treat one another with affection and equality, but it is unbiblical to demand a certain standard of intimacy, informality or cooperative living simply on this basis.[21] This is why an appeal to the church as 'family' is an inadequate reason to reject mega-churches. Likewise, something has gone wrong in our thinking when we oppose plans to plant a new church because it will be "breaking up the family". Emphasizing the distinct integrity and value of the Christian household can restrain some of these negative tendencies.

Much more serious still are destructive religious movements that gain control over their members by entirely removing them from family and friends. By contrast, Christians are commanded to live out their exclusive commitment to Christ in such a way that still honours family relationships, marriage relationships, and even how to live with the terrible reality of slavery.[22] Celebrating the meaningful spiritual formation and ministry that takes place in the household helps to protect Christians against the dangerous, totalizing demands of controlling leaders. Mature churches unite independent adults in common mind and heart by the preaching of the gospel and by the power of the Spirit who lives in us, not by infantilizing and dominating their members.

---

21 Differences between the church and the biological family include the possibility of romantic relationships between brothers and sisters in Christ; the lesser degree of fixity and loyalty to a single local church 'household'; and the normality of hiring (and firing) church staff.

22 See Matt 15:3-9; 1 Cor 7:1-14; Eph 6:5-9. Dietrich Bonhoeffer argues that spiritual community should be built on Christian love and not on mere human affection. But he later insists that this doesn't mean there can be no family or friendship relationships in spiritual community. If anything, such relationships are more self-conscious regarding the difference between human and spiritual affection, and less likely to confuse mere human rapport with spiritual community. I'm not persuaded that these two threads need to be so rigorously interrogated; see D Bonhoeffer, *Life Together* (JW Doberstein trans), Harper-One, 1954, pp 31-39.

Unhelpful attitudes and patterns of household ministry

1. Household ministry can jeopardize our allegiance to the Lord

God's word is not solely positive about households. A very strong strand of thought—especially in the New Testament—qualifies, relativizes and even critiques the biological family. Jesus warns repeatedly about the possibility of the biological family becoming an obstacle to following him (e.g. Matt 10:21-23, 34-39). In his own life, although a godly and caring son (Luke 2:51; John 19:25-27), he did not consider his biological family to be primary. Rather, the temple was his true "father's house" (Luke 2:49), and he understood that "whoever does God's will is my brother and sister and mother" (Mark 3:31-35). So also for us, our first allegiance must be to the Lord, not to our earthly families and households.

The spiritual family of God is a rich theological theme in Scripture. Family titles are used to describe the first and second member of the trinity: the Father and the Son. God's relationship with his people is also described in familial terms: in the Old Testament, Israel was his "firstborn son" (Exod 4:22-23); in the New Testament, we are both his "bride" (Rev 21:2) and his adopted "children" (Rom 8:14-17). As a result of our relationship with God the Father in Christ, we also become 'brothers and sisters' in Christ to one another, with Christ himself as "the firstborn among many brothers and sisters" (Rom 8:29). Further still, although there ought to be no extreme hierarchy among Christians—where leaders are to be called 'father' (or 'teacher', for that matter) in a way that undermines God's ultimate fatherhood and our fundamental equality (Matt 23:9)—the relationships of older to younger (Rom 16:13; 2 John 1, 4, 13; 1 Tim 5:1-2), evangelist to convert (1 Cor 4:14-16) and mentor to trainee (1 Cor 4:17; Phil 2:22; 1 Tim 1:1-2, 18; 2 Tim 1:1-2; 2:1; Titus

1:4) can all be described using parent-child language.[23]

As a natural consequence of these truths, it is fitting for the church to be described as "God's household" (1 Tim 3:15). It is important to give great weight to these biblical teachings to avoid the risks that come with unhealthy attitudes and patterns of household ministry.

2. Household ministry can neglect the broken family, the mixed marriage, the widow(er), the orphan, the bereaved parent, the single, the childless and the disowned

Without paying attention to the many kinds of possible households, a strong focus on 'household ministry' can devolve into a strong focus on 'nuclear family ministry'. In many cases this can lead to an accidental but painful neglect of those who do not fit this model. When the Sunday morning gathering is called 'Family Church' and the Sunday afternoon gathering is called a 'Youth Service', when much is made of Mother's Day and Father's Day, or when children's ministry and marriage support seem to dominate the church programming, then those without a Christian spouse, those without children or those who have lost parents will feel pushed to the periphery of church life. Ironically, then, this attempt to focus on 'families' can undermine our spiritual family connection as brothers and sisters in Christ and as children of the living God.

Each Mother's Day, I greatly appreciate how the pastor of my church leads us in prayer. He always makes a point of praying for those who long to be mothers but can't, those who have lost mothers or children, and those who are estranged from mothers or children (and likewise on Father's Day).

23 Does Paul call Timothy and Titus his 'sons' simply because they were converted through him? Or (as I think likely) does he also suggest that they are his 'sons' because they learned the ministry of the gospel from him? As an aside on the language of mentor and trainee, I have used the word 'trainee' because I dislike the neologism 'mentee', but I would very much love to introduce 'telemachus' as the complement to 'mentor', since the original man named 'Mentor' was a mentor to Telemachus in Homer's *Odyssey*. But I admit that this is both pretentious and obscure.

3. Household ministry can justify investing too much in this world rather than the world to come

While the household is a powerful context for spiritual ministry and self-sacrificial good deeds, it can easily become a place of worldly comfort and ambition. While the Bible teaches that believers ought to give a priority of care to our immediate family (1 Tim 5:4-8), this does not mean we should do this to the exclusion of all others. As those who have been adopted into God's family, we must beware of family-only selfishness that is not open to the outsider.

One way of speaking about the local church is as a 'family of families'.[24] While there is truth in this expression, it can be misleading. The fundamental relationship of all believers to one another is through our union in Christ by the Spirit, not through a network and hierarchy of familial relationships. And although the church should indeed honour and strengthen marriages, families and households, its ministry and mission cannot be entirely ordered and dictated by this. Not only could such an emphasis force the church to structure itself around the worldly needs and desires of biological families; it could even be co-opted to give heads of families too much spiritual power in the home and the church (see point 5 below).[25]

4. Household ministry can be made too heavy a burden

While there is much potential for household ministry, there is no detailed standard to which every Christian must conform. Passionate advocates of household ministry and hospitality ministry can imply or downright insist that truly devout Christians ought to be engaged in a certain (high) level of hospitality and gospel intentionality.

---

24 Vision Forum Ministries, *A Biblical Confession for Uniting Church and Family*, Equip the Family blog, 2002, article VI, accessed 28 September 2022 (dschadt.files.wordpress.com/ 2007/01/a-biblical-confession-for-uniting-church-and-family-vision-forum-ministries.pdf).

25 M Holst, 'The patriarchy movement: Five areas of grave concern', *Reformation 21*, 10 October 2016, accessed 28 September 2022 (reformation21.org/blog/2016/10/the-patriarchy-movement-five-a.php).

For example, Rosaria Butterfield's book *The Gospel Comes with a House Key* describes her family's remarkable work of hospitality, including weekly 'open-house nights' to a broad range of people in the community.[26] She shows how these practices flow out of the gospel, unpacks how her family does things, and urges others to follow her example. But in the process she arguably implies that all faithful Christians and churches should pattern their households after her astonishing example.[27]

In an interview with Butterfield and her husband, Kent, Jonathan Leeman says he is "trying to sympathize with the reader who picks up this book, reads it and just feels overwhelmed ... 'Oh my gosh, I just can't imagine how I would do all of that. I'm stressed out just reading it!'" Leeman then quotes a section towards the end of the book that recognizes the different capacities people have and the need for husbands and wives to work together. And he insightfully comments: "Wonderful paragraph ... [but] it's just one paragraph in 220 pages."[28] Those who are capable of extraordinary work (in this or in any other area of life) sometimes fail to appreciate how extraordinary they really are, and so presume to call people to an overwhelming standard. Those who are passionate about any ministry, including household ministry, can slip into unhelpful patterns of implying that all Christians ought to be more active in this particular type of Christian service.

This is an area where we must uphold freedom and celebrate diversity in the Christian life. The Bible does indeed celebrate hospitality and exhort us to practice it. But as with many positive instructions (like 'be generous'), it does not bring with it a

---

26 Butterfield, *The Gospel Comes with a House Key*.

27 Regular use of the word 'daily' suggests that she is proposing a universal standard for hospitality. Also, Butterfield's beautiful descriptions of her pattern of life suggest (to this reader, at least) that the pattern is being held up as an ideal.

28 J Leeman, *J Leeman interviews Kent and Rosaria Butterfield: On Hospitality and the Gospel* [interview audio file], Pastors' Talk episode 67, 9Marks, 4 December 2018, accessed 28 September 2022 (9marks.org/conversations/episode-67-on-hospitality-and-the-gospel-with-kent-rosaria-butterfield). In the interview, the Butterfields accept this opportunity to reinforce freedom and grace, but I personally felt the point was still conceded rather than fully emphasized.

particular degree. A Christian certainly ought not be *in*hospitable, but should foster the virtue of a hospitable heart. But the exact degree of hospitality will vary dramatically in frequency and intensity, depending on many factors. Different degrees of household privacy can be preserved while practicing hospitality, just as different degrees of private property can be preserved while being generous. Being more prescriptive than the Bible on this, or any other issue, is never right in the end.

5. Household ministry can undermine the structure of the local church

Some households, especially biological families, can become so involving and self-sufficient, even with spiritual matters, that they have little interest in giving generously to the community or to the ministry of the local church (or to the wider gospel ecosystem, for that matter). Even if interested, they might leave themselves with little capacity to be involved. Such families can operate as insular, impenetrable units: they arrive at church together, sit at church together, and leave church together. There is little deep fellowship or service that extends beyond this unit, and that which does tends to be centripetal, drawing others into the sphere of influence of the household.

Worse, households can become hubs of dissent against the leadership and even the doctrine of the local church, allowing an unhealthy, divisive or theologically eccentric ministry to take root.

The Directory for Family Worship warns against these temptations. Part V warns against "an idler, who has no particular calling, or vagrant person under pretence of a calling" who is "tainted with errors, or aiming at division" and who "may be ready (after that manner) to creep into houses, and lead captive silly and unstable souls". Parts VI and VII of the *Directory* warn against households joining together in such a way that leads to total independence from and neglect of the wider church:

> 7. Even though God has clearly used and blessed the gathering together of different families for worship in

times of great difficulty and trouble [when the usual order of things can often be overturned] yet in times of peace and stability and gospel purity, we believe that multiple gatherings of families should not be encouraged. It tends to limit the fuller participation of each family and family member; and in time can prejudice against the need for public ministry, cause divisions between families in congregations, and even split the Church.[29]

Similar warnings could be given about any parachurch activity: they must beware of becoming all-absorbing, subversive or destructive.[30] I know of several instances where something like this has happened in youth and young adult ministries. The group experiences a season of revival under gifted young leaders, and over time the members of the group develop their own vision and values (if not theology) that are slightly divergent from the wider church. This is made worse where there is no compelling leadership from the church pastor, or if the pastor generously gives more freedom and resources to the young leaders but without providing any consistent direction, expectations and accountability. The youth group soon becomes more ambitious in its programs, and loyalty transfers almost entirely from the local church to the youth ministry.

This kind of subversive upheaval can be a good thing. It may be the way that reformation comes to a stale church or denomination. Or conflict might come to a head, leading to a new church being planted, which, although painful, may in God's providence turn out for good in the long term.

Nevertheless, it is crucial that those involved in such groups take care to honour the leadership of the local church, even as they might seek to gently push the boundaries. The more regular,

---

29 Westminster Assembly, *The Directory for Family Worship*. Martyn Lloyd-Jones saw this danger as a major problem with the *ecclesiola in ecclesia* ('little church in the church') strategy of certain Protestant groups in mainland Europe; see Lloyd-Jones, 'Ecclesiola in ecclesia', sec IV.

30 Stuart Piggin gives the example of 'the Fellowship', a sinless perfectionist movement accused of elitism and controlling behaviour, whose members remained part of existing Anglican and Presbyterian churches in Melbourne; see Piggin, *Spirit, Word and World*, p 118.

formal and substantial any parachurch is, the more diligent it should be about conducting itself in a way that honours the local church (see chapter 5). It is also important that church leaders be alert to these dynamics and have the courage and grace to handle them well, rather than tolerate them with benign passivity or smother them through draconian micromanagement.

In the previous section I wrote that strong biological families can be a safeguard against destructive cult-like dynamics in the local church. The opposite can also be true. The *Declaration of the Complementary Roles of Church and Family* rightly says, "We *deny/reject* as unscriptural the concept of the autonomous family in total isolation from or insubordinate to the church".[31] A Christian marriage or family can itself become a context of spiritual, physical and emotional abuse, which can even be justified by distorted appeals to biblical teaching about the importance of family. Reports on incidents of domestic violence in conservative Christian households in Australia showed how the Bible's teaching on 'headship' can be abused in terrible ways—using biblical teaching to justify emotional, physical and sexual abuse, thus adding a further dimension of spiritual abuse.[32]

It is notable that studies into domestic violence in Christian households showed a high correlation between incidents of domestic violence and irregular evangelical churchgoing.[33] Perhaps this is because such a man is close enough to church life to draw spiritual legitimacy for his distorted views of headship, but not close enough to be exposed to the discipleship and discipline of the church community.

Other movements are more explicit in endorsing a strong and prescriptive patriarchal view of family life, where the role of women is heavily limited to the home and where things like ter-

31 Church and Family Life, *A Declaration of the Complementary Roles of Church and Family*', article IX, emphasis original.
32 J Baird and H Gleeson, '"Submit to your husbands": Women told to endure domestic violence in the name of God', *ABC News*, 22 October 2018, accessed 28 September 2022 (abc.net.au/news/2017-07-18/domestic-violence-church-submit-to-husbands/8652028).
33 Baird and Gleeson, '"Submit to your husbands".

tiary education, secular employment, voting and leaving the father's home (unless to get married) might all be discouraged.[34] A commitment to home-schooling in this framework further enhances the power of the parents over the children. We may protect against these dangers with a high view of the local church and with a strong emphasis on all Christian women as not only equally and individually divine image-bearers but also equally and individually 'sons of God', 'temples of the Holy Spirit', prophets, priests and kings.

34 Movements such as Quiverfull and Vision Forum Ministries. See Quiverfull Resources, *Quiverfull.com*, 2022, accessed 28 September 2022; and Vision Forum Ministries, *The Tenets of Biblical Patriarchy*, Vision Forum Ministries website, 3 December 2013, accessed 28 September 2022 (internet archive web.archive.org/web/20131203012839/http://www. visionforumministries.org/home/about/biblical_patriarchy.aspx). These movements give detailed accounts of the husband's role as "head of the wife as Christ is the head of the church" (Eph 5:23) and the exhortations for women to be busy in the home (1 Tim 5:10, 14; Titus 2:3-5). They draw extra weight from Old Testament laws, descriptive texts, and his-torical cultural assumptions present (but not endorsed) in the biblical text.
   A critical response to such views requires several things: 1) separating the cultural context of biblical authors and audiences from explicit divine commands and principles; 2) insisting on great care in application of biblical instruction around gender roles; 3) showing that the inspired authority of the Old Testament law does not mean that it has direct application to New Testament believers in all its specifics; and 4) highlighting complementary biblical themes which correct against strong patriarchal ideas. See, for example, Holst, 'The patriarchy movement: Five areas of grave concern'.

Chapter 14: Charitable, cultural and political groups

W hen the Christian movement is at its healthiest, Christians are active in all sorts of ways to produce good outcomes and meet real needs in the world. These include investment in the following areas:

- Benevolent care: healthcare; education; safety, relief, support and development; animal and environmental protection, restoration, welfare and stability.
- Cultural enrichment: arts; research; community development; ethnic identity culture and customs; recreation and sport; museums and libraries.
- Political advocacy: justice, freedom, compassion; morality; human rights; reconciliation, harmony and equality.
- Funding: trusts, grants, scholarships and awards.
- Support to other parachurches: administration, facilities, transport and compliance.

Not only are there a whole range of opportunities for Christians to do good in the world, but there are also a whole range of ways to go about it: as individual or informal group action; as an activity of a local church; as a denominational organization; as an independent not-for-profit body; or as a for-profit business (where either the whole business or some part(s) of it are devoted to the good cause).[1] We are reminded again that there is much more to the Christian life, and much more to parachurch ministry, than preaching and prayer.

In this chapter I will first analyze the theological motives for and benefits of good deeds. I will then discuss two warnings that are especially relevant for charitable, cultural and political parachurch groups, before considering the question: "when should a distinct parachurch be established?" In the final part of the chapter I will examine issues especially relevant first to charitable groups, then to political groups, and finally to gospel patrons.

The theological motives for and benefits of good deeds

The following points are repeated, with minor adjustment, from chapter 4. They are very much worth repeating at the beginning of this chapter, to celebrate the great value of Christian good deeds and to remember the proper theological framework for these good deeds.

First, the Christian life is founded not on our imperfect good deeds, but on God's gracious love for us. We have the burning need for the rightful wrath of God to be turned away from us, that we might be declared righteous and at peace with God. The gospel itself is about God's supreme good deed for us.

Second, the necessary response to the gospel is wholehearted worship of God and love of our neighbour. Genuine conversion results in a Spirit-led life of love and good deeds. We are saved to live a

---

1   See for example the ethical business practices and external charitable activity of Guinness Brewery, originally inspired by the preaching of John Wesley; S Mansfield, 'The story of God and Guinness: How the faith of Arthur Guinness inspired the vision for his famous beer', *Relevant Magazine*, 25 March 2010, accessed 28 September 2022 (relevantmagazine. com/god/story-god-and-guinness). Or the entrepreneurial activities of John Curtis, who purchased a pizza delivery business, a funeral parlour, a radio station and a tourist mine to support and facilitate gospel ministry and good deeds in Broken Hill, Australia; see Piggin, *Spirit, Word and World*, pp 194-195.

holy life. The God who saved us is worthy of all glory, honour and praise. And our Saviour God is also the Creator of all things, the one who commands us to serve him as his image-bearers— the pinnacle of his creation. God's glory in his very being, revealed in his great acts of creation, justice and salvation, should move us to spiritual adoration and humble service. Furthermore, this love and worship is never purely individualistic; it is expressed in the network of relationships established by marriage, family, friendship, neighbourhood and the church.

Third, our worship of God and love for our neighbour includes the proclamation of the gospel. We rightly worship God by believing his gospel, praising him for his gospel and proclaiming his gospel. Evangelism is part of our holiness. Offering the gift of eternal life is part of our loving concern for our neighbour. Praising God's saving deeds *among the nations* is part of praising God.

Fourth, good deeds give credibility to the gospel. They show us to be sincere and reliable messengers and they reinforce our gospel of the truth and mercy of God. On the most basic level, our good deeds often make us likeable. This is true not only of personal holiness, but also of the loving community life of the local church, as Jesus promised: "By this everyone will know that you are my disciples, if you love one another" (John 13:35). The church is, in that sense, a "hermeneutic for the gospel".[2] Or consider the opposite: "God's name is blasphemed among the Gentiles because of you" (Rom 2:24). In this way, good deeds become a "bridge to the gospel".[3]

Fifth, good deeds provide new opportunities for evangelism. Being attentive to the troubles and needs of others, and being active in meeting those needs, brings us into relationship with wider circles of people: not only those we care for but also those we partner with, those whom we lobby, and even those we oppose. Good deeds allow us to make connections with people we wouldn't reach through friendship evangelism or doorknocking alone.

Christians have many motivations to do good in a whole

2 Goheen, *"As the Father Has Sent Me"*, pp 175-176.
3 LCWE and WEF, *Evangelism and Social Responsibility*.

range of ways. Evangelism and good deeds are no more in conflict than evangelism and holiness are.[4] Godly Christians ought to be committed to doing good to their neighbours in many ways and on many levels. Faithful preaching and discipleship will challenge and inspire Christians in this, individually and cooperatively. In some cases, it may even inspire cooperation with non-Christians. While there have been ebbs and flows to all these kinds of activity throughout Christian history (for a whole range of reasons),[5] good deeds never have been, and never should be, entirely absent.

As I turn now to complex and problematic areas related to charitable, cultural and political activity, I do not want to give the impression that somehow this activity is more trouble than it's worth. Quite the opposite! Such activity is a fantastic outworking of Christian worship and love; it combines in effective synergy with evangelism and edification.

Don't be absolute about values and principles that go beyond the Bible

Christ is the Creator and Saviour of all things, and so he is relevant to every area of our lives. But that is not to say that he has spoken to us equally clearly and explicitly about every area of our lives. The further we move away from the Bible's core doctrines, the more we will find that Scripture provides principles to inform our decisions, but without definitive answers and prescriptions. We will need to consider several issues to decide how to approach opportunities, where to draw lines, and what to prioritize.

For example, in the area of politics there are several steps we need to go through: what the Bible says about government; implications of the Bible's teaching for basic ethical theories;

---

4   Williams, *Relocating Holism*, pp 48-55.
5   For a description and analysis of these ebbs and flows in the past few hundred years in British evangelicalism, see Bebbington, *Evangelicalism in Modern Britain*. For an analysis of the same in Australian evangelicalism, see Piggin, *Spirit, Word and World*.

how the Bible contributes to larger theories of politics and economics; the best application of the Bible's teaching to our
specific circumstances in terms of public policy; and an analysis
of the most ethical or strategic priority right now. The same
kind of process would be needed as Christians think through
how our faith should influence our approach to art, education,
addiction recovery, and many other complex areas of life.

The important thing here is for individuals and organizations
to not be absolute about the conclusions they have reached. It is
fine to have strong convictions about ideas and methods, but
beware of laying them on the conscience of individual Christians, local churches and the wider Christian community as
moral and spiritual obligations. So often Christians have been
too closely wedded to political strategies, social agendas or therapeutic approaches that have turned out to be gravely inadequate.
We must beware of presuming to interpret the flow of history or
of how God is at work in history, for this so often misses the
mark.[6] Over-confidence about the application of the Bible and
interpretation of history will make us too quick to pass moral
and spiritual judgement on other Christians.

Beware of influences that can undermine the mission

Charitable, cultural and political groups pursue practical goals
that are not explicitly about Christian faith and doctrine. These
organizations have great potential to receive funding and build
useful partnerships beyond the Christian community. While
this can be a great opportunity, it also brings potential influences
that can undermine the Christian foundation for their work.

*Opportunities and ambition to grow can undermine an organiza-
tion's Christian identity.* The broader the base of staff, volunteers
and participants, the greater the capacity a parachurch has to grow

6 See the helpful discussion in Goheen, *"As the Father Has Sent Me"*, pp 298-300.

—but the more likely the parachurch will lose its distinctively Christian identity and purpose. And the larger a parachurch grows, the more it can move towards a paid workforce that ceases to mobilize volunteers as it once did.[7] In some cases this paid workforce is likely to include a lower proportion of Christians. There is a difference between a Christian school staffed by professing, churchgoing Christians—a school which proactively seeks to teach within a Christian worldview and model Christian community—and a church school staffed by a larger pool of teachers who nominally agree with the 'Christian ethos' of the school and merely agree to preserve 'Christian tradition' and promote 'Christian values'. It isn't wrong for a church or denomination to run less explicitly Christian parachurches, but it's a great shame when these groups gradually drift in that direction simply in order to grow or maintain operations.[8]

Salaries and operating budgets can easily become bloated. The more that parachurches operate in the same context as secular bodies, the more their standards will be benchmarked by these bodies. Setting salaries and budgets is not a simple business; factors like size, location, purpose, appeal to donors, access to funding and current life-cycle phase all have an impact. Attracting and retaining well-qualified and experienced staff might come at a greater cost, but could bring big gains for the organization and its mission. Spending more on running costs can sometimes create a more effective parachurch organization.[9] All

---

7   Harold Hill describes this phenomenon in the social services wing of the Salvation Army; see Hill, *Officership in the Salvation Army*, pp 277-278.

8   Mayer Zald and Patricia Denton describe the secularization of the YMCA as 'goal displacement' which provides a model for this kind of drift; cited in Belden, *The Origins and Development of the Oxford Group*, pp 16-17.

9   "Low administration costs alone do not necessarily indicate an effective or well-run charity. Similarly, higher administration costs do not necessarily indicate that a charity is ineffective or poorly run. There are inefficient charities with poor outcomes that report low administration costs, and there are charities that spend more on administration and have efficient programs and successful outcomes. In deciding which charities to support, you should look at the work that charities do and the impact that they have" (Australian Charities and Not-for-profits Commission, *Charities and Administration Costs*, ACNC website, n.d., accessed 28 September 2021 [acnc.gov.au/for-public/understanding-charities/charities-and-administration-costs]).

that being said, parachurch staff, board members, partners and donors should be conscious of retaining an appropriate modesty, rather than simply conforming to secular standards.

Funding and contracting arrangements can bring with them restrictions on how the parachurch conducts its work. Sometimes these restrictions can be healthy, forcing the parachurch to comply with good standards and formulate fair and wise policies. But sometimes restrictions undermine what is distinctive about the organization. Such restrictions could include moral and religious inclusivity hiring requirements; being made to provide certain services and endorse certain ideas; and refraining from evangelism. Private donors and grant-giving bodies can also put pressure on parachurches to change their approach. The allure of greater funding or larger influence must be resisted wherever such funding comes at too great a cost. Sometimes these forces are quite subtle, leading Christians to lose their prophetic vision and be co-opted to the political assumptions and priorities of the wider society.[10] There's plenty of space to compromise, but strong and thoughtful leadership is required to know when such compromise becomes capitulation.

The political process can easily undermine parachurch groups because the political process is necessarily about negotiation and compromise. These pressures are felt strongly by groups that lobby the government. This is a good reason to be especially cautious about involving the local church or denomination in political activity.[11]

The marketplace also brings its own undermining influences, as parachurch organizations feel the pressure to stay productive and competitive. All churches and parachurches might feel 'marketplace' pressures as they 'compete' with neighbouring

10 "If all that congregations and other local groups do is stand between the market and the state, in effect acting as a buffer, they will become co-opted and consumed by them. 'Civil society' then becomes an instrument of the ubiquitous market and the coercive power of the nation-state" (Gornik, *To Live in Peace*, p 19).

11 For a helpful discussion of the difference between the church's duties for 'social service' compared to 'social action', see LCWE and WEF, *Evangelism and Social Responsibility*, pp 39-41.

ministries for members or donors.[12] But in some cases these experiences of competition can be much more acute: for example, where organizational running costs are high; where income is derived primarily from payment for services; or where the organization has both Christian and secular competitors.

Many of these groups face a constant pressure: sticking to their principles brings with it the risk of shutting down. This temptation might be related to ethical or doctrinal compromise, but it can also be in the area of organizational culture and practices. Management might become ruthless, marketing might become misleading, or projects might be adopted based on return on investment rather than actual need.[13] It is also possible that a for-profit business might have a parachurch dimension to its operations,[14] but leaders of these businesses will need a great deal of integrity for their commercial interests to not crowd out their spiritual aspirations.

There is a constant risk for charitable, cultural and political parachurch groups to lose sight of their founding purpose and distinctively Christian identity. The price of organizational effectiveness and public recognition can be ceasing to be meaningfully Christian at all.

One basic way to guard against this drift is to ensure that the parachurch has clear and detailed doctrinal statements and strategic documents. It is surprising just how often parachurches are founded—especially those whose aims are not fundamentally about preaching and teaching—with very minimal doctrinal definition. It doesn't have to be this way. The founders may not see a need for doctrinal clarity, but it can prove decisive later on when the dangers begin to rear their head.

---

12 See 'Co-exist, compare, contrast and complement without ruthlessly competing' in chapter 7.
13 For a really thorough analysis of a range of fundraising and project-planning issues, see LCWE Commission on Co-operation, *Cooperating in World Evangelization*, pp 64-95.
14 For example, Mansfield, 'The story of God and Guinness'.

When is a distinct Christian charitable, cultural or political organization needed?

It should be asked whether a distinctively Christian organization is actually needed in any given situation. Christians can meaningfully worship God and love their neighbour as members of secular government and non-government bodies. It is worth asking whether Christian energy might be more effectively used as a part of a larger secular organization. Would it be better to have Christians seeking to work out their ethics and worldview as members of broader cultural groups, rather than creating a parallel Christian subculture with its own sports leagues, arts and music industries, trade guilds, news services, schools and universities, and even political parties? The added benefit of such involvement is that Christians can be a positive influence in word and deed among their non-Christian neighbours.

Sometimes separate Christian bodies are necessary to ensure a Christian stance on certain ideological and ethical matters. Sadly, larger organizations sometimes insist on ideological or ethical positions which a Christian cannot agree with in good conscience. At other times, while there is nothing problematic in the organization's stance, any uniquely Christian concerns are silenced. In such cases, there is a genuine place for charities, schools and other organizations where Christians can participate in good conscience and the insights of God's word can be shared.

This is where 'sphere sovereignty', an idea championed by Dutch theologian Abraham Kuyper, can be extremely helpful. 'Sphere sovereignty' insists that there are distinct, sovereign 'spheres' of human life (such as church, education, family, and politics) that shouldn't interfere with one another. The government should not interfere with the family, the church shouldn't interfere with the government, and so on.[15] While not being explicitly biblical in its details, this framework helps leaders in different spheres to pause and reflect: "Yes, this is important, but is it our sphere's job to do something formal about it?" Free-

15 McGoldrick, *God's Renaissance Man*, pp 62-72, 80-81, 152-154, 158-166.

dom and diversity suffer when the government imposes too much on church, family and education, or when the institutional church does the same. We should encourage the civil government to show restraint and to allow freedom and diversity among non-government bodies.

Distinctively Christian organizations can help Christians work out their faith in all areas of their lives. Sadly it is possible for Christians to be consciously and deliberately Christian only in the narrow 'private' and 'religious' dimensions of our lives. We are Christians at church and home, but not at work, play or study. Christian cultural parachurches can promote and support the process of exploring what it means to be a Christian tradesman, artist or athlete.[16] This is distinct from evangelistic and discipleship parachurches that serve in such contexts, like the City Bible Forum.[17]

Small organizations provide something different to the wider community. Some things are less effective when handled by large-scale bodies. Small neighbourhood writers' workshops, for example, or support groups or activist collectives can engage people in intimate and personalized ways that larger organizations simply cannot replicate.

But *there is the danger of creating an introverted Christian subculture.* Both the Christian community and the wider world suffer from being too isolated from one another. Christian culture can become thin or eccentric without the input of wider cultural insights and intellectual discoveries. And the wider culture is debased when it is buffered from regular exposure to and input from biblical Christianity. A sharp divide between a Christian subculture and the wider community can make evangelism to some groups difficult. It can also create an unnecessarily jolting culture shock for those who have been immersed in the Christian subculture when they are removed from it—as they

16 "There is a need for 'frontier groups,' groups of Christians working in the same sectors of public life, meeting to thrash out the controversial issues of their business or profession in the light of their faith" (Lesslie Newbigin cited in Goheen, *"As the Father Has Sent Me"*, pp 312-313).
17 See citybibleforum.org.

go to university, for example. On the larger social scale, this can create what is called 'pillarization': when different religious subcultures function side-by-side with their separate political parties, educational institutions, media, hospitals, employers and recreational groups, society can be quite divided under its over-arching political structures.[18] At its worst, this can lead to the hardening of social hostilities and inequalities.[19]

In many cases, the distinctively Christian parachurch contribution might work better with a narrower scope. Rather than establishing entirely separate Christian sports leagues, a ministry that supports and advises Christian athletes might be sufficient; rather than a Christian university, a colloquium for Christian academics might suffice.

Some issues especially for charitable groups

It's sad but true that the noble goal of helping the needy can go so wrong. But there are a range of complicated dynamics which begin to operate when individuals or organizations start helping others.

First, helping others can create an unhealthy dependency, where those in need begin to rely upon those providing help, perhaps even forming long-term expectations and patterns of behaviour around this help. This is often exacerbated because those who offer the help can take great satisfaction from being needed and being helpful.[20] A dynamic of patron-client is established, with

---

18 DT Koyzis, 'When we turn inward: Evangelism and the limits of pluralism (part 2)', *First Things*, 4 February 2015, accessed 28 September 2022 (firstthings.com/web-exclusives/2015/02/when-we-turn-inward).

19 For example, the establishment of apartheid in South Africa; see McGoldrick, *God's Renaissance Man*, pp 227-229.

20 In a practically useful, if exegetically stretched, interpretation of the parable of the Good Samaritan, Jeanne Stevenson Moessner points out that the Good Samaritan took the wounded man to an inn, paid for his care, and then continued on his journey. She stresses the importance of this insight, especially for women who over-identify with the role of caregiver and can neglect their own wellbeing in the process. See J Stevenson Moessner, 'The self-differentiated Samaritan', in Dykstra (ed), *Images of Pastoral Care*, pp 62-68.

an in-built power imbalance. To counteract this danger, long-term help must be focused on not simply offering aid and relieving immediate needs, but on working together with those in need, collaborating with them and empowering them.

Second, when practical help is offered together with spiritual ministry, it is very important to safeguard freedom of conscience. Vulnerable people can feel great implicit pressure to profess faith and participate in religious activities in order to receive practical benefits and a sense of social belonging.

Christopher Swift demonstrates how religion was central to the functioning of the early hospitals: patients were absorbed into the life and religious community of the hospital monastery complex.[21] While few modern parachurch organizations are quite so intense (although some halfway-house ministries are quite similar),[22] the same dynamic can still be present. Whether explicitly or implicitly, people may receive the message that to truly belong and to fully benefit from the resources on offer, you must conform to certain religious expectations. This can be even more of an issue where a parachurch has something of a monopoly in a particular region.

The Pontifical Council for Interreligious Dialogue, the World Council of Churches and the World Evangelical Alliance offer some helpful recommendations:

> If Christians engage in inappropriate methods of exercising mission by resorting to deception and coercive means, they betray the gospel and may cause suffering to others.
>
> Acts of service, such as providing education, health care, relief services and acts of justice and advocacy are an integral part of witnessing to the gospel. The

---

21 Swift, *Hospital Chaplaincy in the Twenty-First Century*, pp 9-13, 21-25. He writes: "Those living and working within early hospitals were required to relate to one another as occupants of ecclesiastical space … they were drawn into the subtle politics of salvation, earning the care they received with the prayers they offered for the imperilled souls of the rich" (p 13).

22 Smith, *The Origins, Nature, and Significance of the Jesus Movement*, pp 110-112, 215-216, 224-227, 231-245, 312-313.

exploitation of situations of poverty and need has no place in Christian outreach. Christians should denounce and refrain from offering all forms of allurements, including financial incentives and rewards, in their acts of service ... fully respecting human dignity and ensuring that the vulnerability of people and their need for healing are not exploited.[23]

In 2 Corinthians 4, Paul describes how he has "renounced secret and shameful ways" in his ministry; instead, "by setting forth the truth plainly we commend ourselves to everyone's conscience in the sight of God" (v 2). This commitment arises from an ethic of honest service of others, the goal of genuine repentance and faith arising from the appeal to the individual's conscience, and great confidence in the power of God's word: "For God, who said, 'Let light shine out of darkness,' made his light shine in our hearts to give us the light of the knowledge of God's glory displayed in the face of Christ" (v 6). These deep spiritual values ought to make coercive and manipulative patterns of charity and evangelism repellent to us. There are steps parachurches can take to ward off the dangers. For example, it is helpful to have formal policies and regular communication that lay out people's freedom to disagree on religious matters and to refrain from participation in religious practices or from conversations about personal spiritual beliefs.

Third, honesty and discernment are needed when holistic charitable parachurches evolve into evangelistic and discipleship organizations. A charitable parachurch should rightly be concerned about the whole person, including their spiritual welfare. In some cases this could lead to the broadening of their programs and structures to provide increasingly long-term and in-depth support for its participants—perhaps even broadening to include explicit

---

23 Pontifical Council for Interreligious Dialogue, World Council of Churches, and World Evangelical Alliance, *Christian Witness in a Multi-Religious World: Recommendations for conduct*, Dicastery for Interreligious Dialogue website, 2011, accessed 28 September 2022 (dicasteryinterreligious.va/christian-witness-in-a-multi-religious-world-recommendations-for-conduct-2).

evangelism and Bible study. Such broadening must be managed very carefully, as it could lead to the organization losing sight of its founding purpose, unnecessarily competing with other parachurch ministries and, worst of all, usurping the local church. In some cases, this holistic approach could lead to the kind of unintentional coercion described above. Parachurches need to be restrained and focused in their programming, acknowledging that they needn't attempt to provide every service or solve every problem.

Fourth, discernment is needed when evangelistic and discipleship organizations evolve into charitable parachurches. This is the opposite side of the coin we have just been examining. Genuine concern for those we serve should lead us to care for them practically, emotionally, socially and politically. In many contexts, it is almost impossible to minister the gospel in an ongoing way without being drawn into providing other kinds of care. But churches and parachurches should continue to evaluate whether some of their activities might be better continued and developed as part of a complementary but distinct organization. Otherwise there is a dual risk: either the disciple-making ministry gets submerged in the midst of the charitable work, or the charitable work gets distorted by its close attachment to the church institution.

An extreme and complicated example of the latter is the Salvation Army, which manifests one of the strongest overlaps between church and charity, with no ultimate separation between the 'field work' (of the church or 'corps') and the social work of the various community service centres. John Larsson praises this unity as "one of [the Army's] greatest strengths".[24] Although the Army had a history of practical charitable work alongside its primary evangelistic focus, this only became a major part of its identity and activity when William Booth announced his grandiose plans in his 1890 publication *In Darkest England and the Way Out.*[25] This signalled not merely a shift

24 J Larsson, *Thirteen Astonishing Years That Shaped the Salvation Army (1878-1890)*, Salvation Books, 2019, loc 1400.
25 Hattersley, *Blood and Fire*, loc 6465-7217.

in emphasis and scale, but also a shift from meeting needs to solving underlying social problems.[26] David Taylor observes that because this charitable work operates within the Army's monolithic hierarchical structure, this can have the curious effect of associating the social services more with the operations of the larger institution and its hierarchy—in other words, the social work seems separated from the local church community.[27]

These massive programs necessarily changed the way the Army operated.[28] Irreligious critics of its social work also opposed the fact that their solutions, funded by donations from the wider public, were being carried out under the umbrella of a religious and evangelistic agenda.[29]

Some issues especially for political groups

Even greater complexities arise around those parachurches that seek to do good at the level of influencing government policy and legislation. At this level, there are many uncertainties that mean the best approach is often not clear. Moreover, there are powerful influences that can consciously or unconsciously influence our convictions and decisions. In all of this, we are often more influenced than we realize by presuppositions that come from our

---

26 Hattersley, *Blood and Fire*, loc 189-194, 6469-6474; and Larsson, *Thirteen Astonishing Years*, loc 1393-1421; cf. Taylor, *Like a Mighty Army?*, pp 52-53.

27 Taylor says that, at its worst, service can be distorted to become a career path for an aspiring officer; see Taylor, *Like a Mighty Army?*, p 267. See also Hill, *Officership in the Salvation Army*, pp 277-278.

28 George Railton, who was heavily influential in the Army in its early days (see Hattersley, *Blood and Fire*, loc 3756-3778), was strongly opposed to the Army's increasing use of commercial means to finance the 'Darkest England' social service efforts—even making a shocking public protest, in keeping with radicalism and eccentricity, by turning up to a major public rally barefoot and in sackcloth and using the open testimony time to decry a newly acquired life insurance society; see Hattersley, *Blood and Fire*, loc 7650-7677.

29 Booth insisted that the spirituality of the Salvation Army was necessary both for the motivation of the aid workers and the internal transformation of those in need; see Hattersley, *Blood and Fire*, loc 6813, 7010-7031, 7087-7176.

cultural context.[30] It is very important that political parachurch groups admit these uncertainties and difficulties, both to consciously correct against them and to avoid claiming too much.

Here are a few specific factors to bear in mind:

First, do not claim to speak for the whole Christian community. One of the highest-profile political parachurch groups in Australia is called The 'Australian Christian Lobby' (ACL). The name is unfortunate because it could be taken to imply that the ACL speaks for all Christians in Australia. But the point here is not primarily about the choice of a name, but about overall rhetorical strategy. No doubt there is persuasive political power in claiming to speak for a large religious constituency—to be *the* voice of the Australian Christian voting public. But it lacks integrity to imply such a thing without good justification.

Second, beware of distorting the public reputation of the wider Christian community. Because political parachurches are often very visible in the media, it is especially important for their spokespeople to be above reproach in gentleness, honesty, integrity and concern for the truth. The pressure to make the strongest possible political case can lead political parachurch groups to marshal every possible piece of evidence that supports their agenda and to dismiss legitimate qualifying and dissenting voices. It can be tempting to maintain a strong public profile and so avoid admitting fault or issuing apologies. It can be tempting to demonize political opponents, and even to criticize potential allies, to further sharpen your message. And it can be tempting to avoid criticizing political allies for fear of losing their favour. All these errors do a great disservice to the wider public perception of Christianity.

Third, be open to the wide range of Christian political concerns. Many Christian political groups have tended to gravitate towards ethical issues that may otherwise be neglected: for example, concerns around the sanctity of life (such as abortion and eutha-

---

30 Consider Alec Vidler's critique of the great British Christian philanthropists of the 19th century; see Vidler, *The Church in an Age of Revolution*, pp 91-93. See also Noll, *The Rise of Evangelicalism*, pp 221-247.

nasia) and the sanctity of marriage (such as divorce and a range of LGBT issues). It is certainly legitimate to adopt a narrow set of political aims, but in doing so it is even more important to acknowledge that such a group is not giving voice to a fully formed Christian political outlook. Christians ought to be concerned about every issue in one way or another, and our ethical priorities extend beyond the ethics of sex and death.

Fourth, strive to seek the wider public good, not merely sectarian Christian interests. If we truly want to love our fellow citizens, we need to carefully consider what will be best for the whole of society. We must aim for a 'principled pluralism'.[31] What is beneficial but also achievable in a society that holds wildly divergent views of God, the universe, humanity, freedom and happiness?

Fifth, assess whether to be a prophetic Christian voice or make a persuasive secular contribution. Christians may not always argue for our views by quoting from the Bible or by spelling out our underlying theological assumptions and motivations. This is rarely persuasive when speaking with those who don't share our convictions or when collaborating on what is best for a pluralistic society. A thoughtful Christian will seek to find common ground with others with whom they disagree, and will then reason together on these terms.

Yet at the same time, there is something useful about naming the values and priorities of an unashamedly Christian outlook in the public square. It is unhelpful for society when Christians completely acquiesce to a sharp public/private, sacred/ secular divide—where those with religious beliefs must not speak about them or be influenced by them in public discussion.[32] Both a prophetic Christian voice and a persuasive secular contribution have a place in Christian political engagement.

---

31 McGoldrick, *God's Renaissance Man*, pp 160-162.
32 N Campbell, 'Why (with all due respect) adopting the rules of the "secular" political game and pretending Jesus doesn't profoundly matter to us is a dumb idea for Christians and we should stop', *St Eutychus*, 15 February 2017, accessed 28 September 2022 (st-eutychus.com/2017/why-with-all-due-respect-adopting-the-rules-of-the-secular-political-game-and-pretending-jesus-doesnt-profoundly-matter-to-us-is-a-dumb-idea-for-christians-and-we-should-stop).

Perhaps what we really need is several types of political para-churches. And perhaps the groups that tend more towards secular persuasion need to diversify their approach to occasionally complement their common-ground efforts with a more up-front expression of their Christian worldview.[33]

Some issues especially for gospel patrons

Major Christian donors, along with the trusts, foundations and support organizations they establish, are their own special kind of parachurch ministry that can play a vital role in the whole gamut of activities discussed in this book. Such supporters are able to provide larger amounts of financial support than is normally available through everyday fundraising and other sources of income. In addition to financial support, 'gospel patrons' can also provide many other kinds of support: strategic advice; introductions into new networks; and access to venues, equipment and manpower. They are not merely donors, but genuine ministry partners with those who preach and teach.

What are some of the major issues that gospel patrons should consider?

First, without intending to, major donors can distort ministry priorities through their approach to funding. One of the easiest ways to structure financial support and assess candidates for support is through a project- or program-based model. But it is important to be aware of the downsides of this useful framework. To capitalize on grant opportunities, parachurches might continue to develop new projects and programs so that they qualify to apply for new funding, even if this is not the most strategic

---

33 Nathan Campbell speaks about the need for clean hands (a non-partisan prophetic voice), busy hands (contributing to public life through charitable and cultural work) and dirty hands (willingness to get involved in the political process); see N Campbell, 'Worried about how Christianity gets treated in the political realm? Join a party for God's sake (and your neighbour's)', *St Eutychus*, 5 January 2017, accessed 28 September 2022 (st-eutychus.com/2017/worried-about-how-christianity-gets-treated-in-the-political-realm-join-a-party-for-gods-sake-and-your-neighbours).

approach to ministry. If application and reporting expectations are too rigorous, organizations might be forced to take on large amounts of additional administrative work—even redirecting staff time and energy to satisfy these requirements—that bring no obvious benefits to the ministry itself.

While short-term seed funding that slowly tapers off (e.g. $10,000 in the first year, $7,500 in the second year, and $5,000 in the third year) can be a useful way to prevent organizations becoming dependent on major donors, this approach doesn't work so well where the road to sustainability is much longer. Flexibility and good communication can open the door to negotiations around funding timeframes, applying for subsequent funding and building long-term collaboration.[34] The most enduring and valuable parachurch work is generally the steady, regular work of the core people, funded by their standard operating budget. But alongside the provision of short-term start-up assistance, there is a valuable place for gospel patrons to offer long-term funding—the type of funding that enables an efficient and effective ministry do its work across a decade or more.

Second, gospel patrons need to be open to the fact that they may not fully understand the sector or the local context. It can be tempting for a capable business leader or an expert in strategic analysis to presume to diagnose the problems of Christian organizations and prescribe the necessary solutions. True, all too often a local parachurch leader will say "but that won't work here," simply out of conservatism, lack of imagination or limited leadership competence. Inadequate explanations and justifications or underdone strategic planning from those working on the ground can make it easy for gospel patrons to become impatient.

Yet it is vital that gospel patrons appreciate the work being done and the context in which it is taking place. While the local workers may not always be able to extract and articulate these distinctives, they often grasp them intuitively and simply need

---

34 Thoughtful gospel patrons sometimes invest additional funds in a project that demonstrates merit and integrity, even if they failed to reach the targets of its original proposal.

help to draw them out. Evangelistic ministry and charitable work are significantly different from commercial enterprises. The best gospel patrons uphold the value of listening to and working through the leaders of the organizations they seek to support.

Third, be cautious of the power to usurp those in authority. One of the strengths and weakness of gospel patronage is that it provides extra power to get on and do things apart from formal hierarchies. On the positive side, patrons can free up gifted leaders to get on and try new things. A lot of adventurous activity can be promoted without depending on church funding. But the other side of the coin is that this can become an unhealthy and corrosive pattern that weakens formal leadership structures.

One way for gospel patrons to express humble submission to their church leaders is by submitting their finances to the oversight of their local church. There is no absolute rule here, but this should be considered. Indeed it is sometimes better to take the longer route of persuading the formal leadership, cementing their commitment to new initiatives rather than circumventing their role.

An obvious way in which gospel patrons can usurp those in authority is by threatening to withdraw the funding on which a ministry might depend, effectively holding a ministry to ransom. When such a threat is reserved only for the most serious situations, it can be a proper form of natural accountability for parachurch organizations. But if used frequently, it becomes manipulative. This calls for integrity and restraint from gospel patrons to avoid sliding to these negative extremes; it also requires parachurch leaders to have the courage to confront such tendencies when they become too prevalent.

Where a positive, respectful relationship between gospel patrons and Christian leaders is established and maintained, these partnerships can be tremendously energizing and amazingly fruitful.

∼

There are so many good deeds that Christians can band together to do in the world. Wherever these deeds go beyond the primary purpose and responsibilities of the church, there are good reasons to start new ministries and organizations to move the good work forward. This division of labour preserves the identity and purpose of the local church, clarifies the uniqueness of the work of gospel proclamation, and enables the valuable works of charity, cultural enrichment and political engagement to develop into their own vibrant enterprises.

Drawing distinctions between the work of preaching and prayer and other kinds of good deeds should not mean that we don't value charitable work, secular work and cultural work. Nor should the different risks and complexities of such activity prevent Christians from engaging in it. Such good deeds are motivated by our worship of God and have all sorts of ties to our service of God and his gospel mission: they are the fruit of the gospel, commending the credibility of the gospel and providing unique opportunities to share the gospel. As such, we should pursue these activities with compassion and caution, ensuring, as much as we can, that our efforts do much more good than harm for God's world and for the cause of Christ.

Conclusion

This has been a challenging book to pull together! To cover the theological, historical and practical dimensions of ministry and mission inside and beyond the local church, and to do so in a way that strives to humbly wrestle with the teachings of God's word in light of the complexities of everyday life, has been a huge effort. But sometimes the most constructive path is also the more difficult one. I hope and pray that the result is not merely a heady mix of confusion and enlightenment, but also of resolve and action. I hope and pray that this book can be of practical use for the pastors and deacons of churches, the board members of parachurch organizations, global missionaries, theological college faculty, Christian podcasters, and faithful volunteers everywhere.

I want to finish with some of the strong convictions that have motivated me to produce this book.

Careful theological reflection is both important and useful. Although complex at points, I hope this book gives every reader a deeper appreciation for the local church, for the denomination, for the various parachurch organizations, and, of course, for the universal church. When we merely react from instinct, prejudice and tradition, we won't arrive at the most faithful and effective actions.

Loving relationships are worth the hassle. Putting the effort into communicating, listening, understanding, apologizing, consulting, collaborating and compromising is the godly thing to do. It honours others, builds trust, and adorns the gospel.

The Lord's work in the world can't be easily contained by human institutions. Even though God has ordained the visible church, its offices and its ministry, he has not confined himself to its committees and programs. While much of the Holy Spirit's work happens in and through human activity, it remains primarily the Holy Spirit's work, and he moves wherever he pleases. Our theological and ecclesiological frameworks must include the humble flexibility to recognize this in practice.

There is more work to be done. We have been entrusted with the great riches of the gospel of the Lord Jesus Christ—riches that bring the power of salvation to everyone who believes. As the people of God, we are charged to make disciples of all nations, build up the church into maturity, and live lives worthy of the gospel in all that this entails for our spiritual, intellectual, personal, social, civic and professional lives. Now is not the time for our churches to be complacent, but to have a holy restlessness. And now is not the time to plod along with familiar routines, but to be prayerfully open to bold and creative new ways in which we might better serve our Master as we wait for his return.

Feedback on this resource

We really appreciate getting feedback about our resources—not just suggestions for how to improve them, but also positive feedback and ways they can be used. We especially love to hear that the resources may have helped someone in their Christian growth.

You can send feedback to us via the 'Feedback' menu in our online store, or write to us at info@matthiasmedia.com.au.

One of the oldest and most influential parachurches: religious orders

I onian monks, Franciscan friars, Moravian missionaries, the Salvation Army, the Jesus Movement, the Benedict Option … religious orders have been massively influential in the history of Christianity. To this day, many people writing about missionary work, church life and authentic spirituality will seek to draw on the insights and practices of various religious orders. Studying the weird and wonderful history of religious orders is not only fascinating, but also very practical as we think about what we can learn from their strengths and weaknesses.

Download this bonus chapter at:
matthiasmedia.com.au/thevinemovement/

Miraculous ministries

I n the course of my ministry, I have often talked with those who have attended special meetings featuring traveling evangelists who seek to proclaim the gospel and demonstrate the power of God through signs and wonders. Some come away enthused; others come away troubled. When I meet those who have had such experiences firsthand, they often report how these experiences have made God seem alive to them in a whole new way—as if their former spiritual life was theoretical or humdrum by comparison. What do I say when I am asked my opinion? Why do I not promote such ministries or seek to incorporate their practices into my own work?

Download this bonus chapter at:
matthiasmedia.com.au/thevinemovement/

❤matthiasmedia

Matthias Media is an evangelical publishing ministry that seeks to persuade all Christians of the truth of God's purposes in Jesus Christ as revealed in the Bible, and equip them with high-quality resources, so that by the work of the Holy Spirit they will:

- abandon their lives to the honour and service of Christ in daily holiness and decision-making
- pray constantly in Christ's name for the fruitfulness and growth of his gospel
- speak the Bible's life-changing word whenever and however they can—in the home, in the world and in the fellowship of his people.

Our wide range of resources includes Bible studies, books, training courses, tracts and children's material. To find out more, and to access samples and free downloads, visit our website:

www.matthiasmedia.com

How to buy our resources

1. Direct from us over the internet:
   - in the US: www.matthiasmedia.com
   - in Australia: www.matthiasmedia.com.au

2. Direct from us by phone: please visit our website for current phone contact information.

3. Through a range of outlets in various parts of the world. Visit **www.matthiasmedia.com/contact** for details about recommended retailers in your part of the world.

4. Trade enquiries can be addressed to:
   - in the US and Canada: sales@matthiasmedia.com
   - in Australia and the rest of the world: sales@matthiasmedia.com.au

Register at our website for our **free** regular email update to receive information about the latest new resources, **exclusive special offers**, and free articles to help you grow in your Christian life and ministry.

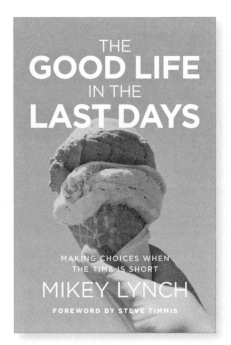

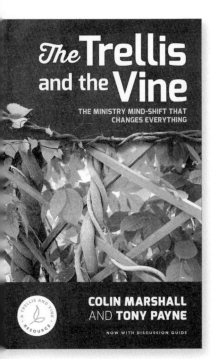

By Colin Marshall and Tony Payne

The Vine Project

In this highly anticipated book, Colin Marshall and Tony Payne provide a roadmap and resources for the church-wide culture change they advocated for in *The Trellis and The Vine*. They guide your ministry leadership team through a five-phase process for growth and change, with biblical input, practical ideas, resources, case studies, exercises and projects along the way. You will be helped to:

- clarify and sharpen your convictions
- reform your own life to express these convictions
- honestly evaluate every aspect of your current ministry culture
- devise and launch key plans for change
- keep the momentum going and overcome obstacles.

The Trellis and the Vine proposed a "ministry mind-shift that changes everything". *The Vine Project* shows how that mind-shift can and must shape every aspect of what you are doing as a congregation of Christ's people to make disciples of all nations.

FOR MORE INFORMATION OR TO ORDER CONTACT:

Matthias Media
Email: sales@matthiasmedia.com.au
www.matthiasmedia.com.au

Matthias Media (USA)
Email: sales@matthiasmedia.com
www.matthiasmedia.com

Craig Hamilton

Wisdom in Leadership Development

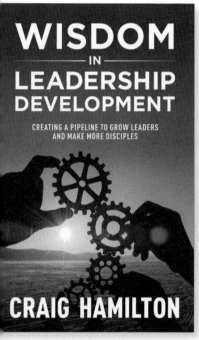

Christian ministries want to grow: they rightly desire to see more and more people following the Lord Jesus as faithful disciples. And so leadership matters, because good leaders multiply disciple-making ministry. Yet many churches and ministries struggle with leadership, and poor leadership ends up hindering their gospel mission.

In *Wisdom in Leadership Development*, Craig Hamilton sets out a leadership pipeline and framework that will help any ministry—big or small—to better understand the various layers of leadership required and to deploy leaders who, under God, will expand the quantity and effectiveness of the ministry being done.

This book is a must for all ministry leaders.